WITHDRAWN

JUN 0 4 2012

eels

BLINKING LIGHTS

AND OTHER REVELATIONS

*For my wife Susan, who always reminds me
that these could be the good old days.*

ML
421
.E35
G75
2011

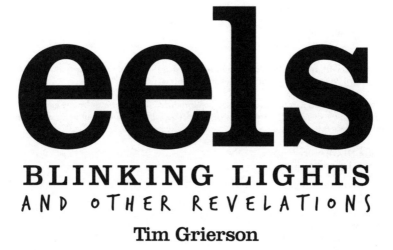

eels

BLINKING LIGHTS
AND OTHER REVELATIONS

Tim Grierson

OMNIBUS PRESS

London / New York / Paris / Sydney / Copenhagen / Berlin / Madrid / Tokyo

Copyright © 2011 Omnibus Press
(A Division of Music Sales Limited)

Cover designed by Fresh Lemon
Picture research by Jacqui Black

ISBN: 978.1.84938.596.1
Order No: OP53724

The Author hereby asserts his/her right to be identified as the author of this work in accordance with
Sections 77 to 78 of the Copyright, Designs and Patents Act 1988.

All rights reserved. No part of this book may be reproduced in any form or by any electronic or
mechanical means, including information storage or retrieval systems, without permission in writing
from the publisher, except by a reviewer who may quote brief passages.

Exclusive Distributors
Music Sales Limited,
14/15 Berners Street,
London, W1T 3LJ.

Music Sales Corporation,
257 Park Avenue South,
New York, NY 10010, USA.

Macmillan Distribution Services,
56 Parkwest Drive
Derrimut, Vic 3030,
Australia.

Every effort has been made to trace the copyright holders of the photographs in this book but one or
two were unreachable. We would be grateful if the photographers concerned would contact us.

Printed in the EU

A catalogue record for this book is available from the British Library.

Visit Omnibus Press on the web at www.omnibuspress.com

Contents

Prologue

On August 3, 2010 at 9pm, E takes the stage of The Galaxy Theatre in Santa Ana, California. For a musician who doesn't particularly like life on the road, the prospect of beginning a two-month, four-continent, 50-date tour would never be a thrilling one, but for the man born Mark Oliver Everett it's even more daunting right now.

It has been more than two years since E completed his last formal tour and four years since he has gone out with a proper band. In recent years he had broken with his tradition of touring after the release of each new album. In the summer of 2009, he put out *Hombre Lobo*, an album of garage-rock and delicate indie-pop ballads, but citing a lack of enthusiasm for touring and a desire not to short-change his audience by giving them a show he wasn't fully invested in, he stayed home. Then at the beginning of 2010, he released *End Times*, a stark, intimate break-up album. Not only didn't he support that record with a stint on the road, he refused to do press for it (although he did finally acquiesce and give a couple of interviews). So as he walks onto the stage by himself to kick off this evening's warm-up show, it's clear that something has changed, and it's not just that he's actually putting in a public appearance. In fact, the full implications of this change won't even be clear to those in attendance until weeks later.

On August 24, he will be releasing *Tomorrow Morning*, the ninth studio album from his band, Eels. Anyone who has followed the exploits of

Eels over the last 14 years can tell you that Eels are a band in the same way that Nine Inch Nails are a band — in other words, it's really just one guy who surrounds himself with a collection of sidemen (some who hang around longer than others) who help out on the albums and tours. Fiercely protective of his privacy, the 47-year-old singer-songwriter has always cultivated an aura of mystery, which is ironic since his music tends to be intensely personal, touching on suicide, depression, death, the end of love, and the struggle to find meaning in the face of life's futility. Eels fans — who, really, are E fans — respond to the juxtaposing impulses of hope and anguish that power the group's best songs, but they're also searching for clues into the mind-set of that witty, sarcastic, peculiar man who created them.

With each new Eels album, E introduces new dimensions to the persona we've come to love: curmudgeonly, caustic, despondent, satiric, romantic, antagonistic. Not only do the records display different aspects of his personality, they also reveal different styles — if he last put out a more pop-influenced disc, the chances are very good that bruising guitars await the listener the next time round. This unpredictability extends to the tours — you can commit a new Eels album to memory and still be surprised by a live performance that has radically reinvented songs that are but a few months old. Consequently, when you go to an Eels show, you're signing a tacit contract with E — he likes to mix things up and constantly keep the material fresh, and he assumes you can roll with that. For fans, this has always been an easy deal to make, and so we attend his concerts armed with a sense of endless possibility. And because it's been so long since he's toured, tonight's show is especially fraught with anticipation.

And perhaps E senses this too. How else to explain the evening's opening act, a painfully unfunny local ventriloquist comedian who includes among his puppets a Sarah Palin doll? Performing a routine that stretches out interminably and contains many off-colour gags, the comedian seems to be E's way of gently torturing his audience who are eagerly awaiting his imminent arrival. And when he does take the stage to a symphonic swell of 'When You Wish Upon A Star' over the loudspeakers, he's dressed in a white jumpsuit and sports a bandana, sunglasses and long beard that conspire to cover his entire face and head. He's back, yet he remains hidden.

Despite the amount of new material to début on this Tuesday evening, the crowd isn't surprised that E starts off with one particular song from the past. Although it's in no way inspired by Santa Ana's Galaxy Theatre, E likes to play 'Daisies Of The Galaxy' whenever he's here, as its last verse ("I'll pick some daisies/from the flower bed/of the Galaxy Theater/while you clear your head") never fails to elicit hearty cheers from the crowd. Soon enough, the rest of the current line-up of Eels emerges — along with E, there are two other guitarists, a bassist and a drummer. And what becomes clear rather quickly is that while the band members attack the songs with pummelling fervour, this might be the most light-hearted, angst-free Eels road show anyone has ever witnessed. Though tonight's set list concentrates on *Hombre Lobo*'s alternately wistful and horny songs of unrequited love and *End Times*' miserable desolation, the band's garage-rock looseness gives even the saddest songs a bounce that makes their melancholy seem a far-off memory rather than a lingering hurt.

This is new for Eels fans, who have followed E as he's negotiated a litany of pain. By this point, those tragedies have been so well documented by journalists that they risk losing their meaning — specifically, the deaths of his father, mother and sister, which left him an orphan at the age of 35. But for much of Eels' lifespan, E's complicated relationship with his family has been the driving force of his creativity, the prism through which the artist has tried to make sense of his world. However, at tonight's show it becomes apparent that E has fundamentally turned a corner; except for a hard-rock version of 'I Like Birds', a cheery nod to his mom's love of the winged creatures, there are no songs that deal explicitly with family matters.

In its place is a celebration of summer. The group rip through The Lovin' Spoonful's 'Summer In The City' and Billy Stewart's rendition of 'Summertime' from *Porgy And Bess*. E throws free popsicles to the audience at one point. Later in the night, he even dances around during the extended funk-like finale of 'Looking Up', making like a white-boy James Brown. Songs as mournful as 'I'm Going To Stop Pretending

That I Didn't Break Your Heart' retain their eloquence, but where previous Eels tours built towards their comforting, hopeful send-off, this show is pure up.

At the end of the night, E comes back to the stage for one last song, his guitarist The Chet by his side. E is not one to talk much during shows, but he takes this opportunity to say a few words.

"We want to thank you for making this a very special, fun night," he says. "It's been a while." The crowd roars in response, happy to have him back. "We appreciate it very much," he adds. And then he goes into the delicate opening guitar chords of 'A Magic World'. The audience knows the song well — it's a story about new beginnings. It's a story about a newborn baby filled with excitement at the amazing possibilities that await him.

Because he uses first-person even when he's singing in the voice of a fictional character, sometimes it can be hard to know what's autobiographical in his songs. But 'A Magic World' is very much taken from his life, inspired by baby photos of himself that he discovered in the attic of his childhood home. It's a song about the bottomless optimism and idealism that children possess when they're born — a rare Eels song to unabashedly embrace such purely happy emotions. It's an intriguing way to end a concert, suggesting perhaps that E has reached a point where he too feels born again, although not in the religious sense. (By all accounts, he remains a devout atheist.)

E has documented the many twists and turns of his emotional journey, not only in song but also on the page. With the publishing of his great memoir, *Things The Grandchildren Should Know*, in 2008, he grappled with the heartbreaks of his life while detailing the musical adventures that helped him transcend those traumas. It's a terrific read, but it only presents one aspect of what E and Eels have meant to their fans. For example, E's autobiography doesn't delve very deeply into the collaborators and friends who have known him over the years and who watched him evolve as an artist and as a person. In addition, *Things The Grandchildren Should Know* obviously lacks the critical distance to examine fully the highlights, challenges and missed opportunities of E's canon, not to mention its outright silence in regards to some E material that ranks with his best recorded moments.

These are but some of the reasons for the existence of the book you're now holding. Some would argue that E's story has been well covered by the man himself, but as any songwriter knows, the experience of a song only half-belongs to the musicians who make it — the other half becomes interpreted, celebrated, re-evaluated and judged by those who listen and take it into their hearts. With this in mind, *Eels: Blinking Lights And Other Revelations* is an attempt to make sense of E's life and enormous creative legacy through the perspective of a music critic and long-time fan, as well as through the memories of those whose personal insights can help create a three-dimensional portrait of one of America's most distinctive, valuable and underrated songwriters of modern times. Twenty years after the release of his first solo record, *A Man Called E*, such a book is long overdue.

After tonight's show at the Galaxy, E and his band head off to Japan and Australia. But for us to understand how E has reached this phase of his life — to understand how he has not just survived but thrived in a creative climate that has become increasingly inhospitable to artists such as himself — we head to Virginia to take a closer look at that newborn who nobody called E. Back then, he was just Mark.

Chapter One

He was born on April 10, 1963 in a hospital in Washington, DC, and at least one of his parents was thrilled at his arrival. Named Mark Oliver Everett, he was the first son of Hugh Everett III and Nancy Gore Everett, who lived in nearby Alexandria, Virginia. He had an older sister, Elizabeth, whose friends called her Liz. She wasn't yet six, a large age gap between siblings, and in truth Nancy had been pregnant once before Mark, but she lost the child in a miscarriage. However, that wasn't going to stop her from getting pregnant again — even if her husband was against the idea.

In a diary she kept many years later, Nancy acknowledged that Hugh didn't much want a family, but for her it was a way to "validate" their marriage. She clung to the hope that perhaps fatherhood would grow on him, "like the pets". It was a funny way to put it, but by all accounts not entirely inaccurate. Hugh had been equally unexcited about the birth of Liz. He and Nancy were dating when she announced to him in the fall of 1956 that she was pregnant with Liz. His response was to ask her to get an abortion. Nancy countered that she was keeping the child, adding that she didn't want to get married if the only reason was the pregnancy. That November, they got married, but as Hugh Everett III biographer Peter Byrne noted, he may never have fully honoured his new bride's request for their marriage to be more than just an arrangement for the child. "Everett was charmed by baby Liz,"

1

Byrne writes in *The Many Worlds Of Hugh Everett III*, "but, consumed by his career and the pursuit of leisure, he left the nurturing to Nancy. If she wanted to raise children, that was between her and Dr Spock."

The career was Scientific Warfare Analyst at the Weapons Systems Evaluation Group, or WSEG. Hugh was working for the Pentagon for a group that, according to a 1979 study prepared by Institute for Defense Analyses research analyst John Ponturo, was concerned with "bring[ing] scientific and technical as well as operational military expertise to bear in evaluating weapons systems... employ[ing] advanced techniques of scientific analysis and operations research in the process." Put simply, Hugh was conducting war games. In the wake of the atomic bombs dropped on Nagasaki and Hiroshima at the end of World War II, nuclear war had become a growing threat, one that the US government wanted to be on top of. Consequently, the Department of Defense (which only recently had been renamed from the Department of War) recruited physicists to calculate the extent of death and damage that would be generated by different war scenarios involving nuclear weapons.

As for Hugh's "pursuit of leisure", it was, ironically, a by-product of the climate in which he made his living. Because of the fear that nuclear annihilation would destroy humanity — and that this would be happening sooner rather than later — American culture began to embrace an anything-goes mentality around its margins. In her book, *I Was A Cold War Monster: Horror Films, Eroticism, And The Cold War Imagination*, critic Cyndy Hendershot touched on this odd phenomenon. "The Cold War period in American history was an age when taboo and transgression became highlighted," she wrote. "As taboos were emphasised more and more in 1950s America the allure of transgression was heightened." Creatively, this shift was signalled by sexually charged horror films, which reached their peak with 1960's *Psycho*, but regular Americans were experiencing it, too. As Byrne observes in his Hugh biography: "If the world was going to end in a radioactive bang, better have some 'fun', reasoned many middle-class Americans."

For Hugh, this meant affairs. And while Nancy tried to appear hip and modern by accepting his dalliances — even trying her hand at being a swinger herself — her decision to stop using birth control and to get pregnant with Mark was at least partly provoked by her annoyance with her husband's promiscuity. But her hope that Hugh would warm up to their children never quite happened. As Mark himself put it in his forties: "I think he thought of us kids as experiments and wanted to let the experiment play itself out." Or as one of Hugh's physicist co-workers recalled to Byrne: "I never met Hugh's kids, and he never talked about them."

McLean, Virginia is about a 20-minute drive west of Washington, DC and 25 minutes north-west of Alexandria, Virginia. Mark and his family moved to McLean when he was two. In 2000, the city's population was nearly 39,000 — in 1970, it was 17,698. "It was a pretty sleepy little place," says Bobby Read, a musician who moved to McLean around the same time as Mark did. "There was very little commercial stuff. There was a small shopping centre. There was a Hardee's, there was a sports shop. There was not very much [there], though I must say it grew very quickly in the years that I lived there."

Part of the reason for McLean's quick growth was the influx of government employees. The Central Intelligence Agency opened its headquarters in nearby Langley at the end of 1961, with the building becoming fully occupied by May of the following year. Read's father was an analyst for the CIA, eventually doing daily briefings for the President. "There were two branches," Read says of the CIA. "One was a covert branch and one was a non-covert branch." Read's father worked in the non-covert sector, but Bobby got to experience the other group first hand. "I actually worked at the CIA for a summer job," he recalls. "You know, pushed a mail cart around. I saw the father of one of my best friends there. And he came up to me and he said, 'Don't you dare tell Frankie you saw me here'."

Hugh worked a little farther away, at the Pentagon, but Mark grew up only knowing that his dad did... well, something secretive for the government. In their basement was a Teletype machine that was hooked in to the Pentagon. If that wasn't disconcerting enough, guns and boxes of food sat in the basement as well, creating a sense throughout the house that Hugh was prepared for the worst and perhaps the rest of the family should be, too. If Hugh's children were rattled by his doomsday strategising, he was too preoccupied to notice. A chronic drinker and smoker, Hugh didn't have much time for Liz or Mark, being more concerned with writing computer code or brewing home-made wine than properly raising his kids or even getting to know them.

"When you're a kid, whatever is going on inside your house seems normal to you," Mark said about Hugh's rather passive form of fatherhood. "It didn't seem odd to me. I didn't find myself longing for my father's attention because it was never there. If it had been there and then taken away from me, that would be different. But it was just never an issue. It was just the way it was." To Mark, Hugh was simply an uncommunicative guy who fell asleep on the couch watching the *CBS Evening News*. "The only time he ever resembled a human to me is when he would get down and play with the dog on the floor occasionally," Mark said in a 2009 interview. "But otherwise, there was no sign that there was a human inside that body. It was more like a piece of furniture or a robot was in the house." It was only later in his youth that he realised that not all dads were like his. "I barely had any conversations with him while he was alive," he said, "even though he was always there. He was always a mystery to me."

His mother, Nancy, was her own puzzle. Almost exactly nine months older than her husband, she was born on February 13, 1930. Where her husband abhorred nature and athletics, she grew up in a family that loved the outdoors — in fact they ran a wilderness camp. Growing up in Amherst, Massachusetts, she rode horses and hiked. Raised in Bethesda, Maryland, his sporting interests were poker, ping-pong and, later, drinking alcohol and chasing women.

In Byrne's biography of Hugh, Nancy's journals suggest that she always thought of herself "as a child trapped in an adult's body". If she thought she was hiding this feeling from her son, she was mistaken. Mark described her as "very childlike in some ways" in his autobiography, thinking of her more like a sibling than a mother when he was growing up. ("Nancy was funny," says musician Mike Kelley, who grew up in McLean around the same time. "That has to be where Mark got his humour — Nancy could crack you up. She would say the funniest things — I'm not sure it was [always] on purpose, but sometimes I thought it was.") Nancy and her husband could not have been a more perfect cliché of a Cold War couple: he was the breadwinner and master of the household, and she was the dutiful wife, caring for the kids while secretly harbouring resentments against a society that looked dimly on women asserting any sort of independence. But that inequality was intensified by the fact that Hugh wasn't just any husband. After all, how many men could claim to have written to Albert Einstein — and gotten a letter back from the revered scientist — by the age of 12?

"I didn't know he was a famous physicist," E said of his father, "because [back then] he wasn't that famous because he wasn't taken that seriously... But occasionally something would happen — I was aware that there were some *Star Trek* episodes and *Twilight Zones* and whatnot that were based on something he had written. And sometimes it'd be something like a neighbour would be playing in a hammock or something next door, and he'd come running over with a science-fiction book he had been reading that afternoon and say 'Hey, Hugh is in this!'"

The "something he had written" was 'On The Foundations Of Quantum Mechanics', a thesis Hugh completed while at graduate school at Princeton. An incredibly complex argument — especially for those of us largely ignorant of physics — 'On The Foundations' was Everett's stab at scientific greatness. To simplify Everett's ground-breaking theory immensely, he postulated, at the age of 24, that there are innumerable universes in which every different outcome for every event is possible. Consequently, each possible outcome causes the universe to split into different branches, one for each outcome or decision. (For those who grew up with the *Choose Your Own Adventure* children's books — in which the reader would be confronted with different decisions for the protagonist, with each choice pegged to a different page to continue on to — Everett's theory espoused the belief that all those different choices were going on in their own parallel realities. The book, in other words, contained all the parallel universes.)

As mentioned, this is an exceptionally rudimentary explanation of Hugh's theory, but for its time Hugh's notion was considered highly controversial, butting heads with the era's leading theory, forwarded by Nobel Prize-winning Danish physicist Niels Bohr, the so-called godfather of quantum mechanics. Bohr believed that everything in the universe behaved according to one of two quantum principles, depending on whether the object was larger than an atom or not. Hugh's theory argued against Bohr's separation of items, instead placing everything under one category of classification in order to determine its behaviour.

Bohr, at the height of his acclaim and standing, disapproved of Hugh's theory and told him so. As cliquish as any other group, the scientific community huddled around Bohr and rejected Hugh, who left academia soon after to work for the government, where he could earn a far larger salary than he would within a university's ivory towers. But over time, Everett's so-called "many worlds" theory began to take hold, particularly in the world of science-fiction writers, who used this radical proposal to construct stories involving parallel universes. (The short-lived 2009 American TV sci-fi drama *FlashForward* paid direct homage to Hugh and his son by, among other things, including photos of both men tucked away inconspicuously in the background of the programme.) Eventually that acceptance spread among the leading physicists, so much so that those who came to agree with his theory named themselves Everettians. ("I think by default I have to be an Everettian," Mark once responded when asked if he believed his dad's theory.)

But mind-bending, cutting-edge physics was not the concern of young Mark. Even on the cusp of stardom decades down the road, he wasn't quite sure how to explain his upbringing. "I don't know, it's hard to talk about without sounding melodramatic or corny," he told the *Los Angeles Times* in 1996. "I just... came from a family where we really weren't emotionally in touch with each other whatsoever. We grew up in this suburb in Virginia, and it should have been fine, but it wasn't. My dad was this genius guy that was just off in his own world. He was always there physically, but to this day I can't tell you anything about him. I just didn't know him at all... There was two kids, me and my sister, and we were kinda on our own basically... We had no idea what we were supposed to do with our lives..."

He and his sister may have had no idea, but at least they had each other. Most people who grow up in thrall to music have an important person in their formative years who turns them on to great songs. Maybe it's a family member or a best friend. For Mark, it was Liz. She introduced him to the albums of Neil Young, whose Seventies records provided a road map for the sort of eclectic, challenging, uncompromising career that Mark would follow in his own artistic journey. "I think one of the concerts that made a big impact on me was when I was 16," Mark said later. "My older sister took me to a Neil Young concert — this is when we lived in Virginia — and it turned out to be the *Rust Never Sleeps* concert, but the album *Rust Never Sleeps* hadn't been released yet…I was just expecting Neil Young And Crazy Horse to get up and jam in front of us but it was like this mind-blowing, theatrical presentation that not only had Neil Young never done before but that *nobody* had ever done before. And it's still maybe the best concert I ever attended."

But beyond her impeccable taste in singer-songwriters, Liz was a kind-hearted older sibling, allowing Mark to pal around with her and her friends, giving a painfully insecure little boy a safe haven. He could not have been clearer about her importance to his early years than when he told *Word* in 2008, "I learned everything I knew from her."

"They were brother and sister without question, man," says Kelley, alluding to their similar sensibility. "Mark had the wit, and Liz had the wit. She was as sharp as Mark."

"She loved Mark," says Timo Goodrich, who met Mark when they attended Churchill Road Elementary. "I found it kind of astounding — if you have siblings, you have a way you interact with them, and then when you see another family and see the siblings, you go, 'Wow, that's strange'. My brother used to give me a noogie every day, but she just adored Mark. She was really very motherly towards Mark, and vice versa. It was quite apparent that they had a special relationship. Whatever might have happened in the household, they would comfort each other."

Mark was lucky to have Liz because, frankly, there wasn't much of anything else around to grab his interest. Beyond the plethora of government employees living in his neighbourhood who had moved there because of its closeness to DC, he felt surrounded by what he referred to as "the real Virginia people", who were to his mind nothing but rednecks.

Granger Helvey, a musician who met Mark in the early Eighties, understands what Mark means about McLean's "redneck" contingent, but only to a degree. "There's so much Civil War history here," Helvey acknowledges. "So you still see a lot of pickup trucks with rebel flags in the back window — or, you know, Stars-and-Bars bumper stickers. There's still a lot of Confederate spirit." But for Helvey, who grew up in Roanoke, a Virginia town much further away from the hustle and bustle of the DC area, moving to northern Virginia was almost culture shock. "I thought [the McLean area] was far from redneck," he says, "but at the same time you didn't have to go far to find a pickup truck either. There was still that element."

Luckily, though, Mark's father's job kept him shielded from the elements of Virginia he detested. "They lived in a kinda upper-middle-class, upscale neighbourhood," Helvey says. "They were not wanting. I don't say that there was a pomposity or an arrogance there, but, you know, I can see where he might think that he was maybe just a cut above the rest."

"I view them as a kind of quintessential Cold War family," says Byrne, who also grew up in northern Virginia. "They weren't really rich or anything, but they were well-off. They could afford everything that they needed. It was kind of a typical nuclear family — you know, the two parents and the two kids and the house and the dog and all that. And having grown up in that culture, I was very familiar with the difference between the outward appearances and what was going on inside the family. A lot of people felt the Everetts were kind of normal."

"You can just say I didn't get enough love," Mark explained in a 1996 interview with the *Los Angeles Times*. "I mean that's the simple way to say it. People like that spend their whole lives working against it, making up their own memories. It's just a really lonely, desperate way to live your life, you know." But while Mark has talked about the lack of discipline he received from his parents, who were awfully permissive of their children, at least one friend of his from that time says it wasn't entirely out of the ordinary.

"Growing up, there were the grown-ups, and then there were the kids," says Goodrich, whose father also worked for the CIA. "And every now and again, we ran into each other. In that environment, so many [parents] were like, 'Oh, [we] have to go to the country club', so a lot of us were running around — there was no focus. Today, I'm noticing parents are *totally* focused on their children. That was not the case back then — they were basically, 'OK, we had you, we wish you well, good luck, we'll see if we can save some money for college'. Parents had their thing going, and they were living their life. So we weren't abused by any stretch, but they were living their life."

Goodrich remembers that when he and other friends went over to Mark's home, Hugh seemed utterly oblivious to what was going on around him. "His dad used to always be smoking Kents," Goodrich says. "He'd walk around in his blazer smoking his Kents and jotting things down and going into some door that we never really knew where it went. And then he would come out, walk into another room, writing something down, look up and say, 'Oh yes, there's five kids in my living room — hi'."

But even if Mark's parents were largely absent as parental figures, in hindsight he realised that they had actually been supportive, even if it was in their own unusual way.

"I do have to give him credit," Mark said about his dad. "He let me play drums in the house every day." The boy had purchased his first kit at a neighbourhood garage sale at the age of six. His parents gave him the $15. "And I wasn't like most kids who buy a toy drum set from the garage sale next door and play it for a week and then lose interest in it. I played them every day for 10 years. And I have to take that as some sort of endorsement that he let me do that in the house. Because I know now, as an adult, that if there was some kid playing the drums every day for 10 years, I'd go insane."

From such humble, loud origins began Mark's interest in playing music. And when Mark reached his teens and started playing in bands, his dad showed enough awareness of his son's activities to borrow the name of one of Mark's groups, Monowave, for a software company he financed in the late Seventies.

Years later, after his father had died, Mark would speak to one of Hugh's closest friends, physicist Donald Reisler. Mark asked him what his father would have made of the fact that he had become a musician. "I think, if your father had had the emotional vocabulary, he'd have been very, very pleased with what you did with your music," Reisler responded.

But that was a long time in the future, when Mark was well into his forties, almost everyone referred to him as E, and his mother, sister and father were all gone. Enough years had passed that when he was writing his memoirs he was able to be nostalgic for the home that had caused him so much grief as a child. "Some nights, all these years later," he wrote, "I'll sit here and think about when I was really young and how great it felt when things were OK and we were all there in the house: my father reading the paper, Liz playing Neil Young over and over in her room, my mom laughing her goofy laugh at something that wasn't that funny to begin with. When I think about the feeling of being in the middle of that, I'm overwhelmed with desire, like I'd give anything to spend a night back there again."

But first, like all young people, he had to rebel against the comforts of home. He did it in two ways — one that opened the door to his future, and another that could have prematurely slammed it shut.

Chapter Two

"There was no artistic community whatsoever," Mark once said about McLean. "Everyone was either a drug addict or a redneck. Or both, which usually ended up being the case and was the worst possible combination. I think I wasted so much of my life there, but I didn't know what to do with my life and didn't really care, like everyone else around me. I was a drummer. That's all I did for years — play drums, from the age of six to 18. That was my entire identity — the young kid who played drums really good with all these older bands."

One of those older kids was Mike Kelley, a local keyboardist who was closer to Liz's age. Kelley's younger brother, also an aspiring musician, was good friends with Mark, and so Kelley got to experience Mark's talent firsthand when he was still just an early teen. "He had this god-awful Plexiglas set," Kelley says. "It's a real harsh plastic drum set, but it was full-sized. My younger brother and him, they were just starting out — they were young kids — and they were beating around playing Zeppelin probably. And I noticed this young kid Mark had a great sense of the backbeat. He was a pretty loud, physical drummer, but he had good metre, and he had something that is kind of fleeting in some drummers: he had some mass to it. He could kick it even as a young kid."

Perhaps not surprisingly, Mark's focus on music caused him to largely live in his head — a trait he later realised he shared with his father. "We're both ideas men," he said in 2008 in an interview with *The*

Guardian. "I understand that you can be so busy sorting our your ideas in your head that there isn't time for much else." However, he didn't inherit his interest for creative expression from his father — more than likely that came from Hugh Everett III's mother.

Katharine Kennedy Everett died around Christmastime the year before Mark was born. In contrast to her son and his wife, she was a bit of a bohemian, divorcing her husband and pursuing a career as a writer, getting published in everything from *Catholic World* to *Harper's Bazaar* to *The New York Times*. She was a poet, short-story writer and teacher. In 2005, Mark would speak a little bit about her poetry's impact on his songwriting. "My grandmother's work is passionate, full of life and longing," he told *The Sunday Times*. "That was an influence on me, that vibrancy is something that I strive to achieve."

But Katharine also had to work as a researcher and secretary in order to support herself. And according to Everett biographer Peter Byrne, she suffered from manic depression. Hers was not an easy life, which prompted Mark's mother to refer to Katharine as "a truly tragic person", someone who could never quite fit in with conventional, traditional society.

Hugh had a chilly relationship with Katharine, living mostly with his father after the divorce, although she tried to instil in him a love of writing. (It didn't take.) But beyond her passion to create art, she passed along to Mark another trait that would factor into his later work: her principal inspiration was her own life, which she returned to again and again in her stories.

Mark was a bit of a lost child throughout his adolescence. Though he was bright, school bored him, and he had a sense of insecurity in part instilled by a first-grade teacher who thought he was cheating on a test and wouldn't stop harassing him until he admitted it. He finally acquiesced just to shut her up, but the humiliating effects of the confrontation have lingered all his life, leaving him with a guilt complex. In addition, he wasn't very athletic and was, according to his childhood friend Timo Goodrich, "kind of an awkward-looking kid". If all that wasn't enough, he had an overbite and big lips, although the overbite eventually developed into an underbite in seventh grade when, as he mentioned in *Things The Grandchildren Should Know*, he was so upset over a girlfriend who dumped him that he "kept [his] mouth in a locked, stone-faced position."

His escape came through his imagination. He staged puppet shows and sold tickets to the neighbours. He pretended to be a DJ on the radio, playing records for his family through a speaker while the rest of them were eating dinner. And in third grade, he made the basement of their two-storey house his bedroom, where he would endlessly play his drums. It began a tradition, that has continued throughout his life, of playing music in the downstairs portion of his residences, far away from the outside world.

Though Mark hated school, his first musical performance happened in the cafeteria of his elementary school when he was still only in first grade. He drummed along to a recording of 'The Star-Spangled Banner'. His mini-concert was warmly received. The lesson he learned from the performance? Music was the only safe way to express himself in the world.

For those who knew him growing up in Virginia, music was Mark's life. But perhaps in part because he didn't have parents who actively or demonstratively encouraged him to pursue it as a career — or maybe because his grandmother Katharine had to have other jobs to pay for her writing aspirations — it took a while for him to seriously consider making music his life's pursuit.

In the meantime, he listened to records, drummed, and got into all kinds of trouble. Twice in ninth grade he was suspended, most memorably for drinking on school property and giving head to his girlfriend. Mark didn't reveal in his memoir exactly when he lost his virginity, although he noted that he and his sixth-grade girlfriend would "take off all our clothes and get under the covers of my bunk bed's bottom bunk where we'd try to have sex". (And according to Byrne's biography about Mark's dad, this behaviour wasn't necessarily frowned upon by Mark's parents, who "allowed [their children] to drink, smoke dope, and have sex with friends at home".) Mark admitted in his memoir that he would skip school and snort coke, although Timo Goodrich remembered him more as a drinker than a heavy drug user. "It's amazing we all lived through some of the *shit* that we did," Goodrich says. "And this was going on on a weekly basis."

If anything, Liz was even more of a handful than her younger brother. "Anything I did, she'd done worse before me," Mark told *Word*. "I was a walk in the park compared to her." Byrne's book mentions that Liz's parents were warned about her behaviour as far back as elementary school, notably on one occasion when she "was running around the building and playing among the cars". She sent obscene drawings in the mail to at least one of her friends. And in her teen years, she was promiscuous — according to Mark's autobiography, "Everyone wanted to fuck her, and probably did."

But while Liz helped usher Mark into the world of beer and bongs, she also passed on her record collection to him. And although she helped get him into Neil Young, he was starting to pick up his own favourites, too. One of these was John Lennon. When Mark was 10, his favourite record was *Plastic Ono Band*, Lennon's stark, unforgiving and candid first solo album. Taking into consideration the musical path Mark would later forge, his affinity for the album made perfect sense — it was a record that turned therapy into art. As an added bonus for an outsider like Mark, *Plastic Ono Band* was a commercial failure at the time, although it has since been hailed as one of Lennon's greatest achievements, on par with The Beatles' best records. In early 2010, he reaffirmed his love for Lennon: "If I had to pick an ultimate favourite," he told *Mojo*, "I would probably have to pick him."

Another act he adored was The Who. In 2007, he got to write the liner notes for the band's documentary *Fragments*, in which he spoke about their impact on his formative years. "When I was 12 years old," he recalled, "my older sister Liz took me to see The Who. I remember Keith Moon standing on his snare drum and floor tom to announce, with mock pomposity, a set of songs from *Tommy*. Then I had a laser blaze straight into my eyes for the first time. Now I wear Coke bottle-thick glasses."

But Mark bore the band no ill will from the incident. Instead, the devotion deepened, as he fell under the sway of the band's *Quadrophenia*. In the same *Mojo* interview, he said: "There's something uniquely teenage-centric about that album that's so comforting, it was like a warm blanket wrapped around you."

He also loved Randy Newman, a distinctive and brilliant singer-songwriter who in the Seventies composed piano-driven songs starring twisted narrators, sometimes grouped together on concept albums like 1974's *Good Old Boys*, a portrait of the American South that Mark especially adored. As an artist, Newman could be poignant, satiric and funny with equal skill. It was a hat trick Mark's best music eventually achieved as well.

Catching a showing of 1978's *The Last Waltz*, Martin Scorsese's superb documentary chronicling The Band's 1976 farewell concert in San Francisco, Mark quickly latched on to the band's drummer, Levon Helm. Hoping to eventually be more than just a drummer himself, Mark loved the fact that Helm both sang and drummed. He started going to Helm's solo shows just to pick his brain.

If his interest in Helm was driven in part by a desire to figure out how to advance his musical ambitions, then so too was the day when, at the age of 18, he read the 1978 Ray Charles autobiography, *Brother Ray*, which a close friend's librarian mother brought him. "[I]t's where I got the best career advice," Mark said 30 years later. "He explained that when he started out he was basically a Nat 'King' Cole impersonator and nobody cared about him and then one night he sang just like himself and suddenly everyone was interested. He said, 'You've got to make it stink of your own manure', which is a colourful way of saying you've got to find what's unique about you and go with it."

It's worth noting that those last two personal heroes of Mark's — Helm and Charles — came about during a time when he was starting to tire of his wayward lifestyle. This was enhanced by a frightening encounter at the age of 14 when he had to appear before a judge over an incident that occurred during the summer of 1977.

By that point, he'd already been quite comfortable taking his mom's Vega (which had a bumper sticker advertising NORML, the National Organization For The Reform Of Marijuana Laws, an example of Nancy's liberal bent) out for rides in the dead of night, even though he wasn't yet 16 and, therefore, didn't have a licence. But on this night, he ran a red light and got busted by the police, charged with both driving underage and car theft since he didn't own the Vega. Within a few days, a pal of Mark's swiped some property from a community centre, leaving behind a jacket Mark had loaned him. When the authorities investigated the burglary, they found the jacket, which had Mark's name on the collar. The cops picked him up at home, Mark unaware what had happened.

Now facing court dates for two separate arrests that, ironically, required him to be at two separate courthouses at the same time, Mark appeared in court for the car theft charges, an experience, he wrote later, that "scared the hell out of me". He was frightened that he might have to go to jail, but luckily that didn't happen: the judge simply gave him a stern talking-to and Mark had to pay a fine. Although he'd dodged a jail sentence, he was determined to change his ways, even if his permissive parents (and permissive sister, who had moved out to live with her boyfriend) weren't interested in reprimanding him. So he grounded himself and swore off drugs. (He still drank, though.)

"I do [remember] him going through, like, a serious phase and not being drawn in so much to the partying scene," Goodrich says. "He was concerned about his dad's drinking, and I think he might've been worried about Liz's drug use."

Beyond pounding away on the drums, Mark was also getting interested in trying his hand at songwriting. He had previously composed poems and songs for girlfriends, but in his later teens his approach took on a greater focus. "Toward the end of high school," he told *The New Times Los Angeles* in 2000, "I got a four-track machine and got into writing songs. They were terrible, but just like now, I kept trying to get better. I'm really not all that talented as a writer or musician, but I do work hard."

Mark graduated from Langley High in 1981, having recently turned 18. His senior picture taken from the Langley yearbook shows a smiling, chubby-cheeked young man with medium-length hair that contrasts with a photo from his sophomore yearbook of an unsmiling but still handsome, thin, long-haired kid. In his senior year, he had become the drummer of The A.S.A.P. Blues Band, a quartet that played a lot of rock covers, including tunes from ZZ Top and The Allman Brothers Band. The group's name might at first seem to be an abbreviation of "as soon as possible", but in actuality it referred to the fact that all the members except for Mark were in Virginia's drunk-driving programme called the Alcohol Safety Action Project. "We may not be *Masterpiece Theatre*," Mark told a reporter at the time, "but we have a good time with what we're playing."

When A.S.A.P. began to flourish, Goodrich (who wasn't in the band) noticed that girls started getting interested in Mark. "He had pretty girls, so we were all kind of envious that he could have any girl he wanted," Goodrich claims. And while Mark's autobiography charts the many heartbreaks he experienced in his youth from unsuccessful stabs at relationships, Goodrich sees the problem stemming from Mark's insistence on finding girls of "substance". "I'm sure Liz set the example of what he was interested in," Goodrich says. "Just someone that he could be honest with and be in a relationship with. I think that's what he was lacking — we weren't at that level yet."

Kelley also remembers Mark as a guy who didn't have problems getting attention from the opposite sex. "If he didn't have a girlfriend, then he was looking to have a girlfriend," Kelley says. "He wasn't shy. He'd call a girl up — he was a friendly guy."

Nonetheless, Mark was finally starting to establish himself as a singing drummer. "People would defer to him," Goodrich recalls. "Everybody in the band, they had egos too, but everybody was taking their cues from him. He wanted to implement things, make things happen. Other people would be talking about it and talking about it, [but] then, next thing you know, they're in college and gone. He was always coming up with the plan." And as Mark's musical confidence was beginning to solidify, so too did a nickname that would accompany this new identity.

Because there were several people in Mark's life who had the same first name as he did, "he [started] going by Mark E," says Granger Helvey. "And a lot of people just called him E — that was his nickname. I don't know so much in high school, because by the time I met him he was already out. But I know that a lot of us just called him E."

And so shall we from here on out.

Chapter Three

Our memories can be powerful, but they're not always accurate. When E published his memoir, he talked about an incident that happened in McLean that profoundly affected him. "Around the time I was 12," he wrote, "a plane crashed in our neighbourhood." To this day, he still remembers that he was watching the sitcom *What's Happening* when he heard a deafening explosion outside. Since this was during the Cold War, he initially assumed the US was being attacked.

He was wrong about it being an air raid, and he was also wrong about when it happened. In fact, he had just turned 14. The crash occurred at around 8:40 p.m. on April 28, 1977, when a corporate aircraft owned by Southern Company Services, a power company, departed from DC and was bound for Birmingham, Alabama. Instead of reaching its destination, it exploded in midair and fell into the Everetts' neighbourhood. All four passengers, including Southern Company Services' president and executive vice president, died. More than a year later, the National Transportation Safety Board released its findings, indicating that "ground witnesses saw an explosion in the sky followed by the wreckage of the aircraft falling to the ground. The sky was overcast and light rain was falling... One residence and two automobiles were destroyed by impact and fire and several other homes were damaged by falling debris." The cause of the explosion was blamed on "a failure or malfunction of an undetermined nature in the pilot's altitude indicating system which led to a loss of control and overstress of the aircraft structure." (Apparently there had been whispers at the time that the crash wasn't an accident but, rather, an act of corporate espionage. The National Transportation Safety Board concluded that, "There was no evidence of either lightning or bird strike damage, nor was there any evidence that an explosive device had detonated.")

But while E had misremembered the time frame of when the crash occurred, one part of his personal recollection was eerily correct. In a piece written by Jeanne McChesney (and assisted by Jean Jonnard) for the McLean Citizens Association, there's a note that one of the Everetts' neighbours, the Dennis Clarke family, "narrowly escaped injury when a section of the aircraft crashed into the back of their house." What were the Clarkes doing at the time? "The family was watching a TV show entitled *What's Happening*, in the family room, when the plane struck."

But the specificity of exact dates or years means less in the grand scheme of things than how those events affect us. And for E, the harrowing scene outside his door would always stay with him. "I ran toward the huge funnel of smoke that was lit up in the night sky by flames and emergency lights," he wrote, "passing seats and ashtrays and body parts that were littered all over the neighbourhood. One house had been completely levelled and there was a group of bodies all lying in near proximity by the park. As my bare feet hit the asphalt, I sped up and thought about how these people were just alive but now they were dead, and how much I felt alive at that moment."

It was an extraordinary juxtaposition of sensations — being surrounded by death yet feeling astonishingly alive. Without his trying to seek it out, it's a juxtaposition that would keep revisiting him in the years to come.

E has dubbed it, with his reliable gift for deadpan sarcasm and mordant wit, "The Summer Of Love". The summer of 1982 was a miserable time for him. A year removed from high school, he was very much adrift. Although he had largely straightened himself out after years of heavily consuming illegal substances, he was living at home and working at a gas station. For the most part, he seemed to like the job, enjoying its ability to give him time to think and be by himself without being burdened with demanding tasks. (And it's funny how gas stations have occasionally popped up in E's lyrics — one appears in the closing track off *Electro-Shock Blues*, while another is featured prominently in a skit that kick-starts the exceptionally hard-to-find *Bad Dude In Love* LP.) Still, he knew that such an existence wasn't enough to fulfil him. A friend and occasional Eels collaborator, Jim Jacobsen, says of E: "He has learned this peculiar little artistic expression of his that he developed as a teenager: 'I wanna be a rock star'. It's what has kept him sane and healthy in the world. I don't know that he would have made it if he was still pumping gas; I don't think he'd be OK."

But E wasn't the only man in his family having problems. During the summer of 1982 the US was in the grip of a crippling economic downturn. In fact, at that time it was the nation's most severe recession since the Great Depression of the Thirties. (For those too young to remember the recession of the early Eighties, the more recent downturn that occurred at the end of the Noughties actually supplanted it in terms of its severity.) Hugh Everett III was feeling the pinch acutely. Juggling multiple car loans, paying two mortgages on his home, watching a travel agency he backed plummet into the red, owning a pricey condo in the Virgin Islands (where he would bring Nancy and other women, whom he'd hit on without apology), Hugh was in serious financial trouble, never mind that the man was still drinking and smoking heavily. Because he was so wrapped up in his own troubles — and also because doting on his children was never his interest — he was blithely unaware of the deteriorating state of his daughter.

Early in the summer one afternoon, right around her 25th birthday, Liz walked into the upstairs bathroom of their home and grabbed a bottle of sleeping pills. She emptied the bottle down her throat. If her boyfriend hadn't phoned the house, which prompted the family to look for her, she would have died that day. Fortunately, the paramedics arrived in time, wheeling her into the emergency room with mere moments to spare.

E recalls that his father's response when he found out was: "I didn't know she was so sad." Reading his response in print, it's hard to know if his comment was made with bemusement, clinical apathy, genuine concern or some combination of all three. And judging from the general ignorance of the comment — equating Liz's commitment to ending her life with being "sad" — it's fair to say that Hugh simply wasn't in tune with his daughter's deep suffering. But to be fair, neither was her mother, who upon finding Liz's unconscious body just assumed she was napping on the bathroom floor during the middle of the day. (She did, however, give Liz literature on Alcoholics Anonymous on occasion.)

According to E's memoir, Liz had by this time already become an alcoholic and was dabbling in heroin. She had a boyfriend — from the way E describes it, just the latest in a long string of losers — who suffered from severe personality disorder and who once attacked E with a knife. Plus, she was changing and, as E put it, "wasn't herself" any more. For the first time in his life, he started to actively dislike Liz, his personal refuge from school and home.

Granger Helvey had met E after that summer and remembered E and Liz bickering a decent amount. But while she was, in his words, "a real hellraiser," Helvey didn't recall at the time thinking Liz was in any particular danger. "We were all partying, we were all carrying on," Helvey says. "If I were to step back and not have been so much of a willing participant in the partying and the lifestyle, I might have been more concerned for her safety. But, being caught up in it all at the same time, she was just one of the life-of-the-party kind of girls, always laughing and having a good time. Of course, not to dime-store analyse it, but a lot of people who are loud and gregarious and wearing the lamp shades and everything, sometimes they're hiding that darker side or that pain — you know, trying to anaesthetise, self-medicating, all of that. But she seemed like she had a good attitude. She wasn't a mean drunk or anything like that. She was just kind of on the wild side. I think that there obviously were demons there that no one that I knew who knew her had any indications of." (For what it's worth, E definitely remembers Liz as what might be described as a mean drunk.)

At 19, E had already experienced a decent amount of death and near-death situations: the plane crash, his sister's almost-successful suicide attempt. Depending on how much meaning you ascribe to the randomness of the universe — a subject which Hugh Everett III spent much of his academic and professional career trying to master — you could say that these previous events were preparing E for what would come next. Or you could just say that God has an awfully wry sense of humour.

On a Sunday night in July, E was doing something he almost never did: talking with his father. With Nancy and Liz away visiting family, the Everett men were hanging out at home. They had little in common, but on this night they chatted about poker, which E had only recently started getting into. (According to two musicians who have toured with Eels, E still enjoys playing cards.) E could probably count on one hand the amount of actual conversations he had with his dad, but tonight was one of them. E went out later that night with his friends, but not before noticing that while his dad was lying across the couch, as was his custom in the evening, something was off. Hugh's head was by the end of the couch where his feet normally were — a small thing but certainly a break from tradition. E gave it a moment's thought, but decided it was nothing and headed out the door.

It's amazing how sharp our memories are when they're attached to intensely powerful emotional moments. E remembers coming home later that evening, flipping on the television and watching a rerun of Charles Grodin's 1977 appearance on *Saturday Night Live*. It would be interesting to know if E also remembers the unusual conceit of that particular episode. During the show's opening, John Belushi expresses concern to Gilda Radner that "this Chuck Grodin guy" has barely shown up all week and even missed dress rehearsal for that night's show. With that setup in place, Grodin would appear in sketches and foul them up, accidentally saying other cast members' lines instead of his own, seemingly flummoxed by a skit's premise, and not realising that the show was live. It was, of course, all an elaborate put-on — and an example of the sort of prankster spirit that E would later incorporate on occasion into his own musical career.

But on that July 18 night, all E knew was that his father had gone upstairs to bed. When E woke up the next morning, he couldn't shake the sense that something seemed weird in the house and he went upstairs into his parents' bedroom. His father was dressed in the same clothes he'd had on the night before, and he was on top of the made bed. E called to his dad. Hugh didn't respond. Terrified, E phoned 911. The female operator told him to put Hugh on the floor so that she could talk E through how to perform CPR on him. He told her that Hugh's body was stiff. She knew what that meant, and he probably did as well, but neither of them said the words.

As his mother and sister were still with family in North Carolina, he was alone in the house with his dead father. The paramedics arrived and removed the body, as E was crying and clutching a copy of *Newsweek*, the magazine his dad loved reading. And that's when it happened: the paramedics took Hugh out of the house in a black bag without the use of a stretcher. One of the great physicists of the 20th century was carted out of his home in something that looked like a trash bag. The scene permanently scarred E. "I've never been able to shake the images of my father walking into his house one night and then being carried out in a black bag the next day," E later wrote.

Dead at the age of 51 from a heart attack, Hugh had finally suffered the consequences of his astoundingly unhealthy lifestyle. His autopsy laid out a grim picture of his physical condition at the time of his passing. He had an enlarged heart and an inflamed prostate gland. He suffered from high blood pressure and arterial sclerosis. If all that wasn't enough, he was also legally drunk.

Nancy was concerned that her son blamed himself for Hugh's death, perhaps believing that if he had done something that night before going out with his friends he might still be alive. So, that autumn, once E had left home and tried (rather half-heartedly) to attend college two hours south in Richmond, his mother wrote to him. After watching a PBS programme on heart attacks, she had deduced that "you wouldn't want to save anyone after the first four minutes anyway." Furthermore, she wrote, "I think he knew it was inevitable, but he also wanted to spare us any worry over it."

Hugh's wishes, unsentimental to the end, were that his ashes be dumped in the trash. Half a lifetime later, E reflected on his dad's unusual request. "I don't have him around physically," he told *Clash* in

2005. "[But] every time I throw something out it's like, 'Hey dad!' It's nice to have him around."

For anyone fortunate enough not to lose a mother or father at an early age, it's impossible to imagine what E's life must have been like in the wake of Hugh's passing. But for at least one friend who knew him at that time, it seemed that even in those early days E was beginning to forgive his father for his shortcomings.

"We never had any in-depth, sitting-over-a-beer kinda conversation or heart-to-heart about it," Helvey says of E. But he said that E "spoke rather reverently about his father. I could see that there was a lot of respect there. He talked about some of his dad's scientific and professional accolades. He bragged on his dad." But as would be the case with others who would know E during future hard times, the young man wasn't looking for shoulders on which to cry. "He didn't go into a whole lot of emotional talk about his feelings towards his father other than just expressing his pride," Helvey says. "I remember asking about his dad at one point, and it was more like he was reading me his résumé."

The year E spent in college at Richmond was highly unproductive, unless you count his short-lived flirtation with skydiving. But like many undergraduates who go off to school in part to learn what they *don't* want to do for a living, E quickly realised that university life (or anything being taught there) wasn't for him. Though he still couldn't comprehend the idea of becoming a professional musician, he returned home to McLean and set about putting together songs on a second-hand four-track. He used an old guitar of his sister's, his mother's family's piano, and his drum kit. Soon, he upgraded his musical arsenal to include a synthesizer and a drum machine, which made him a rarity among his peers who tended to only play one or maybe two instruments. "He was a drummer, but he also played a mean piano and guitar, not to mention banjo," Goodrich remembers. "He had this crazy voice that just sounded good when he sang — he could get that guttural sound."

As for his career plans, E seriously considered starting a tow-truck company since, as with his old gas-station job, it would provide him time to think. In the meantime, though, he worked for a music teacher who dealt with troubled teenagers. He enjoyed working with the kids and playing music with them, and eventually he was hired at another school to perform the same task with younger children. He also did some substitute teaching. The guy who had grown up dreading school was now the authority figure.

Of course, E probably was comfortable in a position of authority because of his family situation. Nancy was still coping with the loss of her husband, a situation that would leave anyone feeling emotionally out to sea but in this case undoubtedly heightened by her distant manner. "His mom was very sweet," Helvey says. "I really liked her a lot," although he acknowledges that "she wasn't your typical housewife. I mean, obviously at that point she was a widow and a single mother with a couple of budding adults. [But] I remember her being just a very pleasant person. She wasn't gregarious. She wasn't particularly outgoing. She was just very friendly and very sweet." As for Liz, she was plummeting faster in her downward spiral. She was raped by a group of black men, which left her harbouring racist feelings towards African-Americans and, according to E, provoked a massive change in her personality. He had come to hate the rednecks in his community from an early age, but now Liz was acting like one of them, which must have been a bitter pill for her brother to swallow.

Liz's suicide attempt during that traumatic summer of 1982 was more startling, but E too had at least pondered the possibility of killing himself. "Sometimes you're in such a bind that you just need some idea that there's a way out of it," E admitted in a 2008 interview with Q magazine, "but I never got to the point where I was planning it out. Not too specifically, anyway."

Besides, he had a better way out of his misery, which was through his music. The son of an atheist who grew up never going to Sunday school or believing in a divine being living up in the clouds, E focused on songwriting while everything else around him seemed utterly awful. But in his darkest moments, he did call upon a higher power. "When I was younger," he wrote, "I remember trying to make a deal with God where, if he'd let me make music, I'd try to help people."

E's father would surely have scoffed at this heavenly deal his son had tried to make. As Byrne's biography indicates, Hugh as an undergraduate put together a "'logical proof' against the existence of God that caused one of his professors to despair of religious faith." Indicative of his willingness to provoke the powers that be — which would continue a few years later when he confronted Niels Bohr with his controversial, nose-thumbing "many worlds" theory — Hugh was attending Catholic University at the time he concocted this proof. Hugh would continue to air his no-God theory on occasion throughout his life, the sort of intellectual puzzle that can't be solved but makes for fascinating dinner-party conversations (or, perhaps, fights). We'll never know if God heard E's prayer for a career in music. But a career he would soon have — although probably not as soon as E would have liked.

Chapter Four

E's last major band during his days in Virginia was The Toasters, a five-piece that came together around 1983 out of the ashes of a number of defunct groups from the area. The line-up consisted of E on drums, Richard Aspinwall on guitar, Mike Kelley on keyboards, Chris Ivy on lead guitar and Granger Helvey on bass. And while other members of the group also contributed some lead vocals, according to Helvey there was no question who was the front man. "Mark was the driving force behind The Toasters," Helvey recalls. "He exuded leadership from the beginning."

The band quickly became popular in the local scene, working up a set list of 40 or so songs they could play on any given night. "We were basically hitting the wave of classic rock that was coming into play in the mid-Eighties," Helvey says. "We were primarily a covers band. We did some J. Geils Band, Outlaws, Doobie Brothers, a lot of Southern California rock that came out of the Seventies, Leon Russell, Commander Cody And His Lost Planet Airmen — classic rock with a roots feel to it and a little bit of rockabilly."

Kelley's memory is that The Toasters were even more eclectic than that, incorporating Willie Nelson, Smokey Robinson and The Jackson 5 into their repertoire as well. "It was a democratic band," says Kelley. "What was cool about the band was we didn't really have any ego problems. Mark was wide open. He was up for anything."

E was already working on his own songs by that point, but to be booked in local clubs one needed to play material the patrons already knew and loved. "The venues were very few and far between that really catered to original music," Granger says. "So you had to focus on those covers that would get you in the door — and then you would slip in your originals. Like out of a 10-song set, we might try to slip one or two originals in there and hope nobody noticed. Maybe they might even like them." And although E was positioned behind the drum kit, that didn't keep him from serving as the host for the evening, introducing songs and band members with a talkative exuberance he rarely exhibited off the stage.

"I remember him smoking and drinking the occasional beer," Helvey says. "He was not a heavy partier or heavy drinker. I don't know that I remember him ever doing drugs. I'm not saying that he didn't take a toke off a joint or try this or that. And I think that may have been one of the things about Liz that caused a rift between them — she was really, at times, off the deep end. And he was much more controlled and under control — sometimes to the point of almost being a little too stiff. When he would let his hair down wasn't through drunken laughter or silly stoned behaviour — it was more when we were playing music. I mean, he would go to town on the drums. He sang from behind the kit, man, and he would just wail. Such a powerful voice. I think that was his release, you know? All this pent-up energy flowed out of him when he was playing."

The Toasters' set list would come together from suggestions made by individual members, who picked songs within their vocal range. Kelley says that E would encourage the band to go with whatever moved them. "If you like a song, just do it," he says. "In other words, don't try to fit a song into the band — just go with your heart." And beyond being a tight, well-loved band, they were also an intricately arranged vocal group, thanks in large part to Helvey's contributions. "Mark was the lead vocalist, and I would be a close second in terms of lead vocal assignments," Helvey says, "but I also liked harmonies so much that I didn't mind singing backup. Mark's voice hasn't changed that much over the years. It's got that sort of raspy, smoky flavour to it. He does a wonderful job with leads, but he wasn't much of a harmony singer.

I don't think it was his forte. I loved being able to organise the others' vocals, who all had good voices. But there are lead singers and backing singers, and then there are singers who can do both. They really are unique skill sets and abilities, and I think that I was better suited to be the sidekick, the backing vocalist, and I enjoyed mustering the other guys together to back Mark up."

The band's rising popularity was clear from the fact that they started opening for nationally touring outfits, such as the late-Seventies North Carolina arena-rock group Nantucket. And their shows' atmosphere suggested the tone E would pursue in his later concerts. "The Toasters was kind of irreverent," Kelley says. "It didn't have to make any sense." According to Kelley, E's attitude was, "This is a party onstage — just enjoy it and don't think too deeply about it. He'll do the deep thinking for you. We had what we called stage gags — you'd bring a bunch of bananas, stick them on the piano, and people would say, 'What's with the bananas?' And you're like, 'Well, I don't know.' You know, we'd dress in a bear costume or something like that."

E's openness to the funny non sequitur onstage was in part inspired by his and Kelley's mutual love of Leon Russell, an iconoclastic singer-songwriter of the Seventies. "He's a little flamboyant," Kelley recalls of Russell. "We chased him all over the local scene for a month, wherever he went. We shadowed Leon's tour. Mark liked — I don't want to say theatre, but he liked that [Russell] didn't take rock'n'roll real serious. By that time rock'n'roll was a little disappointing to both of us. We didn't really like the rock that was coming out."

But despite The Toasters' ability to fill venues with fans and friends, the band didn't last. Within a year, the group had played their final gig, a pal's wedding, and E was looking toward the future. But although he was feverishly working away on new material, an out-of-the-blue opportunity presented itself to him and Helvey around the same time. A club owner who loved The Toasters was working with a guitar-and-keyboard band in Atlanta that needed a drummer and bassist to go out on the road.

"Mark and I talked about it," Helvey remembers. "They were going to put us up in a house which would double as our rehearsal space, and we would get a $200-a-week allowance, which was good money for a guy in his twenties in the early Eighties. We'd be playing music full time." But the two ultimately balked, for very different reasons. "I think I was a little bit chicken to make such a big change in my life — just quit my day job, pack up and move to Atlanta," Helvey admits. "Mark, I think, was more inclined to do it, but the more he thought about it, he didn't want to go be a back-up player for a couple of other songwriters. He wanted to do his own thing."

In his memoir, E talks about that drive to make his own music. Giving up on college, he churned out a wealth of songs, "a weird, naïve mix of pop, country and soul with a synthesizer and drum machine." His autobiography creates the impression that these experiments were simply things he did for himself, but in fact he graduated beyond four-track cassette albums to something more advanced in late 1984. And although he's downplayed its existence for most of his later career, the very first E album to appear on vinyl was unveiled in 1985, seven years before *A Man Called E* (his first official solo record) hit stores.

It is an album called *Bad Dude In Love*, a labour of love E put together with several of his former bandmates and co-producer Bobby Read. Unavailable for purchase, the album came to the attention of Eels fans in 2005 when a copy of it popped up on eBay. The truly fanatic can venture to the Library of Congress in Washington, DC to hear the album on vinyl, but beyond the occasional online torrent leak, the 11-song collection has remained largely a mystery.

A journalist asked him about it in 2010, and E tried to play coy, until finally downplaying the record by saying: "That's just one of, like, a zillion tapes I made when I was in my early twenties that happened to get pressed up on a small quantity of vinyl as an experiment. It's not like actually an album. It's just one of millions of things like that I did."

"I have that," future E collaborator Parthenon Huxley says with clear pride. "I stole one from his house. I found his stash and said, 'What the hell is this?' E said, 'No, no, no, no! You can't have that!'" After Huxley swiped it, he had to hide it at his house because E would come by and try to steal it back.

Perhaps not surprisingly then, E never mentions *Bad Dude In Love* in *Things The Grandchildren Should Know*, although there is one veiled reference to the album. Relating a story from their childhood when Liz stole his drumsticks, he remembers vowing that when he became a musician he would name one of his albums *No Thanks To Liz*.

That moniker didn't become the name of *Bad Dude In Love*, but it appears at the very end of the album's liner notes. But what's contained on the vinyl is far more interesting, charming and revealing.

Combining eight originals with three covers, *Bad Dude In Love* certainly suffers from some dated sonic influences, but it's a consistently satisfying early glimpse into E's songwriting and record-making talents. Demonstrating a sense of humour that would be evident throughout his later work and a playful energy that has rarely been so overt since, the album captures a young man not yet 23 who's trying to shake off the recent death of his father and the misery of his generally boring life with synth-heavy rock and soul songs.

But the album's carefree sound was the exact opposite of E's preparations before the record. Prior to heading into the studio, he enlisted Helvey's help with back-up vocals, eventually crediting him with "vocal harmony arrangements" along with his assistance on bass and percussion. "It was very intense," Helvey remembers. "I think 'intense' is the best word to describe Mark in general — a little bit of a brooding personality even back then." The two hung out at the Everetts' family home, "working on parts and arrangements and whatnot."

Helvey recalls E's mom being a very friendly presence in the home, but the atmosphere was all business as he and E set about working on charts for the *Bad Dude* material. "I'm into the mathematics of the music and the structure and the rhythm and the metre and the harmony," Helvey says. "Harmony is very mathematical. I'm all into the science as well as the art. So I would sit down and make very meticulous notes. He dictated the arrangements, so I was more or less the court reporter recording everything that spilled out of his mouth. And then as far as the harmonies and everything, I threw in ideas about, 'Well, maybe we should do a shadow vocal here, or a straight harmony there'. He made all the final decisions. We worked closely together, just the two of us."

Another crucial collaborator was Read, who was several years older than E and had already begun a career as an engineer and recorder in the area. Living in nearby Falls Church, Read operated his studio Soundscape out of his home. Read had never met E before the *Bad Dude* sessions, and E's interest in working with him was largely based on practicality.

"I was recording a lot of bands in the area," Read recalls. "I was doing sound at The 9:30 Club in DC when it first opened [in the early Eighties]. It was a big alternative music centre, and I guess I just had a little rep around for doing good stuff. And, you know, I was cheap — I had a home studio with an eight-track. There certainly were big, expensive 24-track studios around at that time, but he didn't have a lot of money. So we were a good match in that way."

Neither of them spent any time worrying about getting to know each other on a personal level during the sessions — the work was what was important. E built the songs piece by piece, starting with laying down drums. And if this was the first time he'd ever made a proper record, he certainly didn't let on that he was a novice. Even 25 years later, Read remembers being impressed with how organised and self-assured the young man was during the recording process — something he rarely witnessed even in artists older than E.

"He just was confident all the way through the thing and moved quickly," Read says. "I was able to keep up with him creatively and technically, and the thing came together fast, but he always knew what he wanted to do and just went for it. He clearly had a vision of what he wanted to sound like, and I was happy to go along for the ride."

Bad Dude leads with its freewheeling attitude on the opening cut. The album's first 28 seconds concern a skit in which hapless Mark is running late to his gas-station job and promptly gets fired by his boss, who's tired of his tardiness. From there, a drum machine and synthesizer announce the start of 'Everybody's Trying To Bum Me Out', a line he would use later on 'Flower' from the first Eels record, *Beautiful Freak*. Perfectly capturing an era in which Bruce Springsteen's *Born In The U.S.A.* and radio smashes like 'Let's Hear It For The Boy' and 'She Works Hard For The Money' celebrated the plight of blue-collar Americans trying to make ends meet, 'Everybody's Trying To Bum Me Out' was a giddy, knowingly cheesy nod to working-stiff pop. Buoyant and clearly designed for radio play, the song finds the protagonist explaining that despite all the depressing things around him, he's not going to let it get him down. In this way, the track stands as a mirror image of what E would often do later in his career: rather than making sad songs about trying to hold on to optimism, this was a bubbly number that insisted that the right attitude was all you needed to overcome your blues.

"He definitely made me laugh a lot of times," Read says about the process of putting the album together. "All of the lyrics have some funny parts to them. I mean, there's a couple that are more serious, but I feel like he just has a great sense of humour in all this stuff. A happy spirit."

That sense of naïve, limitless possibility also presented itself on the three covers. Two were of songs previously recorded by The Temptations, 'Too Busy Thinking About My Baby' and 'I Can't Get Next To You'. These were songs that reflected the two sides of puppy love: the former was an ecstatically blissful salute to a special someone, clearly modelled after Marvin Gaye's rendition of the song, while the latter was a pained lament for a woman who won't give the singer the time of day. And while 'Too Busy Thinking About My Baby' was a glorious presentation of Helvey's skills with background vocalists, credited on the album as "The Ever-Etts," 'I Can't Get Next To You' was a showcase for Mark's vocal gymnastics, handling all the different parts as if he was a one-man Motown group.

"He seemed to be coming out of an R&B kind of place," Read says. "And what was great about it is he was, you know, unabashedly a white dude. And I never got the feeling he was trying to sound like a soul singer. He was just being himself, never questioned himself and let himself do all these wacky things that he did."

Bad Dude also featured a version of 'Burning Love', which had been made popular by Elvis Presley, an early indication of E's love for The King. "I'm a fan of all the Elvis periods," he said in a 2003 interview. "You put on any Elvis record — maybe particularly the ones that are considered his worst — and the thing that jumps out at me is the humanness of the voice, the vulnerability. You hear all the insecurity of him. And I love that. That's what I want ... the human experience."

"Mark was a student of rock'n'roll," Kelley says. "I mean, this is before the internet, right? The boy just *knew*. If you would talk about so-and-so [artist], he could talk off the top of his head about their history and discography."

But despite its embryonic artistry, *Bad Dude* contained hints of his later career, perhaps most overtly on 'The Girl In My Neighborhood', a silly love song whose chord structure would later be recycled for 'Rotten World Blues', which was part of a four-song EP included with 2001's *Souljacker*. Look past the Prince-cum-Cars new wave influences, and *Bad Dude* stands as a template for so much E and Eels music that would soon follow: the lilting piano ballad 'I Just Wanna Be With You' in particular contains the DNA for the searching, heartsick material that is essential to the appeal of everything from *A Man Called E* to *Electro-Shock Blues*. All of that was still many years away and perhaps impossible for E to even envision at this point. But according to Mike Kelley, who played on the record, there was a sense that *Bad Dude In Love* sparked something in E.

"You can tell he loved it," says Kelley about the album's recording process. "It was creative, and I think that's the bug that got him. He saw all the possibilities of how he could express himself musically through recording. At that time, all he had been doing was performing and writing his own little stuff and maybe laying 'em on cassette. But now this was a bona fide production. I think that really lit the fire under him."

In the album's liner notes at the bottom, there was an inscription that read "This Record Is Dedicated To Hugh Everett, III." "I remember [E] said, 'My dad made this possible'," Helvey says. "You know, his dad had helped him with drum sets and keyboards and encouraged his music — he certainly never discouraged it. I think [E] was very reflective — the little bit of conversation that we had about his father's passing was, 'God, I wish I hadn't have been such a shit'. I think there was a certain melancholy there because maybe he wished his relationship had been a little better with his dad. He never expected his father to pass away like that."

Once the album was completed, E brought together *Bad Dude's* musicians and supporters for a cookout at his house to celebrate, which stemmed from a weekend ritual already firmly in place. "Every week, he [had] a volleyball thing," Goodrich says. "So everybody would come to his house to play volleyball, which was really kind of neat — nobody else thought about doing something where it was, like, an ongoing event every week. It developed into something big, where we had 20 people on the weekend playing volleyball. That was the place to be, and the thing to do."

Regarding the album-party cookout, Helvey recalls that "It was like a wrap party for a movie project." A group of friends and players (including Helvey, Kelley and Goodrich) gathered near a fence to have their photo taken, which ended up as part of the *Bad Dude* packaging. "I enjoy looking at it from time to time," Helvey says fondly of the picture, which shows E lounging on the grass donning sunglasses, shorts and a half smile. Not in the photo is Kim, E's girlfriend at the time. If Goodrich's assessment of E's early dating woes was accurate — i.e. an inability to find a woman who had the maturity and self-assurance of Liz — then it appears that Kim represented in part a corrective to some of Liz's more extreme traits.

"She was the girl that he dated most of the time that I knew him," Helvey says. "I remember her as being a very cool chick. I remember her being very supportive of Mark's music. You know, a lot of times they're called 'band widows', but she wasn't [the sort of] girlfriend who sat there with her legs crossed, filing her nails, being impatient, waiting for rehearsal to be done. She was all into it, from what I recall. Now, I'm not saying they didn't have their times, when maybe [she felt like] the second fiddle. But my recollection of her was that she was very fun, light-hearted, smiling — I guess you could say a good counterbalance to the more brooding, quiet, introspective Mark. But yet she wasn't also off the handle like Liz — she wasn't a wild-ass party girl. She was just a very friendly and very sweet woman."

Helvey still remembers the day when the first vinyl copies of *Bad Dude* (credited to "Mark Everett") were delivered, saying that E was about ready "to wet himself" with excitement. "I remember going over to his house as soon as I got off work," says Helvey. "I went over there and saw the cardboard boxes full of albums. Getting one of the first albums out of the first box was just beyond thrilling."

Seeing the physical copy of the record might have been deeply satisfying for Helvey, but E was already thinking about the next step. "I remember him saying something to the effect of, 'I'm out of here'," Helvey recalls. "'I'm saving my money, I'm getting my stuff together, and I'm outta here'. He knew that he needed to be in a music town. And DC had a wonderful history and a wonderful pedigree for musicians who had made it big over the ages. But I think he needed a more eclectic audience and he needed to find a place where he could find people of a like mind in greater numbers. So I think he knew when he made this album that it was just so he had a product. He had something: a résumé builder, a calling card."

Still, E was not someone who wanted to appear as if he was obsessed with commercial success. "I'm sure he could have been another Rolling Stones if he wanted to," Goodrich speculates. "I don't know if he wanted to. You know, I think he really enjoyed what he did — he tended to laugh at people who were chasing the fanfare, the glory." Nonetheless, E was enterprising enough to set up a PO box for his newly created Joe Mama Records and tried to promote the *Bad Dude* album by selling "two-sided *Joe Mama Records/Bad Dude in Love*" T-shirts for seven dollars, which included postage.

After the intense period working on *Bad Dude*, Helvey lost track of E and eventually formed a new band. It wasn't long until Helvey learned from mutual friends that E had left town.

Kelley had talked to E right before he took off. "I didn't realise how badly he wanted it until he was just about to move out to California," Kelley says. "He was over at my house, and we were sitting around watching TV. And he said that he was gonna move out to California. He was gonna go for it. That's when I realised that he was really committed. Up to that point, I just knew that [music] was something that he really liked — I didn't know how bad he wanted it. He said, 'Yeah, I'm gonna go out there and make some records. And when I

go out there, I'm gonna call you and you come out and play some.'
And, I'm like, 'Yeah, yeah…'" Kelley laughs. "In my mind, I'm like,
'Yeah, I'll see you in six months when you're broke.' I wasn't gonna
say anything, but, you know, a lot of people wanna move to LA and be
movie stars and whatnot. I'm pragmatic. I'm thinking, my cousin tried
that. And how many people wanted to go to Austin and play music, or
they wanna go to Nashville or LA? But Mark had a — I don't wanna say
a vision, that sounds kinda grandiose — but he had a plan, maybe, and
he had the fortitude. The boy went out there and he showed everybody,
man. I'm just so damn proud of him."

Writing in his memoir, E described his rationale for escaping McLean
for good: "I need to get the fuck out of this suburban wasteland and go
on some kind of adventure." And if he was worried about leaving his
sister behind, that hardly mattered — Liz married her latest boyfriend
in 1987. As further proof that her taste in mates hadn't improved with
age, the guy was a drug dealer. He was also incarcerated when they got
hitched.

When Helvey found out E had left, he wasn't terribly surprised —
the signs had been there since Mark had turned down the Atlanta gig. E
had an album under his belt and a desire to make something of himself
through his music, even if it was not yet fully-formed. "He knew that
he had kind of an unconventional voice — not what you would call
a classic voice," Helvey says. "Even then, he knew that he was going
to be more like Jackson Browne, a great writer. I think Mark knew all
along that he wasn't the best singer, and he might not be the best player
or best songwriter. But he was just going to do his thing. He was the
best Mark Everett."

Chapter Five

When Hugh Everett III was 24, he composed his theory on parallel universes. When E was 24, he packed up his car with all his belongings and moved to Los Angeles to become a musician. While the son's undertaking might seem pathetically insignificant in comparison to his father's — frankly, anyone's would — it did not come about without its share of challenges, risks and courage that were equally momentous.

E knew no one in Los Angeles — he had chosen the city over New York largely because it was further away from McLean. And judging from what we know of his adolescence, the only previous time he'd been in Southern California was when he was an older teenager and had driven his sister's car home from Orange County — she had just ended a disastrous relationship in Hawaii with a guy who was in the army. E had no plan in mind once he got to Los Angeles — he called a sister of an old girlfriend who lived close to San Diego to find a place to stay. But like his dad, whose theory was long ridiculed before eventually being embraced, E simply went for it, consequences be damned.

The exact time of E's arrival in Southern California has been a bit of a mystery, although there are enough clues to narrow down the period when it could have happened. On the Eels' website, his official bio says that he was 24. In his memoir, he mentions "navigating through a terrible ice storm in Oklahoma" on the way to Los Angeles. Shortly after arriving in LA, he relates a story in the book about running into

Angie Dickinson when she was on hand for the dedication of rock singer Billy Vera's star on the Hollywood Walk Of Fame. A cursory glance at meteorological records uncovers that an ice storm pummelled the middle of the country (including Oklahoma) over the last week of December in 1987. And Vera received his star on February 16, 1988. Somewhere in between those two time periods, E began his LA adventure.

His first place of his own was in the Valley, north of Los Angeles in Burbank. The sound of airplanes buzzing by his bedroom was excruciating, so he focused on writing songs, holing up in his closet with his four-track recorder. He worked remedial jobs and, by all accounts, was utterly miserable. But he kept working on music. The way he saw it, what other choice did he have?

But while those early years in Los Angeles were a struggle, littered with endless rejections from record companies, they did have their bright moments. He met Little Richard while standing in line at the post office. "I nervously told him I was a fan of his work and he couldn't have been nicer," he wrote in his book. "He even had God personally bless me."

Then there was the night he bumped into Joni Mitchell at a nightclub. As he told *Billboard* in 2005: "I went up to her, because she was one of the first famous people I'd seen in the flesh, and she was extremely nice to me, and talked to me all night." This was a recurring theme in E's early brushes with celebrities. Whether it was meeting Levon Helm back in Virginia or his first encounters with the famous in Los Angeles, it's striking that there was something about E's demeanour that made these people want to talk to him, which is hardly assured when "commoners" engage with the stars in public.

By early 1989, E had started working for *Music Connection*, "The West Coast Music Trade Magazine" that, as its masthead proclaimed, had been "published every other Thursday since 1977." His title at first was receptionist but he eventually got bumped up to "administrative assistant." Regardless of the title, though, the job was essentially the same.

"Mark worked the front desk," *Music Connection* CEO Eric Bettelli says. "At that time, I think it was 11 to 4 pm. He worked for my office manager, and I think he used to work 25 hours a week. I think his pay was $7 an hour."

There's a picture of *Music Connection*'s 16-person staff that appears in the magazine's year-end issue of 1989. Gathered around a *Music Connection* banner, everyone's wearing a jacket, a button-down shirt, slacks or a suit — everyone except E, who's in the back row wearing a ball cap and a T-shirt.

"He was a moody kid," Bettelli says. "I had a couple of — I wouldn't say run-ins with him, but big disagreements. He was just always down. I mean, I liked the guy. He was a little too moody for my cup of tea. That's the front desk — you know, people would come in the office, he's the first guy to answer the phone. You want somebody a little more bubbly, and he seemed down a lot. I know he had this horrific childhood — his family stuff was pretty crazy." And while Bettelli couldn't remember specifically what E had told him about his family, he remembered it came up in conversation during the two years E worked at *Music Connection*. In regards to E's moody behaviour, Bettelli says that his employee had an explanation for it. "He told me he had Epstein-Barr," says Bettelli.

This wasn't a con E perpetuated on his bosses to mask his total disinterest in the job. Moving to Burbank, he began to be convinced that his new apartment was bad for his health. In the liner notes to his B-sides collection, *Useless Trinkets*, E talks about a song, 'Dog's Life', that was written during the time "I lived near the Burbank airport, which I later learned was a neighbourhood full of poisoned water from the Lockheed plant." A former manager, who remembers E claiming he had Epstein-Barr, says E was convinced "he was living on top of a toxic waste dump." E later moved to a slightly better place about 30 minutes southeast in Atwater Village, where apparently the biggest health concern was gang killings.

E continued to toil away writing songs and trying different styles. If he wondered why his music wasn't impressing anyone at the record labels, he needn't have looked any further than the cover of the first issue of *Music Connection* during his stint as an employee to get some hints. One of the headlines of the January 9-22 issue of 1989 reads, "Anatomy Of

A Hit: Poison's 'Every Rose'." As a trade publication that focused on the business side of the music business, *Music Connection* analysed the chart success of 'Every Rose Has Its Thorn', hair-metal group Poison's breakthrough power ballad, the sort of slick, syrupy, baldly commercial tune that was nothing like the music E was concocting — or was interested in pursuing. "The beginning of 1989 sees Top 10 singles in a state of flux," scribe David "Cat" Cohen wrote, mentioning that the current chart heavyweights included everything from balladeers Chicago to metal band Guns N' Roses to pop singer Anita Baker. In a mainstream marketplace that was splintering as different audiences embraced different genres, Cohen recommended that would-be hitmakers stick to their strengths. "What one needs is an established following in one's genre and a song that widens the market appeal," he wrote.

Reasonable advice for the newcomer, to be sure, but E couldn't have been further from the tenets of popular music at that moment, even though he was quite close to that world geographically. In the two years he worked at *Music Connection*, the company was on Sunset Boulevard in the heart of Hollywood, right next to Sunset Sound, the legendary studio where parts of *Exile On Main Street*, *Sign O' The Times* and *Pet Sounds* were recorded. Manning the receptionist's desk, E worked in a windowless room that was approximately seven feet by five feet. "It was really this tiny little box," Bettelli says. During E's tenure, disposable pop princesses such as Taylor Dayne and Wilson Phillips were on the cover when the likes of Kip Winger, Cher, L.A. Guns or Richard Marx weren't. (One of *Music Connection*'s cover stars did later cross paths with E — The Bangles' Susanna Hoffs would co-write a track for *Broken Toy Shop*.)

But while it was surely a tough time for him, wondering if he was wasting his life as thoroughly in Los Angeles as he had been in McLean, the same publication did provide hints about a possible future niche he could inhabit. In *Music Connection*'s April 1989 "Songwriter Profile" column there was a piece on Aimee Mann, then the frontwoman of the new wave band 'Til Tuesday. The band had tasted pop success with their 1985 synth-heavy ballad 'Voices Carry', but Mann had slowly developed a reputation as a serious, introspective songwriter.

Speaking with *Music Connection*'s Pat Lewis, Mann said: "A song already has its own life. You just have to be sensitive and tune into its life. If you take the time and think about it long enough, it *will* come to you." As for the charge that she wrote in a confessional tone, Mann was quick to deflect that label. "I write honestly, but not really confessional," she said. "I want the emotion of the song to be honest. Quite often I'll start out telling my personal story, but if I have to change details to make sure that that emotion remains pure, I will. There's a lot of fiction that has to go into it." Lewis went on to observe that "Mann is a strong-willed, driven individual. She does not make compromises in her personal or professional lives. She is adamant about her distaste for 'selling out' to become a commercial success." This sort of honest, distinctive songwriting was precisely what E was interested in pursuing — and to further drive home the similarities between Mann's and E's artistic temperament, Mann had grown up just outside of Richmond, Virginia.

About 10 months later — opposite an article about the Latin dance craze the lambada — there was a profile of another Los Angeles-based songwriter whose aesthetic seemed similar to E's. Michael Penn, the older brother of acclaimed actor Sean, had just released *March*, an ornate set of Beatles-inspired chamber pop that featured the breakout hit 'No Myth'. "In high school, I started diving into home recording," he told *Music Connection*, "figuring out arrangements and essentially making my own records." Like E, he wasn't interested in musical trends and was simply concerned with honing his craft. "[W]ithout any expectations, I sent a tape around and figured I was just going to keep writing and doing it this way for a while until some interest generated," Penn said. But unlike E, who wasn't garnering much excitement for his work, Penn was signed immediately, perhaps in part helped by having two famous brothers — there was not just Sean but also Chris, who had become a star through films like *Footloose*.

Michael Penn and Aimee Mann represented Los Angeles songwriters who had a powerful melodic sense but were unwilling to operate in conventional pop forms, instead exhibiting an intelligent, left-of-centre sensibility. (Their philosophical affinity culminated in a romantic relationship, and they married in 1997.) For E, a guy just a few years removed from Virginia, these blossoming artists had to provide at least some modicum of hope that he hadn't made a terrible decision by moving out to California.

But sharing a sensibility was one thing — getting someone on E's side was another matter entirely. "The whole time I was waking up early in the morning, finishing up the four-track I'd started the day before, going to the job, coming home and starting [a new recording]," he recalled in a 2003 interview with, of all places, *Music Connection*. "I was always making these little albums, ultimately to entertain myself. But I'd have a different album every month, and after a while people started to hear them...and didn't like them."

As during other periods of his life when he focused on music to the detriment of everything else, E was deeply lonely, with no social life to speak of. Asked if he remembered seeing E with a girlfriend, Bettelli says no: "He seemed always depressed. He was always down. I mean, it was hard to get, like, a smile out of the guy. He was just that kind of personality. He just seemed to be in his head a lot. He just seemed to always be thinking."

But while the *Music Connection* job was dreary, at least it allowed for numerous opportunities to connect with people working within the industry. "This is like the perfect day job for a musician," Bettelli says, "because he's dealing with musicians and music-working businesses and he's close to it. If you're going to have a day job, working at a music magazine would be a cool day job for a musician or songwriter. We've had a few hundred throughout the years." In addition, the bosses tended to be pretty lenient about low-level employees pursuing their musical dreams. "We never had a problem with that," Bettelli affirms. "It was cool, and actually in some ways it's even better because they can relate more to our clientele, our constituents, than someone who has no clue."

As part of the hobnobbing associated with the job, E attended a record-release party for Stevie Nicks' solo album, *The Other Side Of The Mirror*, during May 1989. On the way out of the party, he met John Carter, an Atlantic A&R executive who had previously been a songwriter, producer and promotion man. He had co-written Strawberry Alarm Clock's 1967 hit 'Incense And Peppermints' and later served as producer and co-writer on then-newcomer Sammy Hagar's first three solo albums in the late Seventies. He had also helped shepherd Tina Turner's comeback, working as co-producer of her 1984 quintuple-platinum album, *Private Dancer*. E struck up a conversation with Carter and gave the executive a tape of his songs.

"I don't remember that," Carter says when asked about their first meeting at the Nicks party. "Of course, at the time I was a mark and met a million people like that. So, to me, I remember having the tape. I was a good A&R guy — I listened to everything." If the specifics of the night elude him, Carter absolutely remembers "immediately reacting to [the tape], immediately calling him, immediately starting the dialogue." E recalls going out for groceries early the next morning and coming home to a message from Carter: "E, it's Carter. Great songs, great lyrics, great melodies. We'll talk." Carter didn't leave a phone number, but E called Atlantic and eventually got in touch with him.

"At the time I was really excited," E told *Music Connection* in the 2003 interview. "It was like, 'Hey, here's somebody who likes it'."

"I remember wanting to sign him when I was at Atlantic," Carter says, "and everyone laughing at me." Carter's bosses didn't see what had clearly so impressed him, in particular E's lyrical sense.

"To me, it's always poetry with a snare drum," Carter says, referring to the appeal of pop music. "I'm always looking for the lyricist. You know, melody, thank you very much — style, yeah yeah yeah. I can recite lots of great players, lots of great melodies — [but] if you don't have a lyric…"

However, despite Carter's enthusiasm, Atlantic wasn't interested. "So once again, the dreams were crushed," E said with a laugh in 2003. "I was used to it at that point."

Even though Atlantic had passed on E, Carter remained sold on the young man's commercial potential. "As far as pop music goes," Carter explains, "you have to appeal to women. Guys will get you eventually, but you've got to appeal to women, certainly as a solo singer-songwriter. And to me, he had the vulnerable male perspective."

Carter would have the opportunity to back up his faith in E when he was fired from Atlantic. In E's memoir, the songwriter says that he persuaded Carter to become his manager. According to Carter, the transition to management had already begun by the time they discussed it. "I was ready to go into management and try that for a while," Carter says. "I had already decided I was gonna move to San Francisco — I still think of myself as a San Francisco guy. I've had a lot of successes with artists there. I wanted to move up there, and I pretty much systematically made that move, knowing that I was gonna come down [to Los Angeles] regularly anyway. [E's tape] happens to be on my desk, and I'm passionate about it — and no one else on earth was talking to him."

The men agreed to work together: the talented novice and the seasoned veteran.

"Carter's one of those unique guys," future E collaborator Parthenon Huxley says, with clear affection. "He's done a lot of different shit. He's really funny, he's really weird, he's got his own tastes, and he's a character — he's a frickin' perfect Hollywood/LA music business character. He wrote 'Incense And Peppermints', so" — and here Huxley assumes the persona of a glad-handing music-industry veteran — "'he's had a number one, baby!' And once you get a taste of that, once you are a hit-maker, it's like, well, 'It can be done, 'cause I did it'."

Spend any time with Carter and you're immediately impressed by his almost scientific approach to the making of hits. He is a man of philosophies and theories, which are backed up by experience and cold hard facts. His demeanour is slightly intimidating without seeming combative — he's larger-than-life, but also quite charming. And by his own admission, he's a know-it-all.

"Over time here in the business, you study, you study, you study," Carter says. "You come up with generalities — I believe in generalities. And I realised a vast majority of short cuts to a hit. I have a big long spiel about proper nouns — it's *amazing* how advantageous it is to call your song 'Peggy Sue'. I see this chart, decades ago, of the Top 40 Jukebox Records Of All Time. Of the Top 40, 30 are songs with proper nouns — 'New York, New York', 'Hey Jude', bang, bang, bang. I was like,

'Oh my God, I get it — proper nouns'. The Rolling Stones' biggest hit? It's not 'Satisfaction' but 'Angie'. It wasn't 'Bridge Over Troubled Water' [for Simon & Garfunkel]; 'Mrs Robinson' was their biggest hit." (For what it's worth, three of the Eels' biggest songs — 'Novocaine For The Soul', 'Susan's House' and 'Mr E's Beautiful Blues' — fall into this rubric, just so long as you remember that "novocaine" derives from the proper noun "Novocain.")

Carter was tireless about getting his new client's music out to people. And Carter also had ideas about how to promote him, capitalising on his one-letter moniker. "I'd send out postcards with pictures of David Letterman," Carter says, "and on the back it would say, 'There's a new Letter Man'. Picture of a gas tank on 'E': 'We couldn't be more empty'. I ordered a thousand of just the Scrabble letter E: 'The Value's Only One'."

Still, no one was sparking to the material E was generating, seemingly unmoved by the pretty pop whimsy of 'E's Tune' or the melodic life-in-LA snapshot 'Fitting In With The Misfits'. After months of pounding the pavement for E's demo, Carter's breakthrough for his client occurred on a Saturday morning when he wasn't even trying.

"I had shopped it a little bit and gotten nowhere," Carter recalls. "I'm having a garage sale — I'm an insane collector of shit. At my garage sale, I'm selling some ghetto blaster and I'm playing my E demo. A friend of mine — record company A&R guy — says, 'What's this?' I say, 'It's E, you passed on him two months ago'." Carter's friend was shocked, replying, "I did? This really sounds good." Carter popped the tape out of the player and gave it to his pal.

The friend was Davitt Sigerson, a songwriter and producer who had worked with The Bangles, David & David and Carly Simon. (Previously, he'd been a rock journalist and critic, interviewing the likes of Van Morrison and Chic.) "A good friend of mine," Carter says. "I had definitely already given it to him — he was that close and someone I would automatically play everything for. [I would] expect him to get the quirky pop sensibility that E was at the time."

If this period was marked by crushing lows brightened by a few flickering moments of hope, the garage sale incident was an indication of E's fortunes possibly changing. It wasn't just the fortuitousness of Carter playing the demo at that exact moment and Sigerson responding to the songs in a way that he hadn't before — it was also that E had just dropped off the tape to Carter at the garage sale moments before Sigerson's arrival.

Speaking about the oddity of Sigerson liking the demo at the garage sale when he had previously been uninterested, Carter suggests that "it's all context," meaning that for any of us who listen to music, it's not always just the quality of the songs that matters. Sometimes it's being in the right place with the right sort of sound system, or hearing it with the proper mind-set. Or maybe — and this is the possibility that's easily the most maddening for aspiring artists trying to win over managers and executives with their songs — it's all one huge crap shoot.

Whatever the reason, Carter's second chance with Sigerson paid off. Sigerson sparked to the material and told E that he wanted to produce the young man's album and get him a record deal. E probably didn't want to get too excited, but he undoubtedly hoped his life was about to change. Before that happened, though, Sigerson's did. After a career in music, whether making it or writing about it, Sigerson was tapped to become president of Polydor Records in early 1991. Suddenly, it became a lot easier for Sigerson to get E signed to a label.

E learnt the news while at *Music Connection*. Carter called its Hollywood offices to give him the lowdown: E would have a two-album deal, although it wouldn't be a lot of money. But E didn't care — it meant he could quit *Music Connection*. ("It wasn't enough money," Carter later said. "I'm sure that he should have kept the day job.")

The last *Music Connection* issue to contain Mark Everett's name on the masthead was February 4-17, 1991. Mariah Carey, hot off the success of her self-titled début, was on the cover. ("I don't aspire to be Whitney Houston," she said in the article. "I'm a singer-songwriter, and writing is a major part of what I do.") After E stopped working for the magazine, Bettelli never saw him again. But shortly after E's departure, his old boss did run into him, sort of.

"I had very little kids at the time," Bettelli says. "My oldest daughter was three or four, and I used to take her to this gymnastic place in

Burbank, where there was a record store that had a picture of E. I went, 'Wow, look at that!' This was like a couple of years later or maybe a year later. I was just very impressed that, you know, a guy that worked for us got a *real* record deal. Not just an indie deal — he got a real deal."

More than 10 years later, E was still struck by the weird and random events that had led him to be "discovered" — without ever playing live, mind you — after years of fruitless struggle. "For all the thousands of people who heard my tapes over the years," he said in 2003, "it just took one who liked it — and who also happened to be the president of a record company."

And now E was finally going to get a chance to make a record — two, actually. And as he had demonstrated when he made *Bad Dude In Love* back in Virginia, he was in no way star-struck by the opportunity. On the contrary, he was charged up with clear ideas and a vision for his career moving forward.

In *Things The Grandchildren Should Know*, he recalled a breakfast meeting he'd had with Carter and Sigerson shortly after Sigerson had flipped for the demo. At the meeting, E laid out his artistic goals. "I had a lot of musical ideas in me and I wanted to grow and evolve, trying different things over the years," he remembered saying. According to E, Sigerson "said he thought I was going to get the chance to do that." E's aspirations were ambitious, certainly, but in hindsight his pronouncement could also have been considered a warning to those who would work with him. He was going to follow his muse wherever it led him, and he wasn't going to let anyone stop him. Coincidentally, Sigerson's response could be considered just as ominous: be careful what you wish for — you might just get it.

Chapter Six

If you talk to Carter about Eels, there's one thing he wants to know immediately.

"Any Eels fan I run into," he says, "I always ask, 'Got *A Man Called E*?' Any Eels fan that discovers the E records loves 'em."

The man who made them doesn't feel the same.

"I don't remember the last time I heard them," he told a reporter in 2005 about the E solo records. "It's the sound of someone who's still growing and not ripe for the picking, particularly in terms of production. The other thing is that the late Eighties and early Nineties were an unfortunate time in recording technology. But the real problem was that I didn't have a strong vision… it was more a matter of soaking things up, learning and, for better or worse, recording that process."

Just a few months after quitting his job at *Music Connection*, E was putting together his first solo record and meeting with music publishers. Landing at MCA Music Publishing, he spoke with Betsy Anthony, who liked his material and wanted to introduce him to one of her company's writers. It was a guy named Parthenon Huxley.

Affectionately known as Hux or P Hux by his friends, Huxley had started working at MCA in the late Eighties, paid to come up with songs that could be hits. It was a nice gig, except for one obstacle. "I don't know what a hit is," Huxley says. "I've always just written songs that I thought were great, and I've always been wrong. You know, I've had four Top 20s, but I'm never about that kind of thing. I just write stuff that I get excited about. I was blissfully naïve — I still thought that 'music' was the most important word in that phrase 'music business'."

When MCA suggested he team up with E, it was a potentially difficult pairing since both men preferred writing on their own. Plus, outwardly they seemed very different. At that time, Huxley was a real sight, sporting a half-beard and what he refers to as a "sideways mullet": a combination of short hair on one side and long hair on the other.

"Oh god, the things we do when we're young," Huxley says now about his early-Nineties look. "To me, it was just fun. I mean, I had half a goatee for six months — it's on one of my passports." Why did he do it? "It was, like, 'Let's do this — I live in LA, I'm in my thirties'. It was just something to do [that was] different... I mean, I had a garden with 'love' spelled out in flowers. I had TVs buried in my lawn. I was being artistic, right? It was another canvas to do weird shit on."

Huxley had been impressed with the four-track recordings E had made of songs like 'Are You & Me Gonna Happen', a beautiful ballad, and once they started hanging out they soon discovered how their writing styles could complement one another.

"I'm kind of a parts guy," Huxley says, "I can create parts all day long just by noodling. I would start noodling on guitar — even just like tuning up and noodling — and he'd go, 'What was that?' And I'd go, 'What was what?' And he'd say, 'That thing you just played — play it again'. And he would run with stuff. What's great about him is he's a finisher — we'd crash something together and then he'd say, 'OK, I want to go write the lyrics, I'll be back in a half hour.'"

One such experience led to a track that eventually became *A Man Called E*'s signature song, 'Hello Cruel World'. "I probably played those first two chords, the E and the F-sharp minor," Huxley recalls. "I was just messing around and he goes, 'What's that? Keep doing it'. We started into the melody — we would just start in, we just dove in. And it worked really, really well most of the time." From there, E crafted lyrics that sounded like a direct address to the misery he'd experienced in his life, managing to offset depression with a resilient, cheerful melody.

Excited by what they'd come up with, they went to the basement studio of MCA at Universal City, which offered a significant sonic step up from E's previous four-track concoctions. "We cut ['Hello Cruel World'] to 24 tracks with a pro engineer and the best compressors and the best everything," Huxley says. "And that's what led to me producing the record — Davitt Sigerson heard our collaboration and said, 'That's you guys working together? Well, why don't you two produce the record?'"

Recorded in May and June of 1991, *A Man Called E* was, like *Bad Dude In Love* before it, put together very quickly. "We didn't have much of a budget," Huxley remembers, placing it at around $20,000 to $50,000. "We had to be economical, we had to be prepared when we went in, to know what we were doing. So there was a lot of pre-production, which is a glorified way of saying sitting around my house or his house working on the stuff and making sure it was cool."

And as when he had made *Bad Dude*, E wasn't intimidated by working in a high-quality studio and with people more experienced than himself. "He was always confident in his stuff," Huxley says. "In his own way, I think he really knew what he wanted. So I don't think this was a mind-blowing experience for him. But I'm sure it was probably a relief, you know, to get some fidelity going and to have some access to a nice studio with somebody who is pretty simpatico to his thing. You know, I really liked his stuff, and we got along well and had a lot of fun. We were laughing our asses off most of the time we were working."

Perhaps just as important for E's development was his introduction to the Echo Park/Silver Lake/Los Feliz crowd who would shape his future recordings. Huxley lived on Baxter Street, a treacherous roadway. *Los Angeles Times* writer Bob Pool summarised it succinctly: "It's a lengthy, 32% grade that climbs a ridge east of the Silver Lake Reservoir, crosses over the top of the hill and immediately drops off on the other side. Unsuspecting motorists gasp when they reach the crest and discover the roadway in front of them has dropped out of sight and there is nothing but empty space in front of their car's hood."

"I drove on that every single day," Huxley says. "You know, you turn into the driveway and everything on your front seat just falls off."

Across the street lived another musician, film composer Jim Lang, whose home studio was used for *A Man Called E* and who played accordion and different keyboards on the record. "I walked over to the studio in slippers sometimes," Huxley said. "I was, like, cup of coffee and let's make a record — isn't LA grand?"

Ask Lang what his special contribution to the record was, and he's defiantly modest. "I had a studio, there were some instruments there, I was across the street," he responds. "I'm a real chameleon — it's kind of the nature of my film-writing thing, or maybe it's just me in general as a musician, but I like a lot of different kinds of things. I've worked on all kinds of different things and so as a consequence my hipster card in the Rolodex really doesn't come up as, 'Jim Lang: He's The Guy That Does *That* Thing'. I was kind of a utility player — I was a good-enough engineer to record the stuff, I had the shit we needed to record it, I was a good-enough mixer to mix it."

Lang's home studio at the time wasn't massively bigger than E's old reception desk at *Music Connection*. "It was two rooms in the basement of my house on Baxter Street," says Lang. "If you look at the house nowadays you'd go, 'There is absolutely no way anybody could record anything in there.' There was one long skinny room that had my console in it — it was a big long console — and all the outdoor gear. And then there was another room that was the recording room, which was also my office."

Beyond meeting Lang, who would add his stamp to several future Eels records, E also got to experience a whole new climate of creative individuals in the Echo Park neighbourhood where Huxley and Lang resided. As opposed to McLean, he now got to hobnob with the legitimately artsy, or at least be around people who were as serious about music as he was. In his memoir, E notes how much he liked "being around people that weren't only interested in pickup trucks and tractor pulls," although E would himself drive a pickup truck in his early years in Los Angeles. Nevertheless, Huxley and his wife, Janet Heaney, a film and television writer, were friends with artists such as X's John Doe and Exene Cervenka, as well as eventual Paul McCartney guitarist Rusty Anderson. "E was almost like part of my family," Huxley recalls.

"I mean, he started meeting everybody I knew, and in LA who doesn't know 55 artists?"

But it wasn't just the exposure to other artists that mattered — it was the opportunity for E to know that there were other people out there in the world that wanted to devote their lives to making music. "I think that probably was a nice thing for him," Huxley says. "I mean, he went out [to LA] completely on his own. He was just working and writing songs, and that was about it. So, making that record and meeting some musicians, it was probably a good social thing for him."

The confluence of different artists to the area was no accident. Echo Park, Silver Lake and Los Feliz were cheap, relatively safe sections of the city for those who were trying to scrape together a living while pursuing their dreams. "In '85, when I moved here into this neighbourhood, we bought the place on Baxter Street," Lang remembers. "It was pretty much the most affordable neighbourhood in Los Angeles. And that was because it was Funkytown. I mean, there were certain neighbourhoods [where] there were still chickens running around in the streets. It was old families who had grown up and raised their kids here — very lower-middle-class, working-class families, the mothers and fathers still living in the house, kids gone off to college and moved out. You know, old cotton-tops driving beat-up cars and then the huge Latino population, and basically that was it."

But while E's world was opening up, Liz's continued to implode. By this point, her situation had become even direr, as she found herself being checked into mental institutions. In October 1991, she wrote to E. "People just don't understand that it has nothing to do with whether things are going good or bad in your life," her letter said. "You just feel like shit, regardless." Later in her letter, she went into more detail about the depth of her misery. "Another thing I've been thinking about is when you were home and Mom said, 'I wouldn't want to be anybody but myself', and we both said that we'd rather be ANYbody than ourselves. I don't know anyone else that feels that way... Anyhow I've had that 'feeling of worthlessness' shit for ages."

★ ★ ★

The majority of the songs on *A Man Called E* were written solely by E. The exceptions were 'Hello Cruel World' and 'Nowheresville', another collaboration with Huxley that once again demonstrated a mash-up of yearning melodicism and distraught lyrics. The album as a whole, at just under 32 minutes, included songs that Carter had fallen in love with when he was trying to land E a deal, including 'E's Tune', the lovelorn 'Are You & Me Gonna Happen' and the touchingly autobiographical 'Fitting In With The Misfits'. Addressing his Ma — which is what he called his mother — 'Fitting In With The Misfits' is nothing less than E's letter home, reassuring Nancy that he's making his way all right in Los Angeles, enjoying the nice weather and digging the city's eclectic, artistic energy. A beautiful example of chamber pop, 'Fitting In With The Misfits' expresses all that E had hoped would happen when he moved far away from home, finally finding some sort of community that he could call his own.

But in his memoir, E said that *A Man Called E* makes him cringe these days, dismissing the album's "cheesy reverb and instrumentation." It's strange that he would disparage the material because, as Lang notes, he was clearly making the creative decisions for the project.

"It didn't seem like a first record at all," Lang says. "He has always been incredibly organised as a producer and as an artist — always a really active listener and an active, active, active participant in the production process. Very specific about his likes and dislikes. To my way of thinking, he was a very mature artist with a pretty good idea of what he wanted the songs to sound like."

In regards to E's dismissal of *A Man Called E*, Lang adds, "I don't know if he would say this in exactly the same way, but I think he kind of repented of this material because it was way more pop. You know, it was sort of lighter fare than where he ended up in later years. That having been said, I think he really knew where he wanted to go with it. [*A Man Called E*] is a real pop record, and a really, really well-made pop record, very deep in terms of the songs on here. I also have to make this disclaimer: I haven't listened to it for at least 10 years. But, you know, some records you work on, and as soon as you walk out of the studio you couldn't tell anybody how any of the songs go. These songs were in my head for months after we finished. Just looking at the titles, I can probably go back and sing you a bunch of these songs. So to me, it had that quality of a real pop record in the best — and, maybe for him, worst — sense of the term."

Whether or not E dislikes the album because of its pop sheen, what *A Man Called E* offered, especially for those only familiar with his Eels work, was a singer-songwriter who could wield a disarmingly genuine streak, something that would be somewhat obscured in later years by irony and wit. Instead, the first E solo album wore its heart on its sleeve, not just in the plaintive, self-explanatory 'Are You & Me Gonna Happen' but in songs like 'I've Been Kicked Around' and 'Pray', in which the sentiments were purely and simply expressed with a lack of self-consciousness. And the arrangements, though adorned with toy piano and synthesized strings, had an equally small-scale, home-made simplicity to them that was delicate without being precious. "He loved the toy piano," Huxley says. "He liked kooky, little cheap instruments — like we all do."

E's singing reflected the album's overall openness, his voice full of Beatles-meets-Beach-Boys sweetness that displayed no trace of sarcasm. It was, in essence, a smart indie pop record very much in keeping with similar efforts at the time, such as Michael Penn's *March*, The Posies' *Dear 23* and Matthew Sweet's *Girlfriend*.

In addition, *A Man Called E* helped establish E's musical persona, which Huxley refers to as "the lonely sad guy". "The E theme has been there since the very beginning," he says. "He hasn't varied much from that — it's 'Everything sucks, but there's a ray of hope and I'm going to make the best of it'. If you could encapsulate E, that's kind of his thing." Picking from a group of 20 to 30 songs, E narrowed the track list down to 11, including the tiny instrumental 'Symphony For Toy Piano In G Minor' that served as a sort of halfway-point intermission, a technique he'd use on subsequent Eels albums. In the liner notes, he thanked, among others, "all my friends & family in Virginia" before adding that the record was "Dedicated to everyone who rained on my parade; thanks for the inspiration."

On February 4, 1992, two months shy of his 29th birthday, *A Man Called E* was released, a time in which Nirvana's *Nevermind*, Garth

Brooks' *Ropin' The Wind* and Michael Jackson's *Dangerous* were fighting for supremacy on the *Billboard* album chart.

"I'm just trying to reconstruct in my head what our aspirations or what our hopes were for the record," Lang says. "I mean, I think we all felt like we made a really good record and there were things on it that were really tuneful. Honestly, I'm so kinda disconnected from what's going on in the music business in general and always have been. I couldn't really tell you what we were up against at that point and what was happening and what kinds of songs were, you know, big and what kinds of songs weren't big."

Polydor put advertising muscle behind the record, taking out a full-page ad in *Spin* that featured its positive reviews, including one from E's old employer, *Music Connection*, which declared: "It is, unquestionably, one of the more vibrant pop débuts of recent vintage." Others praised his "miniature pop symphonies" or called him "a talented songwriter, the kind that comes along once in every hundred albums you hear." (And in an early example for E of how the press could mangle his biography — even though they were saying nice things about him — *The New Yorker* complimented the début from "the mysterious young man from San Francisco", misunderstanding Carter's San Francisco PO box address within the album's liner notes as E's city of residence.)

In addition to the album's good reviews, 'Hello Cruel World' became a hit, peaking at number eight in early May on *Billboard*'s Modern Rock chart, nestled between U2's 'One' and Red Hot Chili Peppers' 'Under The Bridge'. And although growing up in Virginia he would downplay his interest in being a big success, E admitted in his memoir that, yes, he did call his girlfriend in excitement the first time he heard 'Hello Cruel World' on the radio.

A few months later, E was asked to open for another up-and-coming singer-songwriter, Tori Amos. E had become accustomed to playing live as a singing drummer in his old Virginia bands, but this was going to be an entirely different proposition — and not one he was particularly looking forward to.

"It was something that we always fought about," Carter says. "He didn't want to play live." Before the Amos tour, Carter had forced him to play some shows, but the resulting gigs were, according to Carter, torture. "He was so introverted and weird," he says. "It was terrible. This little guy and his little electric piano — where you gonna play in LA?" Making matters worse was the West Coast's geography, which didn't do any favours to a new act. "On the East Coast, there's a college in a town every 10 miles," Carter says. "There's a gazillion people. On the West Coast, it's a long way from [LA] to Santa Barbara, a long way to San Francisco, and after that, there's nothing — you're gonna drive to Oregon? It's just hell."

But opening for Amos presented a new opportunity in which he would be backed by Huxley on guitar and *A Man Called E* musician Jennifer Condos (or, later on the tour, Chris Solberg) on bass. The trio were far from certain it was going to work, though. "That was the exact question: *How the hell are we gonna do this?*" Huxley remembers, laughing. "*How are we gonna make this work live?* Our little dog-and-pony show was probably the most successful weird thing I've ever done."

"It was a big moment for E," Carter says, "playing in front of that many people as opposed to a hundred people." But E didn't seem to be nearly as resistant as he had been to Carter's previous suggestions about playing live. "It's easy when you know people aren't there to see you," Carter says. "You're [just] the opening act. He pulled it off, and I think it was a big turning point for him."

"I think all we did in preparation was just learn the songs and try to make 'em sound good," Huxley recalls of the trio's rehearsals before the Amos tour. "Like, 'OK, this part is too big on the record — we gotta do something with this little tiny unit to make it work this way.' So we rearranged them so that it could work."

Their live set-up was equally spartan and pragmatic. "We had no drums," Huxley says. "We had E sitting at a little electric keyboard and, I think, there was a blanket draped over the front of those dogs playing cards. And I'm acoustic guitar and maybe a little electric. Basically it was like, when we were small it was just E and piano, and when we're big we added some bass and acoustic guitar to get to the chorus. But we had harmony vocals, and the songs are short, they're solid — there's no muss or fuss, there's no jam-band element in E's stuff at all."

But the trio's aha moment came about from something non-musical: the shared sense of humour that Huxley and E had developed while making the album. "What ended up really making it work — and we had no idea this was what was gonna happen — is we had this repartee on stage of, you know, Johnny [Carson] and Ed [McMahon], or Conan [O'Brien] and Andy [Richter]," Huxley remembers. "The comedy aspects of the show, it was so over the top. We were just doing the stupid jokes and having a lot of fun and harassing the audience. And then we'd do these songs — and for some reason, it worked. There's something captivating about his music, obviously. It was quiet, so people had to shut up to listen — it kind of worked to our advantage. And then we'd loosen people up and make them laugh in between, and then they'd pay attention. That was completely unplanned — I didn't know we were going to be funny *and* sad, but that's kind of how it worked. And it worked really well. We went out with 30 shows or something with Tori Amos, and we got 2,000 people laughing and weeping."

One gag in particular Carter remembers quite fondly: "They would do 'Free Bird' and for the solo, Parthenon would just light two big lighters." Carter pauses, thinking about it. "Just fantastic, just fantastic. It was just too good."

The tour ran a little over a month, starting in Kentucky and stretching from Florida to Oregon, with several stops across California near the end. Improbably for an opening act, the band would even be asked back for encores. "I don't know why it went over so well," Huxley says, still amazed. "I honestly don't. It was this little thing, but I guess the songs were just really reaching people. We got a standing ovation in Sacramento, some big 2,000–3,000-seat place. We went back [out] and I was like, 'Holy shit'. It was at the end of the tour. It was one of the last dates, and I was just flabbergasted — it felt so great. And it was just our little tiny thing."

One such person affected by their show was *Rolling Stone* music critic David Wild, who himself had just recently moved to Los Angeles when he went to the Tori Amos show at the Henry Fonda Theatre in August. "If I ever had any interest in Tori Amos, I lost it after [E's] first song," Wild recalls. "I just absolutely loved this guy onstage. To this day he's one of my favourite songwriters of all time. Also, it's something that sometimes got lost on some people, but he was also incredibly funny. He's one of those guys who's like a [more] heterosexual Morrissey — he could combine misery and great wit. I just loved him, he was brilliant." Interested in picking up the artist's album, Wild went into the lobby after E's show and met him. The two immediately hit it off. "I never went back in," Wild says. "I never saw Tori Amos."

They became fast friends, the musician and the music critic, which created some fun opportunities for E to meet some of his heroes. "From the first time I heard him that first night, he struck me as every bit the equal of Ray Davies," Wild says. "And in fact, weirdly around that time I interviewed Ray Davies for *Rolling Stone* for a little Kinks story. And I remember, somehow [Davies] asked me to drive him to the airport and I said, 'Can I bring my friend E? He's a fan'. So, you know, we drove Ray to the airport, and I remember Ray said, 'Could you help me with my luggage?' And E said, 'People said I wasn't worthy of carrying Ray's luggage — but it turns out I am worthy'."

But it wasn't just E's humour and talent that impressed Wild — it was also his decency. "Especially being in LA, I've gotten to know a lot of the quote-unquote sensitive singer-songwriters of a few generations," Wild says, "and, as a rule, they are not any more sensitive — and perhaps slightly less — than the average person. But if you put E in this sort of post-sensitive singer-songwriter bag, he is one of the most thoughtful and sensitive individuals. Beyond the craft of him just being a great tunesmith and a really smart lyricist is his depth as a person with real character that comes across in his best stuff." Wild also helped bring out an unexplored talent in E: wedding singer. When Wild and his wife got married, E, one of Wild's groomsmen, played 'In My Life' for the couple, then surprised them with a rendition of 'Mrs Brown, You've Got A Lovely Daughter', which he changed to 'Mrs Church', Wild's wife's maiden name.

Wild wasn't the only LA journalist from that time who was taken with E. Music critic Bill Holdship recalls being introduced to him by Wild in the early Nineties. "After that, any time we were in the same room anywhere, he'd make a point to come up to me and say hello and always knew my name," Holdship said, "even after he became a 'pop star' briefly." Indeed, when Holdship interviewed E in 2000 in connection with *Daisies Of The Galaxy*, the musician was thoughtful enough to offer his condolences to Holdship, being aware that the critic had just endured a traumatic fire that had destroyed his home. "I always appreciated that and think he's just a great guy," Holdship said.

During the time E was beginning to establish himself as an artist, there were also other like-minded musicians who were trying to make small, intimate albums in Los Angeles, but they were badly outnumbered by the glut of terrible groups chasing trends. "I moved to LA in '91 and was shocked because these legendary clubs were being played by, like, rich kids' bands who were paying to play," Wild recalls. "Just depressing leftover hair bands that were trying to go grunge — it was kind of a pitiful scene. And then something real started to emerge out of places like Largo — actual songs by actual singer-songwriters."

Started by Dublin-born Mark Flanagan in his mid-twenties, Largo opened in 1992 on Fairfax, across the street from Canter's, a 24-hour deli whose Kibitz Room had been a meeting place for infamous LA bands like The Doors and Guns N' Roses. Largo wasn't about Hollywood rock'n'roll excess — instead, Flanagan focused on distinctive songwriters with no major interest in bowling over the music business.

Shon Sullivan, a songwriter and guitarist who credits Largo with helping launching his career, says: "Flanagan was always like, 'You know, the drinks are OK-priced, the food's good, but the music is *great*.' He's the Irishman that didn't drink who ran a bar."

"I've always appreciated people who can really tell good stories or write good songs," Flanagan said in a 2009 interview. "I had no interest in opening a bar or restaurant. The kitchen at Largo was the bane of my existence. I had to learn how to run a restaurant through 40 different chefs... But all I really wanted to do was just put Jon Brion and others onstage!"

A producer and songwriter, Brion became Largo's in-house muse, eventually holding a weekly Friday-night show at the small 120-seat club. "We're all song sluts here," Brion explained in an interview with the *Chicago Tribune*'s Greg Kot. "That's what brings people to Largo."

A beloved figure, he was decidedly modest, always putting the focus on the importance of making music. "Why do I love songs? It's three minutes of condensed storytelling, of trying to collect your thoughts lyrically, musically and emotionally," he said in the same interview, "and when it works there's nothing on earth like it. Think about it: Airwaves of sound move the little hairs and bones in your body, enter your brain and make your neurons fire off skyrockets. No matter how much you look at the math of it, it is beautiful, it is mystical beyond words. I only have to think about a song like 'Waterloo Sunset', and my physiology changes. What's not to love about that?"

"Jon Brion was this somewhat pure, ethereal, monstrously talented spirit who so clearly didn't care about all the buzz and heat about him and all the critical acclaim," Wild says, adding with a laugh, "I don't know if he ever quite got it together to put a record out. He just refused to play any other game. I think he sort of inspired a sense of improvisation within popular music."

That improvisation carried over into the mentality of booking guests for the club. Sullivan met Flanagan while playing guitar in indie songwriter Elliott Smith's band, and pretty soon Flanagan was inviting Sullivan to start coming by on his own. "You'd be [backstage]," Sullivan recalls, "and he'd say, 'Hey, you wanna do a couple of songs?' You'd go out and do three songs. And it was never very planned — he really did like to have it that way. He'd call me up the day of or the day before: 'Hey, so-and-so's going to be in town — why don't you come down and surprise them and do a couple of songs with them?' It was just amazing, like this one night I was playing, and we had a keyboard player — and I look over and it's Benmont Tench from Tom Petty And The Heartbreakers jamming on one of my songs. That's, like, whoa!"

"There were some pretty spectacular nights at the old Largo back in that period," local producer and mixer Greg Collins says. "Like '96 to '98 or '99 was considered a period of amazing stuff happening at Largo on Friday nights. I got to see a lot of those and I remember if I missed one I'd be bummed. I was working in a recording studio at the time, and I'd sometimes have to work until three in the morning on a Friday night — if I had a session that was like that, I'd just spend the whole night going 'Ah, I bet Elvis Costello's up there [at Largo] right now doing a duet with Fiona Apple'."

The emphasis on organic collaboration and surprise pairings helped build Largo's reputation, not just in the world of indie music but also alternative comedy, which was then sprouting up in Los Angeles. For every Aimee Mann and Michael Penn who graced the Largo stage to play a song, there was also a Zach Galifianakis or Patton Oswalt who was fine-tuning his stand-up material.

"Comedians want to roll with musicians, and vice versa," comic Greg Proops told the *Los Angeles Times*. "That's been the most fantastic part of Largo — interfering with each other's worlds."

For Wild, though, the connection between the two types of artists also reflected an apathy about the commercialism of the city they lived in. "LA is the mass production line for sitcoms and for very mainstream comedy," he says. "But those clubs were becoming the centre for people who were actually trying to amuse themselves with comedy." Disinterested in becoming platinum stars — or, at the very least, seeming like that was their sole objective — Largo songwriters behaved similarly. "Aimee Mann had already been through 'Til Tuesday and been through the hit-single machine," Wild says. "They were just a bunch of people who were actually trying to amuse themselves and one another as much as trying to please the beast of the music industry."

By the time E was preparing to make his second album, he was firmly a part of several scenes — Largo, Silver Lake — and had recently moved into Huxley's old house on Baxter. But the excitement of releasing *A Man Called E*, producing a hit single, and enjoying a successful tour didn't keep him from experiencing one of the most common of life's heartaches. He had been dating Jocelyn, the sister of Huxley's wife Janet, but they had broken up.

It appears that she was E's first significant girlfriend since he'd been embraced by the Silver Lake scene, and not surprisingly she was an artist and writer herself. When E had been seeing her, he and Huxley's lives more closely intertwined. "We went on double dates together," Huxley says. "I mean, Jocelyn and Janet were born on the same day nine years apart, so we'd go on birthday things." One night, they ended up riding around in grocery carts on Hollywood Boulevard. "We'd spend Christmases together," Huxley continues. "When Janet and I got married, he came to our [wedding] in New Hampshire — I think that's when he and Jocelyn first kind of hooked up. We were very tightly woven together."

But after Jocelyn dumped him, E decided to pour that heartbreak into *A Man Called E*'s follow-up. And if his first record had been a relentlessly poppy album, then *Broken Toy Shop*, as its title suggested, was a more sombre and nuanced affair.

In some ways it was a fairly predictable collection of tunes detailing E's sorrow, but as with *A Man Called E* he demonstrated that, at least at this early stage of his career, he was seemingly incapable of writing songs that weren't chiefly concerned with a twisty, melodic accessibility. Distraught he may have been, but even when the album kicks off with the darker pop textures of 'Shine It All On', there was a welcome lack of the tortured angst that was prevalent at the time thanks to grunge's rapid ascension in the pop mainstream. Rather, *Broken Toy Shop* was all luxurious melancholy — the songs rarely containing a cruel word for the woman who had crushed his spirit. "I always described him as Charlie Brown with a guitar," Carter says, and that pithy portrayal works exceptionally well in suggesting the gently, deeply likable main character who populates so many of the songs on *Broken Toy Shop*.

Songs called 'The Only Thing I Care About', 'The Day I Wrote You Off', 'Permanent Broken Heart', 'She Loves A Puppet', and 'A Most Unpleasant Man' hinted at his approach, which was a mixture of sad-eyed direct addresses to his ex and vaguely fatalistic reports on his state of mind. And if *Blood On The Tracks*, Bob Dylan's seminal 1975 record, is the yardstick by which all break-up albums are measured, *Broken Toy Shop* was more 'Buckets Of Rain' than 'Idiot Wind', the songs a tour of a man gradually accepting his fate as the one left behind.

But even if he was nursing a broken heart, the album showed little signs of pretentious or self-indulgent articulations of that pain. Its most noticeable sonic advancement was the use of real strings, which were arranged by E and John Philip Shenale, a composer and arranger who had worked on Tori Amos' 1992 record, *Little Earthquakes*. "I always hated not having real strings on the first record," E told *Billboard* shortly after *Broken Toy Shop*'s release. "With more of a budget, my priority was to get real strings. It was probably the coolest moment of my life to hear my songs with a 22-piece orchestra." In addition, there was a move toward more ornate pop structures. 'Mass', which E co-wrote with childhood friend Sean Coleman, was buttressed by trombone and violin, while its melody echoed John Lennon's White Album composition, 'Sexy Sadie'. And intentionally or not, the album consciously returned again and again to scenes from E's childhood.

The most overt example was 'Tomorrow I'll Be Nine', a peppy full-band track in which the preadolescent E describes his unhappy home life, deciding that he needs to find that special someone out there who understands him. That search for sanctuary continues in the next song, a ballad called 'The Day I Wrote You Off', but here the mood was much more melancholy. Now an adult, E tells of buying a photo of a smiling family at a thrift shop: "I feel better now when they don't call." Presumably, the face he sees when he's staring at the ceiling is that of his former girlfriend, but his admission that he "always dreamed that one day I'd leave home/and now I do it again and again" complicates the song's meaning, suggesting that, as for a lot of people, finding love was a way for E to reclaim the comforts of home while correcting the misery that it brought into his life.

Even more so than on *A Man Called E*, *Broken Toy Shop* found E starting to concentrate on song sequencing, creating a thematic, emotional journey through the precise placement of different tracks. "When you're making a record and you're the writer and creator, no one knows this stuff better than you," Huxley says. "It's also a journey for the artist to put it together. Like, when I sequence my records, it seems like I know what the songs are about or what the hidden story is. But we learn a lot about the songs when we sequence them — it's kind of like, 'Ah, look at this.' So it's kind of a learning process for us, too." Add to the fact that on the album's back cover there's a photo of E's feet with the words "HI MOM" written in ink and that the CD photo of E is credited to his father, and *Broken Toy Shop* starts to become not just a break-up album but also an acknowledgment of the unresolved trauma of his family life. It was the first time a record made by E would feature a commingling of romantic strife and childhood pain — but it certainly would not be the last.

But E wasn't just looking back — he was also proving himself to be a fine chronicler of his new home. The jaunty, conga-enriched 'L.A. River' documented the city's pseudo-river — "actually a graffiti-riddled aqueduct often used for the dumping of gang-related murder victims' bodies," he wrote in his autobiography — which he lived nearby when he was staying in Atwater Village before landing his record deal. It's nothing original for an indie-minded artist to satirise the fakeness of Los Angeles in his lyrics, but E discovered a novel way around the cliché, using the empty river as a light-hearted metaphor for his own disillusionment. A very different song, the moving piano ballad 'Manchester Girl', also displayed E's observational skill. Within a loving ode to Jocelyn, he managed to provide a little local colour, mentioning the gun violence going on right outside her home, a snapshot of the crime that was common enough in areas of the city where starving artists could afford to live. ('Manchester Girl', incidentally, was a song he wrote for her birthday, and according to E, she hated it, a sure sign that there was trouble in that particular paradise.)

Beyond E's collaboration with Shenale, *Broken Toy Shop* reflected his involvement with other LA-based performers. Patrick Warren, Michael Penn's chief collaborator on his first two solo records, played chamberlain on several tracks. Winston Watson, who had just joined Bob Dylan's touring band and was an associate of Huxley's, played drums when E wasn't manning the kit himself. The musicians he had toured with — Huxley, Solberg and Condos — were on the record as well, and Bangles beauty Susanna Hoffs co-wrote a track, the folk-pop 'Someone To Break The Spell'. If you could label both albums as chamber pop, then E ensured that at least they felt and sounded different. As he told Sigerson at their first meeting, E was trying different things and letting his instincts drive him.

As part of that evolution, he chose not to produce again with Huxley — although they had written three songs for the record — instead going with Michael Koppelman, who had recently worked as one of the engineers on Prince's comeback album *Diamonds And Pearls*. Prince was a favourite of E's, and Koppelman's connection to The Purple One surely made him an attractive choice. "I met with a lot of different producers," E told *Billboard*, "and they all told me they wouldn't change a thing from my demos, so I decided to co-produce it with a really great engineer. As with the last album, a lot of the songs stayed like the demos — in fact, some of the tracks *are* the demos."

It was a decision that did not sit well with Huxley. "I foolishly probably assumed I was gonna produce the second record since we'd done the first one," Huxley says. "It did really well, we had an alternative hit with 'Hello Cruel World' and I was in his band. You know, why not?" And in addition to co-writing some of the *Broken Toy Shop* material, he'd also played instruments on other tracks. But while working on tunes for the record at Sunset Sound — the studio E used to see every day going to and from work at *Music Connection* — Huxley suddenly discovered E was moving on without him. "I did a song," Huxley recalls, "and after we finished it, he goes, 'Pack your bags, Huxley'." Huxley pauses in his story and laughs. "I'm sharing with you the one moment that I really hated with him. He'd already made up his mind — he was working with whoever produced that record, some guy he met out of nowhere from Minnesota or whatever. It's like, 'OK, why'd you do that? He doesn't even know your stuff'. I think he wanted separation. And I respect that — I get it. But that didn't feel real good."

For what it's worth, Huxley doesn't feel that E and Jocelyn's break-up had anything to do with E's decision not to have Huxley produce *Broken Toy Shop*. Ultimately, E ended up remaining friends with both Jocelyn and Huxley, but not until Huxley let E know his displeasure. "I think I told him a year later: 'You know, that kind of sucked'," Huxley recalls. "And he goes, 'I know'. He acknowledged it — he said, 'Yeah, I could've handled that a lot better.'"

Broken Toy Shop was released December 7, 1993. At least from the sounds of Polydor executives, expectations were high for his sophomore record. "Retail was very supportive of the first album," PolyGram Label Group product manager Diana Fried said at the time, "and they will be tremendously important in helping us break this album and build a grass-roots campaign." But despite the optimism there were also some dark clouds on the horizon. "The fourth quarter is, of course, brutal for a developing artist, but we wanted to get the album out before the holidays to start in-store and radio play," Fried added. "But in terms of radio, the single and the video, we're really thinking of it as a January release." A video was shot for the first single, the Huxley co-written 'The Only Thing I Care About', which starred E strumming a guitar in a room filled with papers and cats being harassed by cops and doctors.

In addition, a tour was planned, one in which E and Huxley would go out with a drummer and bassist. After auditioning different players, they settled on Jonathan Norton, a 35-year-old pony-tailed drummer who had moved to Northridge after attending the California Institute Of The Arts (or Cal Arts). "He was a big bear of a guy," Huxley recalls. "He had a little bit of that artistic, hippie-drum-circle sort of vibe to him. He was famous for taking anything that made a sound and turning it into a piece of his drum kit. He was just kind of a wide-open guy. He loved playing. My impression is that it didn't really matter what it was to him — he loved playing. He was kind of an arty percussionist and definitely not just strictly a rock drummer at all."

To prepare for the formal tour, the group went up to San Francisco in early 1994 — right around the time a 6.7-magnitude quake shook Northridge — to play a few shows. This was the first time E and Huxley played with a drummer together, and Huxley remembers that although it was clear Norton's artistic bent was more eclectic than theirs, it was a pairing that worked.

"I probably would have thought of him as a guy you would have to rein in a little bit and be pretty specific [about] what you wanted," Huxley says. "At first glance, it wouldn't have been a perfect fit musically, but [Norton] is such a lovable guy that you wanna be around him. He's just a great guy — great attitude, a really good player. Sometimes you get into situations where it's like, 'Well, we can make this work, even if it's not obvious we're cut from the same cloth.'"

They never had the opportunity to develop that onstage bond. Soon after, E got a call from Carter. He was being dropped from the label. There would be no *Broken Toy Shop* tour. Norton went off to find other gigs. Huxley, unhappy about E's decision not to have him produce *Broken Toy Shop*, started focusing on his own material. "We were kinda moving in different directions," Huxley says.

Everybody else moved on. E was stuck. Actually, he was probably worse than stuck. A couple of years earlier when he was distraught, at least he could fantasise about what it might be like to have a record deal. Now he had experienced what it was like to have one. And just like that, it was gone.

Chapter Seven

"That was a very dark period. I was crushed of course. All I ever want to do is be able to keep doing this, 'cause I don't know what else to do. I was always writing songs and always recording them. I really liked having a record deal and being able to keep puttin' 'em out."

E was sitting in a Silver Lake restaurant with *Los Angeles Times* writer Richard Cromelin. It was 1996, and he was reflecting on the days after he had released *Broken Toy Shop*. His whole world had collapsed — he had been booted from Polydor and he needed to decide what he was going to do next. So one morning, he went for a drive. About 40 miles later, he was at the Pacific Ocean, standing in the sand. He flirted with the idea of simply walking out into the water, giving up on everything. But he couldn't go through with killing himself — "I don't like cold water," he explained in his memoir — and instead he drove back home.

Not having any better idea of what to do, he poured his energy into writing more songs, no doubt aware of how hard it can be for acts who lose their label deal to end up progressing in the record industry. Beyond that, though, he was also looking for a new creative direction.

It's interesting, then, that while his E solo albums were products of a rejection of what was popular at the time — those were the waning days of hair-metal and the ascension of grunge, country and high-sheen pop vocalists — the next phase of his career saw him firmly tapping into the musical zeitgeist.

Specifically, it was thanks to 'Sour Times'.

Portishead were a Bristol band who were part of a wave of UK artists of the mid Nineties who specialised in a genre named trip-hop, a reference to its merging of hip-hop textures with trippy atmospherics. Portishead's 1994 début, *Dummy*, became an early touchstone of this musical style, earning critical and commercial success in their homeland. KROQ, an influential Los Angeles alternative-rock station, started playing the single 'Sour Times' in 1994, helping give the group a following among hip American audiences. The song eventually peaked at number 53 on the *Billboard* Hot 100, and at some point during its run, E heard it while driving in his pickup truck.

'Sour Times' combined loops and samples, creating a sense that the song was both ancient and cutting-edge at the same time. The song enraptured E, but it also made him nostalgic. "It reminded me of the fun I used to have making strange little sound collages on a tape recorder for my sister," he told a journalist more than a decade later.

The "strange little sound collages" were funny, odd tapes that combined classical, rock and vocals. He'd send them to Liz when she was living in Hawaii and dating the army man. (That had actually been the first of two occasions she had lived in Hawaii — she would move there later with her drug-dealing husband after his stint in jail.)

But 'Sour Times' suggested a way to make those odd experiments resonate. "I realised when I heard Portishead that I could incorporate some of that spirit in my songwriting," E told an interviewer in 2008. "In my mind, there were endless possibilities."

Fittingly, he would wield this new approach for a song that tackled head-on his uncertainty after being dropped by Polydor. Inspired by snippets of lyrics he had jotted down at different times, he hooked up with songwriter and Jackson Browne guitarist Mark Goldenberg (who was married to E collaborator Jennifer Condos) to put together some drum loops. Kicking off with the sound of a needle on vinyl and a beat that harkened back to the 1961 Fats Domino tune 'Let The Four Winds Blow', 'Novocaine For The Soul' was radically different from anything on E's solo records. Edgy, hip and modern, 'Novocaine' tapped into the alienation expressed in so much alt-rock of its era, although the agony was undercut by self-deprecating sarcasm, a tool that the period's better songwriters, such as Nirvana's Kurt Cobain, were also utilising. "'Novocaine For The Soul' sounds detached because it's about detachment," E explained in 1997. "That's what I think is so great about that song, and on that level I think it's almost genius. It's detachment personified. I'm singing about numbness and I'm numb. It's about having too much feeling."

And where his earlier records had leaned heavily toward a pop aesthetic, this was unabashed modern rock. "I was rocking my paisley Telecaster pretty good considering the rinky dink set up I had in my teeny tiny studio in Echo Park," he wrote later in the liner notes of the best-of collection *Meet The Eels* regarding 'Novocaine'. And while no one would confuse the song with the fury of 'Smells Like Teen Spirit', it was certainly a more musically aggressive direction for E, despite the toy-piano instrumentation that's noticeable in the background.

As for the lyrics, they were a combination of clever wordplay and seemingly autobiographical lines that caught the listener short: how else was one to take E's insinuation that his mother had told him that her pregnancy with him was an accident? ("I don't know if I was actually a mistake," E confessed to *Melody Maker*, "but I always felt like I was. I think my mom wanted to have a child when she had me but I think my father was completely not interested.") Sung by somebody who sounded like he had a chip on his shoulder, 'Novocaine' was confrontational, confessional and desperate. It was also as catchy as hell.

Around the same time as E was putting together 'Novocaine,' he met musician Jim Jacobsen, who had been suggested by Huxley when E was looking for other collaborators for his new sonic vision. Like E, Jacobsen had moved to Los Angeles (from Chicago) to break into the music business. "I was in a band, and we were shopping for a record deal," Jacobsen says. Patrick Leonard, who made his name producing some of Madonna's biggest Eighties hits, "had heard our stuff and said, 'You guys are amazing — the only problem is you're not in LA'. So, we're like, 'OK, we'll move down to LA and we'll become rich and famous'.'" Things didn't quite work out for the band, though. "We all lived in this big horrible house," he recalls, "and within a few months, you know, beer bottles were being thrown around. I mean, it was a fucking nightmare — and that was the end of the band experience."

Jacobsen stayed in Los Angeles to do film work but mostly did library music. "I have spent so much of my career doing whatever the job description is," he says of creating library music. "'We need something that sounds *exactly* like this, but doesn't sound like this'. So that's often the job [description], or sometimes it's more general, which is much preferable — 'something that sounds kind of like Kings of Leon'. And then, you know, the good news is I've got a job — the bad news is I have to listen to Kings of Leon in order to prepare."

The chance to work with E came about through Jacobsen's manager, who played Jacobsen E's solo records. "My manager was a fan, so I knew who he was," Jacobsen says. Then he adds, laughing, "and I knew that he was nuts because I was working with Parthenon and he told me about his great and funny friend. E is one of the funniest people in the world."

Jacobsen's preferred process was to put together a track first, letting his collaborator add vocals, lyrics and melody if he liked what he'd come up with. But at one of their first sessions together, they developed a song by both bringing in ideas they liked. E was interested in using a soulful piano riff from a mid-Seventies Gladys Knight And The Pips hit called 'Love Finds Its Own Way'. Meanwhile, Jacobsen had developed a drum loop he liked. "One of the things that he liked about working with me was that I actually crafted the loops," Jacobsen explains. "I didn't just buy a loop and have a sampler play it back — which is an OK thing to do — but I actually knew how to use the samplers to cut the loop up and move things around to make it work in the song. He thought that was cool."

On top of that, they shared a fondness for the indie band Soul Coughing. "That's why I used the upright bass with the loops," Jacobsen says, a nod to that group's Sebastian Steinberg, who played a similar instrument on their songs. The effect of mixing the elegance of old-school bass with cutting-edge loops and an R&B sample was charming and engaging. When E went about writing the lyrics for the song, he decided to dedicate it to a former girlfriend, crafting a first-person narrative in which he walked over from his place to hers. He named it 'Susan's House'.

"Susan actually lived in Pasadena," E would later write in the liner notes for an Eels best-of collection, "which was way too far to walk to from Echo Park." Despite his fudging of the actual facts, though, 'Susan's House' was another early example of his eye for the details of lower-middle-class life in Los Angeles. While the titular home offers a respite from the ills of the world — hardly a groundbreaking lyrical trope — E used his journey to illustrate the crime, poverty and malaise that swallow up so many lives in major cities. On his walk, he sees, among other things, an insane elderly woman, a teenage murder victim, a kid selling crack and people mindlessly watching *Baywatch* in their home. While some of the details were invented, some were real: "There IS a donut shop," he wrote, "and a kid was killed there on the sidewalk and the paramedics did take his clothes off as they put his body in the bag." Beyond its different musical textures, 'Susan's House' was both comforting and horrifying, pulsing with the tension of living in an unsafe part of town but dreaming about a safe haven in the world.

It was a terrific start to the E/Jacobsen partnership, although Jacobsen acknowledges that 'Susan's House' "was the first and last time that I ever used a sample from somebody else's record on a record. I would rather shoot myself in the foot than do that again. When we were mixing the album, they still hadn't cleared the sample, so we got screwed — we lost so much of the copyright because of that sample."

The Susan of the song worked at Warner Bros and had dated E after his break-up with Jocelyn. To Carter's mind, she would have been an ideal mate for his mercurial client — and a welcome relief from his usual romantic pursuits. "He was such a weird-looking total dork, and just embarrassing," Carter says of E's dating prowess at the time. "He was such a pussy. 'Oh my god, E, get real — you don't stand a chance with this one!' He believed that guys with glasses get more pussy and that all you had to do would be weird and a really beautiful girl would fuck you one time just for the experience. And that was kind of his life, which was, you know, being shit on by a lot of women he had no business with, you know? Except for Susan, who was a little dork like he was. Totally sweet. Totally great. He should have married her — his head was someplace else."

E and Susan may not have lasted, but they remained friends. She would also have a starring role in another new track, 'Beautiful Freak', as touching a song about being a proud weirdo as has ever been written.

Jacobsen and E also came up with the track 'Flower', one of E's early examples of direct addresses to a god he didn't believe in. As a nice satiric touch, the track was dominated by the heavenly voices of an angelic choir. "I had this great sampled women's choir of nuns singing," Jacobsen says. "I had this really interesting set of samples, and I just started working on the progression. And as soon as he heard it, he said, 'Oh yeah, that's really cool, let's do that'." The two sat together to develop the mandolin part that served as a vulnerable counterbalance to the nuns' ethereal, almost spooky presence.

On a different sonic wavelength, the downright rocking 'Rags To Rags' very much incorporated the soft-verse/loud-chorus technique that was the defining hallmark of alternative rock in the Nineties. The track was another snapshot of the artist at a crossroads after the end of his record deal. Pondering the realities of the industry he was (barely) a part of, he described his life as an attempt to live out the classic rags-to-riches storyline, except that it had all gone horribly wrong. 'Rags To Rags' fluctuated between arrogant resilience and world-weary cynicism, and these mood swings were offset by thoughts of his Virginia childhood, a place he knew he'd had to escape but which he still felt a fondness for. The song's structure might have been familiar, but the sentiment was uniquely E: there was no home to return to, so he was going to have to figure out a way to make things work in Los Angeles.

This new batch of songs seemed different to E. They were more direct, more urgent. Maybe it was because he had nothing to lose, but he felt that he was digging deeper within himself to be as honest as he could. And the songs kept coming. On a lark while hanging out at E's house one day, Jon Brion gave E a challenge: write a song in 30 minutes. A half-hour later, E had 'My Beloved Monster', a silly but charming Beatles-esque ode to an unlikely lover. It seemed almost like an afterthought in comparison to several of the other daring tracks he'd been developing. But it had a big future ahead of it.

Meanwhile, Carter loved the new material and was convinced he could find another deal for E. But the same response kept occurring. "I took his new songs out and shopped it," Carter says. "Got a very polite, 'I've always really liked E...'. Pass. So I go back to E. I said, 'All right, I'm not getting anywhere like this — I gotta reinvent you. You know, we got to pick a band name, find a couple of other guys, we're gonna take a photograph. Band is the way to go, singer-songwriter is hell — no record company wants it. All it means for them is they've got to pay for sidemen. The cost is three times as much to market a solo artist as it is a band'."

Jacobsen also picked up on that industry sentiment. "It's, like, a male solo artist had to be Michael Bolton," he remembers. "You had to be in a band. You were a guy and you wanted a record deal? You had to be in a band."

According to Carter, E "kicked and screamed and kicked and screamed" about the idea of going out as a band, but eventually he relented. And that's when Jonathan Norton, the drummer from the aborted *Broken Toy Shop* tour, came back into his life.

The way E tells the story in *Things The Grandchildren Should Know*, he was resistant to the idea of having Norton drum in this new outfit because of his long ponytail and penchant for world music — put bluntly, he "looked like a roadie for the Grateful Dead", which was not meant as a compliment. But when he saw Norton later, the ponytail was gone, an indication in E's mind of how much he wanted the job.

Norton was indeed someone who wasn't a traditional rock'n'roll drummer. His style developed at an early age in Northern California. "I started with listening and tapping out the beats on leather suitcases to my mother and father's record collection in the early Sixties," he told an interviewer. His parents listened to a little bit of everything: swing, classical, country, Latin, pop. As he started drumming in bands, he began experimenting with his kit, adding more percussion instruments to his set-up. But though he felt an affinity for other musical styles, "my heart was realistically in rock/pop/soul — the song and lyrics." He went to Cal Arts where he dabbled in many different musical pursuits, everything from film scoring to theatre to Indian tabla. During that time, he did just about everything but play on a kit. "I studied percussion and delved deep into that," he said later. "My goal was to soak in and perform as much as possible."

Despite the change in his physical appearance, Norton still had to convince E, as he later said, "that I was young and cool enough to be his drummer." Whatever Norton said must have worked because the first rehearsal for the duo took place on June 16, 1995, in Norton's garage in Northridge. The session lasted four hours and the group was identified as The Mohammed Chang. The significance of the name? "The two most common surnames in the world," Norton explained to *Drumhead* magazine years later. The two men played together on four different occasions over the next three weeks, with Norton's unconventional approach to rock songs giving their rehearsals a freshness. E's new tunes, with their loop-heavy beats, resonated with Norton. "Back in the Seventies I played all the funk stuff, and then I've always been a thrasher on that side of things," Norton said. "[E's material] encompasses classical for me. It encompasses funk, it encompasses R&B, it encompasses some jazz... and then it encompasses the total thrash. It's great."

Then, on July 8, a third member came along.

A Southern California native raised in the Valley in Westlake Village, Tommy Walter had been playing in a band called Mrs God and had jammed with E one night at a local club, The Mint. "I just said, 'You know, I'm looking for people to play with all the time'," Walter remembers telling E. "'Let's get together sometime.' I just kinda threw that out there because I was trying to network and meet people." Soon after he got a present from E. "He dropped off this tape at my house," Walter says. "I still have this cassette tape, and it had early demos of what became the record. I just learned a few songs. I thought 'Novocaine' was awesome — that was on there." Next thing Walter knew, he was invited to hang out at the garage to play with E and Norton. "I didn't know it was an audition, but apparently it was," Walter says. "It was really fun and we had a good time just playing — that's what I was looking to do anyway. It was funny, E was kinda sitting at a desk by the front wall. And he just said something, really casually, like, 'So, let's just start doing this every so often'. And kind of like, bam, a band is born."

On July 23, the trio for the first time was called the Eels. The name was Carter's idea. But it wasn't the only new name to surface. Tommy decided that Norton should be nicknamed Butch. E loved it, and so it stuck. It would not be the last nickname an Eels member would pick up during his or her time with the band, and it's worth pointing out that E hasn't escaped getting his own nickname. He's known affectionately as Grandpa. ("He was a curmudgeon," Carter says. "He was an old man before his time.")

Now dubbed Eels, the trio started working to adapt the new songs for a three-piece band that could play local gigs. "I think from the get-go, the three of us had a really cool chemistry," Walter says. "Personality-wise, we all had fun together and we meshed well together. Butch has got that fast-and-slow thing that I have — he can be instantly really quickly aggressive and then, like, pull it back. So, dynamically, we meshed well that way. And E's doing his thing, and it's intense and it's emotional, so I think to have that energy from us behind him was a really cool thing."

"The live shows were fabulous," Lang says. "Always really fun. You know, it's kind of like it is now — you're definitely not gonna see the normal 'get up on stage and do 10 songs and say goodnight' thing. You're gonna see a bunch of different weird instruments, and E's gonna be weird. I remember going to see 'em play [as a trio], and there was French horn and timpani — they brought a lot of different stuff to the party. I didn't go see a ton of live music, but I remember thinking, 'This is not what everybody is doing right now'."

For Huxley, who had played with E when he was a solo act, there was a definite change, especially with Butch as the drummer. "It was like, 'Oh wow, look at Butch,'" Huxley says. "He'd made this transformation into this integral part of Eels. He was more hard-edged and became the foil of all the inside gags. He became kind of a star of the show, which I loved. I loved that whole transformation that he did —

the haircut, the aggressive playing. I thought that was just great — that's a versatile musician going with the programme and seeing an angle and having fun with it."

"Butch was a monster," says Jacobsen. "He was just an absolute monster, and he could take over tons of the show and carry the whole thing great — it wasn't like listening to [Cream drummer] Ginger Baker play a 20-minute solo."

The trio may have immediately clicked, but they were three very different individuals in certain regards. E had never been much of a student and certainly never went to school to pursue music. Butch had attended Cal Arts for just that reason, although like E he had started drumming at age six. As for Walter, he received the nickname "the professor": he had gone to the University of Southern California, a prestigious (and expensive) private school to study music. Unlike Butch, though, Walter had finished his degree.

In a 1997 interview, Walter explained why he wasn't apologetic at all about his college education, despite the ribbing he got from his bandmates about his schooling. "A lot of people who don't understand music theory will tell you that they are glad because theory will somehow destroy their creative muse," he said. "I never found this to be true. You are only limited by your own attitude. My BM in composition taught me how to listen. I think this is the most important skill you can [have] as a musician. Listening allows your mind to be open to new possibilities."

Good luck kept coming E's way. Hanging out at Santa Monica's Third Street Promenade, an outdoor mall a few blocks from the Pacific Ocean, he ran into Chris Douridas, a DJ he knew who worked at the city's most influential independent public radio station, KCRW. "I first met him when he was doing his solo stuff," Douridas recalls. "He already had *A Man Called E* out, and we played it moderately." E had performed on KCRW during the *Broken Toy Shop* promotional rounds, which was when Douridas and E met. They had stayed in touch since, and their chance encounter at the Promenade proved advantageous. E mentioned that he'd been working on new material, and Douridas asked him to mail a tape over to the radio station.

"He sent me a DAT," Douridas says. "I remember exactly what the DAT looks like — it was just a few songs. I started playing songs from that immediately." Most memorably, Douridas played 'Novocaine For The Soul', the first time the song was played on the radio. Soon after, Douridas, who was host of the popular morning weekday show *Morning Becomes Eclectic*, asked E to come and perform. On November 22, E, Butch and Tommy played at the station's Santa Monica studio. The performance clinched it for Douridas. "I remember thinking he was on to something with his new project," he says. "It's really funny going back and listening to *A Man Called E* — even at that point, you can certainly hear the early shadings of what became the Eels trademark in his recordings. I remember thinking at the time that he was a very good songwriter who had a great knack for a pop hook and, yet, underneath all of that workmanship was a rather smug and sometimes irascible character that is an unlikely resident of a typical pop song, which altogether I found appealing."

Chatting with E before the band performed, Douridas told the artist: "I think you're really on to something with this." And while it's E's habit to deflect praise with self-deprecating or sarcastic comments, Douridas says that "he looked at me and he goes, 'Yeah, me too'. He had this look in his eye — I remember that very distinctly — when I said that to him. He had this sort of electric glint in his eye. He seemed excited to have that confirmation from [the station]. He was setting up about to perform live and début this stuff on the air, and I could just sense that there was more to this Eels thing that I didn't know yet. All I had was a handful of songs, [but] I felt a very palpable sense that there was a deep well to mine here."

November was also a fateful month for the band because it was the time when Carter's efforts to cultivate interest in E's new songs finally began to bear fruit. One of the first label execs to respond was Lonn Friend. The former executive editor of *RIP* and host of *Pirate Radio Saturday Night*, Friend had decided to make a career change in the summer of 1994, signing on to work in A&R for Arista Records. "This was the hottest time in the label's history," Friend recalls. "Don't forget, they had TLC, Ace Of Base — everything they touched was selling. They had the Puffy Combs deal, they had Bad Boy Records — I mean, the label was making hundreds of millions of dollars... with zero imprints in alternative music." That's where Friend came in — his marching orders from label head (and industry icon) Clive Davis were to bulk up Arista's rock roster.

Unfortunately, Friend enjoyed little success in his first 12 months, unable to change either the culture at the label or the industry impression of Arista as a rock lightweight. That's when a tape arrived at his office.

"This demo comes in from a guy named John Carter," Friend remembers, "and there was a note that said, 'You'll get this'. I popped it in the deck and the first song was 'Novocaine For The Soul'. I called everyone into my office and I played it again — they all went, 'Wow'." The other two tracks on the tape were 'Rags To Rags' and 'Susan's House', a song that Friend says "just blew my mind."

And while others who fell under the spell of E's songs compared him with The Beatles or The Beach Boys, Friend heard another similarity. "I've been a passionate fan of Peter Gabriel my whole life," he says. "And 'Novocaine' was very Peter Gabriel. It had that melancholy atmosphere that Peter Gabriel's solo albums had, especially the *Security* record. That's just kind of what hit me. Anyone that can come along that can even approach Gabriel — 'cause to me it's just so unapproachable — then I'm paying attention."

Friend wanted to see the band live, which brought him to the group's show at a small club called Luna Park. "I just was floored," he says. "The music was so dark and cool live, just as much as it was on the record. And he pulled off 'Susan's House' on stage, which I thought was really tricky."

No doubt it's a compliment that would have pleased E. When the Eels trio started up, he quickly realised he didn't want to concern himself with mimicking the instrumentation of the original recordings onstage. "We play straight," he told a reporter about a year later regarding the band's approach. "We don't use any samples because I feel that would be like cheating. I don't want it to be a Milli Vanilli concert. I want it to feel like what you see is what you get. Besides, it makes us have to reinterpret the songs in new ways and that opens our eyes a bit."

ark Oliver Everett (aka E) photographed in 1996. MONFOURNY/DALLE/RETNA PICTURES

Mark Everett, back during his McLean days. He wore a jacket and tie for his senior year high school photo but was a lot more casual for his sophomore portrait.

Hugh Everett III, E's father.

Before E made it as a songwriter, he worked for Music Connection in Los Angeles. He's seen here posing with the rest of the staff in 1989. (E's the guy wearing the hat.) COURTESY ERIC BETTELLI

working on *A Man Called E* with (from left to right) John Carter, Parthenon Huxley and Jim Lang.
URTESY PARTHENON HUXLEY

he Eels at Neil Young's Bridge School Benefit in October 1998 at the Shoreline Amphitheater in Mountain
iew, California. TIM MOSENFELDER/GETTY IMAGES

The original Eels line-up in Los Angeles, 1996. FRANCK COURTÈS/AGENCE VU/CAMERA PRESS

A collection of concert posters over the years. When E started his touring career, he opened for Tori Amos (under the name A Man Called E).

Eels at Pukkelpop Festival in Hasselt, August 1997.
NAEPS/LFI

E blows his harmonica during the *Shootenanny!* tour.
CAMERA PRESS/TRISTAN FEWINGS

The Eels (Jonathan "Butch" Norton, Mark Oliver Everett and Tommy Walter) in April 1997.
E. CATARINA/RETNA UK

Eels have their share of celebrity fans. During the 2000 tour, they met up with Los Angeles Lakers head coach Phil Jackson (back row, with glasses and no hat). COURTESY OREST BALABAN

E, Butch, David Hlebo and Spider hanging out in Venice, Italy. Spider would die of a drug overdose on tour with Eels in August 2000. COURTESY OREST BALABAN

Eels in January 1999. From left: Adam Siegel, E and Butch.
BETH HERZHAFT/CORBIS

Asked how the band managed to translate the songs to the live setting, Friend answers, "It was all about him. He just had something." But the trio as a whole impressed as well. "Butch was really funny — like the happy drummer, in a Ringo Starr kind of way. He and Tommy were a great rhythm section — it was a very tight trio that followed the leader and didn't step on what was going on there lyrically. And the songs, because they were so unique, required a little bit of patience with the rhythm section. But on a song like 'Rags To Rags', it kicked ass."

After the show, Friend introduced himself to E and explained who he worked for. "I go, 'What are you doing, like, tomorrow or the next night?' He goes, 'Nothing'. I go, 'Well, let's hang out'."

They went to a Mexican restaurant and then headed to Tower Records on Sunset. "I had an Arista expense account at Tower Records," Friend says, "and I walked through the store with him. I go, 'Pick out anything you want'. I remember I found Todd Rundgren's *Something/Anything?* I go, 'This is one of the records I grew up with — artists like you who play all the instruments'. And I got that for him."

Their time together convinced Friend that E was something special. "That evening with him so solidified my belief that he was a unique, eccentric, and gifted artist," Friend says. Now he just had to convince Clive Davis that Eels were worth signing. On January 28, 1996, the Eels played a showcase for Davis. The industry mogul wasn't impressed. In Friend's memoir, *Life On Planet Rock*, he says that Davis told him, "The songs are interesting but he's not a star. I can see 'Novocaine' getting modern-rock airplay and possibly 'Rags To Rags', but the front man is not compelling. Arista signs stars, Lonn."

It was a crushing disappointment for Friend — both as a rejection of his taste and for the fact that he wasn't going to be able to support a band he loved. But after letting E and Carter know that he was passing, he got a small measure of revenge. "About a week later, I was asked to play golf with Tom Whalley, the president of Interscope," Friend says. "I pulled a cassette tape out of my golf bag, and I gave it to him." It was the Eels demo. "I said, 'I couldn't sign 'em but I'd like to fuck with this. I'd like you to listen to this — just take it back to the office.' He played it for [Interscope co-founder] Ted Field. Ted Field lost his mind."

Field wasn't the only one. Douridas was at the same time being courted by a new label, DreamWorks, to join its A&R team. As a sample of his musical preferences, he brought Eels to the attention of one of the label heads, Lenny Waronker.

Waronker, like Clive Davis, is one of the hallowed names within the music industry. The producer and former president of Reprise and Warner Bros Records, he was instrumental in signing and cultivating such acts as Neil Young and Randy Newman in the Seventies. (He'd had a hand in producing several Newman albums, including *Good Old Boys*.) And it was his reputation as an artists-first executive that helped lure indie-minded bands such as R.E.M. to the label in the Eighties. In October 1995, Waronker — along with his fellow WB execs Mo Ostin and Mo's son Michael — had announced that they would be landing at DreamWorks Records, which was part of the new film, television and music company formed by Hollywood titans Steven Spielberg, Jeffrey Katzenberg and David Geffen. They were looking for artists when Douridas suggested Eels.

"Chris Douridas came over to the DreamWorks office and played four or five songs," Waronker says, "including 'Novocaine For The Soul'. We became really interested. The songwriting was tremendous. And the way he presented the songs, in terms of how he made them, also stood out. I mean, he got incredibly creative in the way he approached making [the tracks]. The overall quality of it, from vocals, songs and production — it was just special."

The irony, of course, was that these songs were no different than they'd been when Carter was shopping them as an E solo act. Well, there was one difference — it was packaged as a band now.

"I didn't change anything," Carter says, "just put a picture and a name on it. Couldn't get *arrested* as a singer-songwriter, couldn't get him a fucking job. As the Eels, we were packing clubs around here. They were as hot as a local band can get — I mean, nights where eight record companies were in the audience."

It was a nutty time. The hysteria and hyperbole of the period is probably best encapsulated by a moment during an Eels show Friend attended after giving Interscope the band's tape. "The room is full of label people," he recalls. "Namely, Ted Field and a bunch of Interscope people. He's standing next to me as the band's playing, and he says to me, 'This is the most excited I've been since Bush!'" In retrospect, the comment's even funnier — though enormously popular for a brief period, Gavin Rossdale's band was never considered an artistic juggernaut. But Field's sentiment also reflected an odd irony about E's sudden burst of popularity: Eels were immediately embraced for their fresh sound and creative arrangements, but the fervour surrounding them was as much about their commercial potential as it was their artistic prospects.

Soon, the suitors were winnowed down to two serious contenders: Interscope and DreamWorks. Interscope was a powerhouse of the industry; DreamWorks was a plucky but untested up-and-comer. And according to Carter, Interscope was offering a quarter-million dollars more than DreamWorks was.

Around Valentine's Day of 1996, E decided to sign with DreamWorks. A big part of E's reasoning was that he admired Lenny Waronker and Mo Ostin. Turning down the more lucrative deal didn't faze him because, as he wrote in his memoir, "the biggest money offer would've expected the biggest money return, not the best music I could make to my ability."

"We really tried to convince him that DreamWorks made the most sense for a number of reasons," Waronker now says. "And a lot of what we were talking about, I think, were the things that he was looking for. Like, a label that was small — and, in our case, incredibly small. Also, being one of the first artists on the label was a benefit. I think he liked us and felt comfortable with us. And he knew of us — you know, he and I actually got along quite well. He was a big fan of some of the records I produced, especially Randy Newman. And he felt that he would be understood because of that. And I think that those were the main factors — he really wanted to be in a place that he felt would understand what he was doing and not interfere."

"Part of why he ended up at DreamWorks is that they wanted him as a lure for other artists," Jacobsen says. "There are more commercial artists than E that they were able to sign because those people thought that he was so hip — they thought it was so cool that DreamWorks was so supportive of him. So he made money for them in sort of indirect ways that were pretty significant."

"When you're a young company, you're really trying to find artists that make a difference," Waronker says about the label's rationale for signing him. "And I think that in our mind, the potential audience was really large — you know, at the time there was alternative radio that meant something. And then there was pop radio, and I thought we'd get it all. But that was just part of it — the real issue was that he was that good. And I think it was a great way to start a label when you're associated with somebody who's doing something as special and different and [has] his own musical point of view. If you're starting a label and you sign an artist like that, that's a message to the artist community that we really are serious about what we were talking about. He was, in my mind, the real deal."

Distraught about losing Eels to a competitor but happy for the band, Friend did something rare for a person in A&R: he congratulated the victors. In a fax to Lenny Waronker and Mo Ostin on February 16, he wrote, "My envy is only superseded by my confidence in [Eels'] future success and the delight you and [the] great people at DreamWorks are going to have making and breaking their records."

Fourteen years after the deal was signed, Carter remains bewildered by E's decision.

"It killed me that we had a much better deal from Interscope," he says. Citing reasons for E's choice to shun Interscope, Carter suggests: "Some musician told E that Jimmy Iovine was an asshole. And of course Mo Ostin had seen him at the cafeteria [at Warner Bros] and had said hello to E when E was having lunch with Susan one day. He heard all these great stories about Mo Ostin: 'I know it's not as much money, but I want to be on DreamWorks'." Carter shakes his head. "You kiss-ass starfucker — what a bunch of bullshit. Mo Ostin, my ass — what, is he gonna have you over for Hanukkah or something, E? Bunch of shit. Interscope was red hot. DreamWorks was going through Geffen, who was ice cold. I didn't give a fuck about Lenny Waronker — I knew him, I knew he was a fucking airhead. It just blew my mind. Blew my mind."

As should be obvious, Carter was indifferent to E's belief in Waronker and the Ostins as patron saints of revered Seventies artists. As Carter puts it: "Are Randy Newman stories worth a quarter-million dollars? He was blowing off a chunk of money. I think it was literally a hippy, dippy decision."

As for E's assertion that going to Interscope would have put pressure on him to produce hits, Carter believes there was equal pressure signing with DreamWorks. Speaking sarcastically, he says, "Oh no, first act on a label like DreamWorks — oh no, no expectations there." E's choice to start his Eels career "wanting to keep the ceiling that low" still bothers Carter. "I had somehow got us to this point, and E was gonna shoot us in the foot by going with the lamer, the slower of the two horses," he says. "We were gonna try to win the race, and you want the mule instead of the thoroughbred? I preach it to every act I work with: [the record companies] wanna have success — they wanna have a success as bad as you do. They're signing you to fail? They're signing you to look stupid? No, they want to be successful." And although Carter acknowledges that DreamWorks was supportive of E's vision, "I knew that Interscope was going to give the same piece of art a better chance, ultimately. They were in a position to cut a deal at Tower Records to get more product in. At some point, it really does come down to getting the record in the store — or at least back in the old days. But it does matter — being in the record store, the tone of your advertising, a promotions man that, you know, someone's taking their phone calls. That stuff counts. But to be with a label that's got nothing else going on…."

And as Huxley discovered, it wasn't as if the DreamWorks contract was for mere pennies. "If Interscope's deal was that much [bigger]," Huxley says, "then it must have been gi-fricken'-gantic. I saw an advance cheque on E's kitchen table by accident, and my jaw dropped. He said, 'Oh, you weren't supposed to see that'." Huxley won't say how much the cheque was for, but it was in the six-figure range.

With the decision to go with DreamWorks made, now there was the little matter of actually making the album. Or, to put it more accurately, remaking it.

"The whole record was done — he had basically recorded the whole record himself," *Beautiful Freak* co-producer Mike Simpson says. "We were all pretty happy with the way it sounded, but someone — you know, I don't remember whose idea it was — [wanted] to go in and re-record all or most of the songs. And that's what we did — we ended up just sort of re-recording them."

Simpson was probably at the height of his acclaim when he came aboard to help bring *Beautiful Freak* to fruition. As one-half of the cutting-edge producing team The Dust Brothers (along with John King), he had helped oversee The Beastie Boys' evolution from frat-boy rap-rockers to sophisticated artists on 1989's sample-mosaic masterpiece, *Paul's Boutique*. In 1994 and 1995, the duo worked with another Silver Lake resident, Beck, on the sessions that eventually resulted in *Odelay*, an album that would beat *Beautiful Freak* into the marketplace by two months. By 1996, Simpson was doing A&R work for DreamWorks, although he was very hesitant about it when Mo Ostin first offered him the job. "At the time I had a lot going on — I had The Dust Brothers thing going, and we had our own label," Simpson remembers. "So I said, 'Wow, I'm really flattered, but I've got my plate sort of full right now and I've made commitments to artists and other people.' And I was reticent — I'd never had a corporate job before, and I'd sort of always seen myself as being on the other side of the fence. It was a little bit scary to me, the whole prospect." After Ostin agreed to Simpson's conditions, which included not having to come in to an office and being able to do outside projects, he signed up, excited by the new label's mantra. "They were pitching it as they were gonna break the mould of the traditional record company," he says. "They were gonna go about it a completely different way and it was really gonna be artist-driven."

When Simpson met up with Eels to re-record some of the songs, he quickly became aware that, while they were a band in name, E was the one who was in charge. "It was pretty much a fun time," Simpson recalls. "I mean, there was a lot of teasing." He laughs at the memory. "E would definitely give those guys a hard time when he could, but it seemed like it was all in good fun. But at the same time, E always let everyone know who was boss, you know? Not in an overt way, but it was always clear that it was E's deal. Butch was just very happy to be there — he was really super-good-natured and just stoked. He put up with E's teasing and just was really excited about being able to play the drums. Tommy, on the other hand, he had ideas. He had ideas for the band and for the music that E didn't really care about. So I think there was a little bit of a struggle there between Tommy and E — Tommy really wanted to exercise his ideas, or he wanted to feel like he had more of a force in the band. And E was always very quick to just shut that down."

Eels and Simpson recorded in what Simpson refers to as "a makeshift home garage studio" in Burbank to get the trio's dynamics on the album for more full-band songs like 'Mental', 'Not Ready Yet' and 'Rags To Rags'. They then went to Conway Studios in Hollywood, where Simpson had also mixed *Odelay*, to tweak E's original recordings. It was a lesson in the absolute commitment E had in seeing his vision carried out.

"E had these cassettes that were sort of old," Simpson says, laughing, "some of which were two or three years old — just cassette mixes of the songs that were to become the album. And, you know, the cassettes were pretty much degraded — he had been listening to them in a $50 cassette player in his old beat-up pickup truck. The playback quality was severely compromised from the original recordings, but this is how he had become accustomed to listening to these songs. And he sort of fell in love with the way everything sounded in his truck on these beat-up cassettes on his crappy cassette player. And so, we ended up going into Conway — one of the most expensive mix rooms in the city — and then every time we would do a mix, E would go out to his truck and he would listen side-by-side [between] our new mix and his old beat-up tape. Basically, we were just trying to match the sound of these old cassettes that he had, and it was a painstaking process — we would feel like we'd gotten it to sound really good and then he'd go out to his truck and he'd be out there for sometimes over an hour. I mean, this is just on one song, and he'd go out there for an hour and then come back with five or six pages of very detailed notes of how our new mix was slightly off from his old beat-up cassette. You know, the running joke as he was out in the truck was that we would wait for the white smoke, like when they were choosing a pope — and so we referred to his truck as The Popemobile. The engineer, the second engineer and myself would just sit there twiddling our thumbs, waiting for the verdict. We had these beautiful, rich, perfect digital recordings and then we were at this really expensive studio trying to make them sound like a fucked-up cassette."

Jacobsen was present during these Popemobile sessions as well. "I have always had complete respect for his way of working even though he drives a lot of people nuts," Jacobsen says. "Those mixes took for-fucking-ever. There was a famous quote — E got really frustrated at some point and he said, 'I hear things that no one else will ever hear'. And we all looked at one another — '*exactly.*'"

But although both Simpson and Jacobsen were clearly tormented by how long the mixing process dragged on, they stuck it out because of E's artistry. "He never bullshitted," Jacobsen says, "he never pretended to know something he didn't know. When he said, 'I hear something no one else will hear', I never doubted him. So my job, I always felt, was to try to hear the thing that he's talking about. He just never compromised, he never bullshitted. He never went, 'Oh, I don't know what to do here — just put some crap on it.' Which is what you do all the time — like, if something isn't working, we'll put some crap on it and it'll work. He never was willing to do that. And he does drive people crazy — and he has at times driven me crazy. But I've never thought that it wasn't worth it."

Because DreamWorks already essentially knew what *Beautiful Freak* was going to sound like — and because its own A&R man was serving as the album's co-producer — the label bosses mostly left the band alone to finish the record at Conway. ("When the record company would come down," Carter says, "it was my job to take Michael Ostin into the other studio and kick his ass in ping-pong to get him out of the room, because he always made such stupid fucking remarks.") And from the sounds of it, there was also plenty of time for practical jokes.

"Oh man, we had some fun down there," Jacobsen says. "One of the popular things was to call the reception desk and give them a message to give to someone, make up the name of some plastic-surgery place or some boutique and say that they were ready for your anal-waxing appointment for two o'clock that afternoon. These horrible, embarrassing things — it was kind of mean to the receptionist, but the comic payoff was really worthwhile. I would come to the gate and say I was coming for the [Eels] session and they'd say, 'Well, who are you?' I'd say, 'I'm Tina Turner'. And so they would have to call in and say, 'Tina Turner is here'." He chuckles. "It was like hanging around with a bunch of four-year-olds in one way — and, of course, very serious at the same time because it was a big deal. We were trying to make a good record."

The combination of sophomoric jokes and intense mixing sessions resulted in the nearly-44-minute-long *Beautiful Freak*. E has said over the years that the album was whittled down from 70 songs to the 12 that made the final cut. "Some of them were just too dark," he told the *Los Angeles Times* later that year about the songs that were left off. "About my family and stuff. I didn't put them on the record because they were just bleak, they were just relentless. I wanted to have stuff that was dark yet hopeful. Even if it's just barely hopeful."

The album was set for release on August 13, 1996, and expectations were that it could be a major hit, especially in light of *Odelay*'s breakout success earlier that summer. Wally Gagel, a producer who worked with The Folk Implosion and later with Eels, still remembers the Beck album's initial impact. "I was in Hotel Nikko and heard *Odelay* for the first time — 'Devils Haircut' or something like that," Gagel says. "And I went, 'Oh my god, this record's *so good*.' I was just absolutely blown away, just like 'I want to make a record this good'." Beyond its sonic novelty — mixing hip-hop, folk, pop, country and rock into a hipster-cool cocktail — was the fact that *Odelay* became Beck's commercial breakthrough, proving that his earlier left-field hit, 'Loser', wasn't a fluke. "Here's an artist doing exactly what they want to do and having a hit record," Gagel recalls thinking at the time. "I had a little taste of that 'cause I was involved with The Folk Implosion and 'Natural One' — that song was a Top 40 hit, which to me still to this day is 'How in the hell did that happen?' It's just so not what a Top 40 hit's supposed to be — that's why it was so great. It was such an exciting time."

In some ways, *Beautiful Freak* wasn't viewed as just E's coming-out party but also a further validation of a Los Angeles music scene. "One of my favourite E stories," Carter says, "is when I'm having a big party, I guess to celebrate the [DreamWorks] signing, and Aimee Mann comes to the party. She steps inside and E's there. She says, 'Hey, E, I hear you got a new record — I sure hope it doesn't suck.' *So* Aimee Mann."

In a *Billboard* interview right before its release, Geffen executive Robert Smith talked about the album's commercial prospects. "Every once in a while, you have a certain reaction," he said, "and this feels much the way that Beck and Garbage did." In addition, 'Novocaine For The Soul' was already making its impact felt on radio, débuting at number 31 on the Modern Rock Tracks chart. Using record-industry terminology, an Atlanta programme director told *Billboard*: "We've hyper-rotated ['Novocaine'] for the last two or three weeks. We thought it sounded different, and it has so many hooks. That's what makes it so special."

What wasn't mentioned anywhere in the *Billboard* profile was that E — who had wondered if he would ever land another record deal and was now, unbelievably, at the brink of stardom — had his mind on things other than music.

About a month earlier — July 11 — Liz had committed suicide in Hawaii. It had been her ninth attempt in 14 years. Overdosing with a bottle of pills, she had just turned 39. In the note she left behind, and excerpted in *The Many Worlds Of Hugh Everett III*, Liz specified that she wanted "no church stuff" at her funeral, asking that her cremated remains be put "in some nice body of water" or the garbage, which had also been her father's wish for himself after his death. Liz clearly understood the significance of her wish to be thrown out in the trash: "maybe that way I'll end up in the correct parallel universe to meet up w/Daddy." E found out the news after receiving an answering-machine message from his mother, in which she talked vaguely about Liz taking some pills — when he phoned her back, she told him that she was dead.

Those who were close to E during that period tend to deflect questions about E's mind-set after his sister's death. Part of the reason is a desire to protect his privacy, but it's also, they say, because E is not one to open up in that way. Of course, another explanation why E's colleagues aren't very forthcoming is that the answers to such questions are obvious. Liz had been such a rock for him in his childhood, turning him on to music and defending him from bullies. And even though they had butted heads more in their twenties, he still loved her dearly.

In October of that year, her death still very much a fresh wound, he told *Los Angeles Times* writer Richard Cromelin: "I got an unexpected perspective from [Liz's suicide], because it's made me be really appreciative of music in my life. . . . I was starting to take it for granted, and I don't take it for granted at all now. . . . 'cause if my sister had had something like this, it would have kept her going. It really is the only thing that's kept me going. Without this I may have given up too." And while therapy seemed to do little for Liz, E revealed that it had been a huge benefit to him. "A lot of artists fear therapy because they think they're gonna get happy and they're not gonna have anything to write about any more," he told Cromelin. "It's done the opposite for me. 'cause I realise I'm not just gonna get happy, I'm just gonna become more aware and learn how to deal with things a little better."

Unable to pull her daughter out of an abyss of her own making — no matter the AA meetings she encouraged Liz to attend, and the amount of money she and her husband sent Liz's way when she was holed up with yet another questionable boyfriend — Nancy wrote Liz a eulogy that read, in part, "We regret we could not help you more."

Asked by Q magazine in 2008 if he thought he could have done anything more for his sister, E replied: "No, that's the problem. You know, we all tried everything we could, but you can't really save people. It's a wonderfully romantic notion but in my experience they have to want to save themselves."

Liz's funeral was in Honolulu. Attending the service of your only sibling would be hard enough, but the funeral parlour's terrible job of making up Liz's face for the open-casket viewing made her look inhuman. Additionally, he has said that Nancy seemed to him to be regressing into a child-like state of denial about her daughter's suicide, which undoubtedly left E feeling very much alone in his grieving, without even his mother to offer much comfort.

There can be little wonder that with such a heavy emotional burden on his mind, commercial success and critical acclaim wouldn't mean much to him. But both came his way nonetheless.

'Novocaine' enjoyed a two-week stay at number one on the Modern Rock chart in October, its single use of the word 'fuck' censored for the radio. (This wouldn't be the last time he would lace a potential radio hit with a pungent curse word.) Boosting the song's popularity was its beautiful accompanying video, a simple but striking black-and-white clip featuring the band levitating in an alley in downtown Los Angeles. Especially in retrospect, it's startling how quickly director Mark Romanek established each member's personality in the video: E was the caustic, brooding front man; Walter was the suave, handsome bassist; Butch was the jokester drummer.

"When I met E, he had this T-shirt on that said 'Grandfather Of The Year'," Romanek later recalled in an interview about the video. "He's just this character — he's like a 20-year-old curmudgeon. For some reason I thought of him as, like, Buster Keaton or something, and I started thinking of him in terms of a silent-movie icon, and I think [the video] has that kind of quality."

Inspired by a childhood love of *Mary Poppins*, Romanek hit upon the idea of having the trio fly, held up by harnesses that were digitally removed after the fact. It was a two-day shoot and not a cheap one. "DreamWorks spared no expense," Butch said later. Romanek, who later went on to prominence as the feature filmmaker of *One Hour Photo* and *Never Let Me Go*, was especially in-demand at the time, having recently helmed the Michael Jackson/Janet Jackson sci-fi video for 'Scream'. The 'Novocaine' clip went on to receive two MTV Video Music Award nominations — for Best Special Effects and Best Cinematography — but lost in both categories to Jamiroquai's 'Virtual Insanity'.

"Probably because of this video is maybe the only reason that anyone's ever heard of us," E later said, with a cutting laugh.

Meanwhile, *Beautiful Freak* garnered positive reviews. Writing in the *Los Angeles Times*, music critic Robert Hilburn said: "Eels' maverick vision reminds you of all the great Los Angeles bands, from The Flying Burrito Brothers to X, that have chronicled the outsider, underdog attitude in the shadows of a record industry that never embraces them commercially." (The album ended up at number five in the paper's year-end poll of its critics.) In her mostly glowing notice in *CMJ New Music Monthly*, Heidi MacDonald compared the album with everything from Soul Coughing to R.E.M'.s *Monster* to Tom Petty. And it was inevitable that because of the Mike Simpson connection, E had to endure many reviews that talked about his similarities to Beck.

"There are definitely similarities," E acknowledged later that year, "but I don't think it came from the Dust Brothers connection. We never even heard [*Odelay*]. They came out at the same time. I've worked on the songs for about two years now and they were almost complete before we met Mike. I can understand someone saying that, but I think Beck is more groove-oriented while we are more song-based. What really turned me on to Michael was his work on *Paul's Boutique* and the stuff he did with Tone-Loc. I thought that was a good example of pop music moving forward."

The notion of creating something new was also a talking point in his *Billboard* profile. "I got pigeonholed into this retro-pop category of musicians that I never intended to be a part of," he said, referring to his E solo records. "I always want to evolve and change through the course of my career." He also expressed ambivalence about being part of a so-called "Silver Lake scene". "My whole life, I've been an outsider," he declared. "I have this thing where I'm not part of the crowd, but I must be, because I live here, and I'm in a band."

Jacobsen also noticed the conscious effort to de-emphasise E's pre-*Beautiful Freak* work. "When we were doing the Eels record, it was like a top secret thing to keep people from [finding out]," he says. "They basically wanted to pretend that he'd never had a solo career. I don't think it really came from E — I think it was everybody else. They were hoping to break the band huge, and they just didn't want any baggage associated with records that hadn't been successful."

As someone who loved the solo records, Wild was amazed by the *Beautiful Freak* material, although he remembers being thrown somewhat at first because it was so different from the songwriter's earlier work. In retrospect, he came to understand what this "giant leap forward" (Wild's phrase) for E represented. "I think he was smart enough and savvy enough to realise he didn't want to be just another power-pop darling," Wild says. "I think he wanted to be engaged in what was going on and not just a nostalgic rehash of anything."

And although E and his team tried to keep his solo career quiet, he and the band would play 'Hello Cruel World' during their early shows. "I would like to do a couple of the songs from the solo records when we have more time in our show," he said in October during a session at KCRW. "I'd like to do 'E's Tune' off the first record... and there's a couple on the second one I'd like to resurrect." Then, he added with typical deadpan wit, "or I'll just maybe save it for my solo tour... Butch and Tommy will be the band." (Surely not wanting to miss out on tangential record sales, Polydor reissued his solo records after *Beautiful Freak* hit.)

When *Beautiful Freak* came out, Jacobsen was overseas, but he got a sense of the Eels' commercial potential. "I was in Paris," he recalls. "I'm out just wandering around. And that record was the toast of the town — every record store you went into, there were these huge displays of *Beautiful Freak*. And I just thought, 'We're going to take over the world'."

That was especially true in the UK, where *Beautiful Freak* went Top 10, generating two Top 10 singles in 'Novocaine' and 'Susan's House'. Nic Harcourt, who replaced Douridas as *Morning Becomes Eclectic* host in 1998, told E during a KCRW performance: "I remember going over to England [when *Beautiful Freak* came out] and seeing the album right there in the front of the store in the point-of-sale display. I mean, prime positioning. I was like, 'Wow, this is so cool'."

Certainly expectations were just as high in the States, which E discussed in the *Billboard* interview. "It's a double-edged sword," he said. "It's really great that we are the first band to come out on DreamWorks, because they are really focused on us, and it's good timing, but there is also that pressure, because DreamWorks got so much media attention because of the big moguls that started it. Everyone has that 'show me' attitude."

"That was the kind of talk about the band when they first came out: 'This is the new thing — this is the next big thing'," Jacobsen remembers. "And then, um, and then it wasn't the next big thing."

Beautiful Freak never cracked the *Billboard* Top 100 in America, with 'Novocaine' failing to cross over onto the pop charts. And while one could be disappointed that the album wasn't quite a smash in its homeland, the truth is the success of its lead single could almost be looked at as one of those freak occurrences that happen when a really great, really weird song actually becomes popular. A quick glance at the number one Modern Rock Tracks of 1996 reveals two trends: a preponderance of artists (Bush, Pearl Jam, Oasis) working in traditional rock formats; and a handful of quirky, almost novelty hits. In the second category were songs that incorporated hip-hop ingredients, such as loops and samples. The Butthole Surfers' Gibby Haynes did a Beck-like rap on 'Pepper', while a one-hit-wonder band called Primitive Radio Gods grabbed a sample from a B.B. King song for the soulful, despondent 'Standing Outside A Broken Phone Booth With Money In My Hand'. About a month later, the ascension of 'Novocaine' seemed less surprising, reflecting the modern rock audience's interest in catchy tunes that sounded old and new simultaneously.

But rather than lamenting what could have been for this supposed "next big thing", perhaps Eels fans should marvel that E was ever saddled with such a label.

"With the Eels, he tried to meet alternative modern rock halfway," Wild says of E's transition from solo artist to *Beautiful Freak* darling. "I don't know if, to my ears, it was as 'groundbreaking' as it was just good — really good. It's like he took [Tom] Waits and Beck, along with all the other early influences, and added an industrial strength version of what he'd always done."

"His vision is very singular," Jacobsen says in retrospect, "and I don't think it's ever gonna be everybody's cup of tea. I think that if they had been able to have a string of videos that were as cool as 'Novocaine', then maybe people would have gotten it. If you get a buzz going around something, even very strange things can sometimes [cross over]. But there was a narrow window there, I think, when that could have happened."

E had his own unique take on the album's reception. "After we played in Manchester recently," he said in early 1997, "I was signing this one guy's CD and as a joke I said, 'Tell all your friends about us.' And he goes, 'I don't have any friends.' So I said, 'Well, when you get some, tell them.' And I thought, 'We're probably never gonna be really big because there's not gonna be any word of mouth about us 'cause our fans don't have any friends.' I'm kinda proud of that in a way. It's kind of nice to have the outcasts. A lot of the outcasts are really intelligent people."

And as far as DreamWorks was concerned, patience was the important thing. "Our experience over the years was that most of the successful artists that were signed at Warner Bros didn't start out as pop artists," Waronker says. "They ultimately got there because their audience kept growing and growing until pop radio had to play it. There were certainly times where records are made that went right on the radio. But most of the artists wanted to feel like they had the possibility or potential to have a long-term career."

With all of this said, though, it's important to reiterate how hot Eels were at that moment, a fact that wasn't lost on Walter.

"My best friend and I were in the car just driving down the street," he recalls, "and Jed The Fish from KROQ was playing each track from the album and talking about it." Walter laughs, adding: "Clearly, a different era. But he was really into it and talking about it. And I was like, 'This is *us*'. He's talking about the whole story about E and just dissecting the record on the air. And I was like, 'This is interesting...'"

Later on a trip to Seattle, he hung out with Dave Dederer, a member of The Presidents Of The United States Of America, an indie-rock band who had had a huge success on modern rock radio the previous year with their single 'Lump'. "I just remember him looking at me," Walter says. "He's like, 'Get ready, Tommy'." It was then that Walter started to understand just how much his life was going to change because of

'Novocaine'. "[Dederer] had already done it, and he was still going through it," Walter says. "And when he looked at me, it was like, 'Get ready for this'. He'd been there and seen what it's like. He wasn't saying this as, like, impending doom — he was saying that this is going to be fun and a lot of work and this is fortunate. And I got that."

Some of that extra attention came in unusual ways. For instance, one day E got a letter from actor Nicolas Cage. "He says he really loves our record and 'Beautiful Freak' is his favourite song," E told *Melody Maker*, "and he doesn't even realise that it was inspired by one of his films. I wrote 'Beautiful Freak' the day after I'd seen the film *Birdy*. There's a line about flying inside. That made my day. It's one thing to get a letter from somebody famous, but to get a letter from somebody famous that does work that you really admire — that's a big thrill."

But when the band started touring to support the record, the different personalities within the band, which had helped energise their live shows, started to cause friction. "My world music influences were not something I was supposed to mention [in interviews]," Butch told *Drumhead*, "and I almost didn't get the gig because of that."

Additionally, while E was a staunch atheist, Butch had a brief flirtation with Scientology back in Northern California as a teenager as a way to kick his pot habit. A bandmate at the time had suggested Butch attend a Dianetics Counselling Group meeting, which had worked wonders for him.

"I went for a meeting and they were talking about getting me off the pot by taking a communications course," Butch told an interviewer. "So I paid 50 bucks, did the class, gave up the pot, started running every day and I enjoyed listening to the basic principles that L. Ron Hubbard was talking about. It seemed very harmless. The root of his thing is that people misunderstand so much. The basis of that made total sense, so I started going back to them, started reading more books than ever before."

He told his parents that he had quit pot, figuring they'd be pleased. And they were… until they discovered what had inspired the turnaround. "My parents freaked," Butch said. "'You're in a cult?!'" After his folks threatened to kidnap him and have him "de-programmed", Butch used their concern to his benefit, convincing them to pay for his studies at Cal Arts. They complied, and Butch never went back to another Scientology meeting.

As for Walter, he recalls a feeling of being belittled when he did Eels interviews. In particular, he remembers a Q&A that was conducted with all three band members where a reporter "asked us about a certain song, like 'My Beloved Monster' or something like that, and I said, 'E, isn't that somewhat tongue-in-cheek in the way that you deliver those lyrics?' I was just asking him — I was answering the question, but I didn't want to step on him. And he just looked at me and said, 'No'. Like, 'You idiot'. And he totally embarrassed me in front of these interviewers. That really tears somebody down."

(A sense of this can be heard in the band's October 1996 appearance on KCRW with Douridas, in which E was discussing how he likes to challenge himself by playing instruments he's not comfortable on, such as his then-recent evolution to lead guitarist in a rock trio. "I'm kind of against the idea of music school," he said by way of explanation. "If you want to be a musician, I think it's a good idea. But if you want to be an artist, if you want to write songs, I don't know if it's such a good idea." Obviously sensing how his words might be received by Walter, he added, "Just my opinion." When Douridas asked Walter what he thought of that, E offered, "Well, Tommy is one of the rare exceptions.")

For Walter, the problems ran deeper, tracing back to the suggestions he made for *Beautiful Freak* that were shot down. Walter saw Eels as an all-for-one band, partly because (according to him) that's how the idea of Eels was initially sold to him. "Carter and Butch at one point when they wanted me to join the band had said, 'Look, this is not [just] E's thing'," Walter recalls. "'You're gonna be a band member. We want you to be part of this band.' Later, I sorta realised that E never really wanted a band. He always wanted to be a solo artist, and I think he was sort of hesitant about having a band and [later] resentful of having a band, even though all of us realised that he was the main force behind everything." By comparison, Butch, even at the time, understood that Eels was a way to service E's creative pursuits. "He is the master behind this whole thing," Butch said in 1999 about E's attitude toward Eels, "and he pretty much has his definite ideas. This is his child and I would be like the surrogate mother coming along."

The philosophical difference between E's bandmates about the group cut to the heart of their divergent temperaments. Butch, as was suggested by Mike Simpson and Parthenon Huxley, was very happy to be part of the team and go along for the ride. "The challenge for me is to help E achieve his vision," Butch told *Modern Drummer* at the time. "That's what the deal is in this situation. In other situations, with other bands I've been with, I might have more of an active role or less of an active role to a certain degree. He comes in with ideas and things that are set, and I'll play along with them. I might take them in a different direction, but the way it works is if it doesn't fit his vision, it ain't going to cut it. This is a specific thing where he knows what he wants, and 99.9% of the time I'm completely right there."

As for Walter: "I just don't automatically pledge allegiance." When E published his memoir, he said that the bassist "was always rubbing people in our caravan the wrong way", a comment that stung Walter and demonstrated in his mind how misunderstood he was in the group. "E's got one of those personalities [where] people really gather around him and they follow," Walter says. "The crew, the road manager — basically, he could do whatever, and everybody would just be like, 'Yes, sir'. That's not my personality. So, to say I 'rubbed people the wrong way'? Growing up in my family, I'm the one who would say, 'Actually, you're not being very nice right now'. So, is that rubbing people the wrong way? Or is it like I'm callin' you out?"

Carter looks at the conflict succinctly: "It's always about the lead singer. It's always about the songwriter." Still, he agrees with some of Walter's frustrations about being underappreciated in the group. "He was a talented guy," Carter says about Walter. "He was not taken full advantage of. E had someone who could play bass, sing and play tuba — he should have co-written a song, should have done one of his [own] songs. E was a fucking idiot not to know that he had a really good little band."

E has pointed to the vast age difference between Walter and the rest of the band as contributing to the friction that occurred during their US and European tours, which ran from early October 1996 through late August 1997, with very few breaks in between. (Carter remembers that Walter "acted out" on tour. "He would disappear after a show and miss the bus the next day.") And while Walter is, understandably, defensive about always being singled out as "the young guy", he does admit it was a factor, if only in terms of perception. "I think if we had all been closer to the same age it would have been different," he says. "E was seven or eight years [older], and I think Butch is 12 years older than me. I think they kind of looked at me like, 'Oh, he's the young guy, he doesn't know anything'."

Soon, Walter felt isolated from the rest of the band and the road crew, which wasn't helped by the fact that Walter had developed sciatica — a pinched nerve in his lower back — while on the road. ("They probably thought I was a super-grumpy guy," Walter says, "when I was actually just dealing with a lot of pain.") Beyond the physical pain, though, Walter was irritated by what he saw as E's attempts to focus more of the attention on himself. "We used to do a stage set-up where I was stage left, E was stage right, and of course Butch was in the middle," he recalls. "And then, all of a sudden, E moved his microphone to the middle of the stage." There was never a conversation about it: this was just the way things were going to be from here on out. "I don't really think of myself as a difficult person," Walter continues. "You know, 'I want more stage space' — I didn't really care about any of that stuff. But there definitely was a shift — all of a sudden, it's like, 'Oh, we're growing in popularity, and E wants all the credit'."

By the end of 1996, tensions were so bad that the band (with Carter) had to have a sit-down meeting. "If the tone of the sit-down was different," Walter says, "things would have changed that day. If it would have been like, 'You are appreciated, we do love you, we want to keep this going, we love what we have going here, why are you struggling, what can we do for you?', I probably would have been more open to it. And then I would have been like, 'Well, what can I do for you guys? I'm really sorry — I am struggling. I am a little bit freaked out. This is all new — I've never done this before. You guys are older, I don't know what I'm doing,' But instead it was a little bit more like, 'This is E's thing — you can be replaced.' And that doesn't feel good." He laughs. "I remember hearing that and thinking, 'This is not a nurturing environment'."

It only got worse for Walter the following year. "Towards the end of the tour, [E and Butch] would go out to dinner and not invite me," he recalls. "I think at one point I was calling Butch's room and the line was busy and I was calling E's room and the line was busy, and it'd been busy for half an hour, and I was like, 'Uh oh'."

If Walter was feeling some bad vibes, there seemed to be plenty to go around. In the summer of 1997, Eels were invited to play as part of the travelling Lollapalooza tour. It was the last year that the heralded alternative-music festival was an annual touring event before being re-launched in 2003. E mostly hated the experience, forced to confront what he called the festival's "sea of teenage jocks in backwards baseball caps" who made up a large part of the audience. If this was what "alternative" meant, he wasn't interested in being part of the scene. (He did, however, get to hang out with Snoop Dogg's dad during the tour, who he thought was a pretty nice guy.)

After Lollapalooza, the band played more shows in Europe. As the Eels tour was finally nearing completion, Walter tried to remain upbeat. "My own feeling was, 'Yeah, we went through some rough times but overall this was fun'," Walter says. "And I was looking forward to settling down, getting home, getting grounded and starting up again. But I had a feeling it was coming."

Walter's final show with Eels happened at a private party after the official tour had ended. "It was somewhere in Beverly Hills," he says. "Somebody had hired us to play." On a lark, Butch decided to do the show naked, which Walter didn't know until they were about to perform in front of a crowd of about 50. "I just remember coming on stage and getting my bass, getting ready to play, and Butch passed me going, 'Excuse me', and being completely naked," says Walter. "Of course, he thought it was hilarious and great, but I was like, 'Really? You just did that?'" To Walter's mind, Butch's stunt was something the drummer and E had discussed behind Walter's back. "They thought it would be really funny," he says, "and they probably both knew that I wouldn't be into it." (They were right: "That's not something I would ever want a band that I was in to do because I don't think [people would] take us seriously.")

Walter's firing happened that fall. It was quick and businesslike, as he recalls: "They sent me a notice in the mail saying, 'You're out of the partnership'."

Shortly after being booted from Eels, Walter did an interview in which he had few kind words to say about his former associates. "The more shows we did and the more popular we became, the more E wanted the focus to be on him," he said. "The focus was on him anyway. Why did E have to go around telling everyone that this is 'my band'? Who cares anyway? That only served to be divisive. It's the typical rock'n'roll clichés that destroyed this band. I never got bored, but in the later shows I hated being pushed towards the role of 'the dumb bass player' while E was acting like a solo artist. That is a waste of my time and a waste of the band's potential. It's a real shame."

"I was pretty low after that," he says 13 years later. Getting fired "was a really difficult time. You know, it's just like the floor falls out from beneath you." Eventually, he moved on, making his own albums and starting his own project, Abandoned Pools, an indie-rock collective praised for their guitar melodies and stylistic scope. "I think that the problem with E and I if you really boil it down," he now says, "is that we weren't reaching out to each other in a way that we should. Maybe I was overwhelmed — he was too. He was having difficulty adjusting to this level of success — it wasn't just me. And he was dealing with a lot of issues with his family, his sister, and things like that. I think he was going through a really difficult time. And so maybe I was having trouble listening and he was too. I think our biggest problem is not communicating to each other and reaching out to each other and saying, 'Brother, what do you need from me?'"

Walter did, however, take some comfort in one moment from the contentious meeting he'd had with his bandmates and Carter a year earlier. "The one tiny little nugget in that little sit-down session was when E said, 'I know I can be difficult sometimes'." Walter laughs. "And I was like, 'Oh my God, he said it!'"

"Eels really wouldn't have happened without Tommy and Butch," says Greg Collins, a producer and friend of E. "It wouldn't have happened the way it did. E is no doubt a talented, brilliant guy — an artist in the truest sense. But that first Eels record and those guys — what they sort of represented and the way they were able to give E an outlet outside of what he had been doing as a solo artist — you can't put a price on that. You can't devalue it in any way, even though that core band only lasted a short period."

Still, Walter's point is a fair one concerning E's own personal issues possibly contributing to the downfall of the trio. After all, his sister's death was still very recent. And, sadly, the family troubles weren't over yet. In the March 15, 1997 issue of *Melody Maker*, E was taking stock of his life in the wake of *Beautiful Freak*. There were reasons to be happy, but also reasons to be concerned — specifically, about his mother.

"I have one sister," he said. "She was older than me and she committed suicide and that was it. My dad died when I was 19 and now my mom's really ill." He then came to grips with what that meant. "I'm looking at being the last member [of my family] standing. It's pretty weird to be this young and to be in the position where you'll have no family. It's weird that all this is happening so fast."

Which brings us to more heartbreak, firings, great songs and the next chapter.

Chapter Eight

Some artists like to get feedback from those closest to them when they're finishing a record, be it from family, friends or collaborators. It offers an outsider's perspective that can be helpful to the creative process and allows the artist to realise what's not working on his album.

E is not that type of artist.

"He doesn't bounce ideas off of anyone," Jim Jacobsen says. "He has ideas, and then he tries to see if he can get people to do what he wants — and he usually succeeds. I was thinking, I don't know that he ever said, 'I could do the phrase like this or I could do the phrase like this — which do you think is better?' He will ponder that on his own and come to that decision."

But there was one person E contacted for feedback and comments — and he did so quite a lot.

"E called me 10 times a day," Carter says. "We would talk for 30 minutes, hang up. I could count to five and the phone would ring again. It was a constant, intense, seven-day-a-week, really, really, heavy, heavy, heavy relationship."

What was he calling about? "Just whatever thought he had in his head, or business things — a million things. I mean, we might talk about the new Neil Young record. We certainly might talk about the song he wrote yesterday that I'd gotten in the mail the next day. Certainly, we talked about E, E, E. As far as he was concerned — as all artists are —

you're his manager in the business of you. And I'm a know-it-all, so I was very preachy about [the music business]."

E has said that Carter was a father figure to him, especially early in his career when he was trying to find his artistic equilibrium. Carter seems somewhat sheepish about accepting that title from E. "I take that term kinda non-literally," he says. "I was a successful songwriter, I was a successful producer, I knew about the record company side — I knew about a lot of stuff, so I always had the trump card on him in those conversations: 'I'm telling you what it's like'. So, 'father figure'? I don't think it was that way."

The two would argue if Carter didn't like a particular song E had just come up with, the manager insisting it needed, say, a better second verse or a different solo. As Carter acknowledges, part of the intensity of their relationship during those early years was his own fault, resulting from his management style. "A lot of acts are looking for an asshole," Carter says. "They wanna be the good guy and they're looking for a bad cop to make them money. And then there are other managers — and I'm one of those — who are all-consuming and worried about every bar, and every word, and the art, and the act, and the sequence, and the haircut. All of that. I've warned the artists that I've been involved with that I'm not just the agent booking the shows and 'let's keep our fingers crossed'. This is a deep science, and you're under the microscope at all times. So, he enjoyed that, and then with him being a very strong-willed artist, he struggled with that too."

As Eels were experiencing their first real brush with fame, E tended to wield an ironic, dry sense of humour when dealing with journalists and their repetitive (and sometimes idiotic) questions. One can go online and find clips of the band — E and Butch, in particular — teasing and harassing clueless foreign journalists whose grasp of English and sarcasm was iffy at best. But E could also burnish a dark comedic streak when talking about his family. When he spoke to the *Los Angeles Times* in the fall of 1996, his sister had just recently killed herself and he was asked about his difficult childhood. "Well, it is hard to talk about because not everybody in my family's dead yet," he said. "But almost." He laughed, but then stopped, adding, "I've just got to laugh, 'cause either you cry or you laugh, and laughing feels better sometimes."

He would again be faced with that choice when, in January 1997, he found out that his mother had been diagnosed with lung cancer, almost certainly due to being around his father's insatiable smoking habit. (Ten years later one of Hugh's closest friends, Don Reisler, developed lung cancer, also probably because of Hugh's ever-present Kents.) Doctors gave Nancy two years tops before the disease would claim her. So as the band's relationship with Walter continued to deteriorate over that year during a gruelling touring schedule, E was also weighed down by the thought that he soon would be the only member of his family left alive.

But it wasn't just his sister's shocking death and his mother's imminent demise that were on his mind. Around the same time as Nancy's diagnosis, Parthenon Huxley's wife, Janet, died from brain cancer at the age of 38. By all accounts, Janet was a fun-loving, vivacious person. And then one day, she was just gone.

Huxley, who would write candidly about her passing a few years later on his album *Purgatory Falls*, didn't fully grasp at the time just how much Janet's death had affected E, who wrote about her fondly in his memoir. "I didn't realise there was such a parallel with his mom," he says. "My perspective [of that period] is quite different from his. I was in a different place — I met this guy E, we wrote some songs, and then my wife's story is, obviously, a hell of a lot more meaningful and impactful to me. I have my very vivid memories of how that whole thing went down, but I didn't know all the details about his mom."

As with his sister's suicide, E didn't talk to his colleagues much about his mother's grim prognosis. Even Carter, whom E spoke to constantly, says: "I suppose I consoled him, but he wouldn't involve people in his life like that." Instead, E focused his grief and worry into his music, which, as should be obvious, was how he dealt with almost everything in his world.

At first, though, he wasn't sure that he wanted to write songs about these family traumas, or if he even wanted to make another album. The carnival surrounding *Beautiful Freak* had left a bad taste in his mouth. Plus, he worried that writing about his family would simply be too personal. But then he got inspired during one of his many trips back to McLean to check in on his mom. Lying in bed in the basement, just as he had when he was a kid, he decided that writing about these experiences might be just what he needed. Maybe from all that misery something positive could be generated.

Without necessarily explaining his approach, he started holing up with his chief collaborators to bang out songs for what would become *Electro-Shock Blues*.

The album was put together in bits and pieces whenever E had the time, what with bouncing back and forth between Virginia and Los Angeles. As a result, the approach helped give the record its herky-jerky, almost schizophrenic quality, its moods and sounds clashing rather than complementing each other. It was going to be a concept album, and a rather prickly one at that, about his sister and mother and his relationship with both of them. And it was the first album E made that, to be truly understood, would need to be listened to in its entirety, in order.

Its first track, 'Elizabeth On The Bathroom Floor', introduced a technique that would be continued on several other songs later on the album: singing from his sister's perspective. "It's like, here's this gift I can give her," he explained 10 years later about his thought process. "It's too bad she couldn't do this for herself but I'm going to let her be an artist here. It's like putting a frame around her."

Opening with delicate guitar, 'Elizabeth On The Bathroom Floor' retold the story of Liz's first suicide attempt during the summer of 1982. But it wasn't just that he sang the song in first-person from Liz's viewpoint — there was a dramatic component to the narrative, incorporating an *in medias res* storytelling style that gripped the listener immediately as we discovered the Liz character lying on the bathroom floor while the family cat tries to revive her. Using a sample of an angelic chorus, the track was both comforting and frightening, alerting the listener to the fact that *Electro-Shock Blues* was going to have an almost theatrical flair to it.

The album then segued in to the atmospheric, lo-fi industrial blues-funk of 'Going To Your Funeral Part I'. The story was no longer being

112

told from Liz's perspective — now it was E talking to his dearly departed sister while at her funeral.

"I think he had just finished touring the first record, and he called me up and asked if I had anything new," Jacobsen remembers. "I had a guitar part that Parthenon had played for a TV show that I was the composer on. I'd had him do a bunch of improvising, and he played this simple riff — he tuned the E string of the guitar down to an A. I loved it. And I thought, 'That [riff] is so much better than this show', which got cancelled anyway. So I had that part. Then I had the idea of putting the whole song as a triplet against a straight beat thing. And I was really hopeful that E would be cool with that — he thought it was great. The song has an unusual rhythmic feel to it — I have actually never heard anything that quite feels like that."

"Jim is fearless like that," says Huxley, who had no idea that Jacobsen was going to use his old bluesy riff for the song. "You know, he throws stuff up on the audio canvas that's just very fearless and really cool."

"He came in and loved everything I had done," Jacobsen says of E's response to the track. "And it's never much more than a day's work with him. If it doesn't come together in a day, his head will explode. Sometimes it doesn't all happen in one day, but if you add it all together it's a good day's work. And then it's time to mix."

For the lyrics, E dealt with the horror show of his sister's funeral, particularly the irony that the ceremony dedicating her ashes was held on an utterly gorgeous day in Honolulu. E's only solace was to think back to happier childhood memories when he and Liz were still close.

The sorrow of 'Going To Your Funeral Part I' gave way to the snarling, almost incoherent anger of 'Cancer For The Cure', a clattering mash-up of funky keyboards, sampled sounds, piercing industrial-rock guitars and percussion that seemed constructed from rusty old metal pipes. It was a collaboration between E and producer Mickey Petralia, but the bones of the song seemed inspired by an E hero. "I think E was always a big Tom Waits fan," Jim Lang offers, "but I wonder when he really fell seriously under the spell of Tom Waits. Tom Waits is such a great storyteller and a *phenomenal* stylist." (In fact, Waits was someone that, like Neil Young, Liz had loved as a kid.)

With its aggressively combative tone and jarring sounds, 'Cancer For The Cure' suggested prolonged exposure to *Bone Machine*, the 1992 Waits record that signalled the iconic singer-songwriter's transition from drunken-pianist balladeer to full-on junkyard rocker. "Waits did those very sort of deconstructed recordings," Lang says of *Bone Machine*, "kind of a lo-fi ethos. In terms of people who had a lot of stature, he was really kind of an early adopter of that — he was fearless about what he would do in the studio and, I think, inspirational because he really kinda pushed us over into the need to fuck things up, to distort things. I think E really went to school on Tom Waits' recordings in a way that really informed his recording practice."

To reflect the track's musical chaos, E delivered lyrics seemingly built from free associations. Kids digging a hole, a grandfather with a porn addiction, a suicidal father — 'Cancer For The Cure' was the sound of a young man so losing his shit over his grief that he was hardly coherent any more. For a songwriter who had previously prided himself on poetic expressions of his pain that felt precisely calibrated, 'Cancer For The Cure' made an unholy ruckus, surrendering to all that he couldn't control.

The hyperbolic 'Cancer For The Cure' turned into 'My Descent Into Madness', a deceptively pretty song about a narrator who's locked away in an institution with a straightjacket. Sung in the first person, 'My Descent Into Madness' doesn't match Liz's biography, but it was nonetheless a deeply empathetic portrait of a young person who can't get the help she needs. Perhaps most heartbreaking of all were the series of "la la la la" melodic choruses that dominated the track, hinting at either a heavily medicated bliss or a complete psychic break from reality.

The track was put together by E and "The Good, The Bad & The Ugly". This mysterious collective was actually Mike Simpson and two other renowned hip-hop producers, Dan "The Automator" Nakamura and Paul "Prince Paul" Huston, a duo who would a year later form Handsome Boy Modeling School, the masterminds behind the avant-garde hip-hop album *So...How's Your Girl?*

"Dan had this idea that the three of us should just lock ourselves in a room for a week with three turntables and a stack of random records,"

Simpson says. "We were supposed to just grab a stack of records and not go through them to see which records they were. It was sort of an experiment, and we put together probably about 25 tracks all in various stages of completion. That was to be the groundwork for our group, The Good, The Bad & The Ugly, which was also signed to DreamWorks, but we never actually finished the record." When the time came for Simpson to work with E on *Electro-Shock Blues*, he used one of the trio's tracks — with Nakamura's and Huston's blessing — to form the basis of 'My Descent Into Madness'. "We didn't add a lot to that, actually," Simpsons says. "That one was pretty much The Good, The Bad & The Ugly." In retrospect the unusual origin of the track makes sense, considering that Handsome Boy Modeling School's work was always a mixture of sophisticated pop and playful, jazzy samples — the perfect counterpoint to E's melancholy ode to a lovely but lost soul.

E transitioned from fiction to reality for the next song, '3 Speed', which had come together after E had been playing with Sean Coleman in his buddy's San Francisco rehearsal space. Written in a motel room shortly after the jam session, the first-person Liz track detailed, as he explained in *Things The Grandchildren Should Know*, "when she was a little kid and things were starting to change for her."

The album's first overtly accessible melody, '3 Speed' was written and produced solely by E, and like 'Elizabeth On The Bathroom Floor' the song was intimate and dreamlike, the product of one person's life filtered through the impressions of another person's. With subtle strings backing a strummed guitar, the tune juxtaposed innocent childhood memories — riding a bike, hanging out in the woods at the outskirts of McLean — with a nagging (and growing) sense that there's something not right underneath the idyllic images. Liz keeps asking the same question: "Why won't you just tell me what's going on?" It's seemingly innocuous, but its repetition proves troubling, especially when she asks it after seeing herself in the mirror: "All I saw was a pretty blonde," she says, a reflection that most young girls would be thrilled to see. But eventually E reveals her dilemma, which in many ways could be his as well: "Life is funny/But not ha ha funny/Peculiar I guess/You think I got it all going my way/Then why am I such a fucking mess?" '3 Speed' drapes its pretty arrangement around a lingering dread that's all the more poignant because the listener knows full well that it will only get worse for young Liz as she gets older.

After that, it was time for another sonically adventurous song. 'Hospital Food' started out as a Butch drum track that E presented to Lang, who added bass and Wurlitzer to it. Then, Lang recruited Bill Liston, a saxophonist he worked with on his scoring gigs, to wail on top of the track.

"I remember at the time I was working on it, I was thinking, 'Well, what I'm doing here may not fly'," Lang recalls. "Jazzy's not exactly the right word, but it was not E's harmony, not his chords like he would normally use. And the lines that I was writing underneath were a little more angular. I guess he heard it and it worked for him — it ended up flying."

Indeed, E embraced the ironic-jazzbo nature of the song, even including an exchange between himself and Butch — "Butch?" "What?" "I can hear you" — into the track.

"Butch, being the Cal Arts guy that he is, really is very adventuresome about what he'll bring to bear in terms of percussion tools," Lang says. When they were working on 'Hospital Food', Lang recalls, "Butch had a toy train that had a whistle sound that you couldn't even tell was supposed to be a whistle. It was just a super-distorted digital sound." They threw it into the song, its high-pitched *wheee-wheee-wheee* adding another element of dissonance. "That's pure Butch to me," Lang says.

'Hospital Food' also felt Waits-ian in its incorporation of a seemingly refined musical arrangement that was systematically ripped apart until it felt like some ferocious mutant variation on the typical genre tropes. On top of this bizarro jazz, E delivered menacing words about the creeping inevitability of death and illness. The song's moral: no matter who you are, eventually you're going to end up in a hospital.

"I was spending a lot of time in a lot of different hospitals for a lot of different reasons," he told a reporter at the time. "I started to develop an interesting point of view about it all. That song is about taking responsibility for yourself. Hospital food has a bad rap — no one wants to eat it. But at some point most of us do end up eating it. And, um, I started thinking about why we get sick... Is it inevitable or do we bring it on ourselves?" The song's lyrics also hinted at a theme that would emerge later on the record: we should appreciate what we have now, because it may not last.

The clatter of rude horns ceased, and the next sound was stark, calm, eerie tones repeating. "Based on writings by Elizabeth," the liner notes indicated, 'Electro-Shock Blues' was inspired by a notepad Liz's family found after her death. She had been given an exercise to write the phrase "I am OK" over and over again. This, apparently, was a way to create a sense of self-esteem and normalcy in her, but it didn't work: eventually she just wrote "I am not OK."

The short track was dominated by those repeating tones, which had the effect of suggesting a losing battle with sanity and a growing madness. His vocals distorted so that they lost all warmth or personality, E portrayed his sister as a lost cause, the opening verse's "I am OK/I am OK/I'm not OK" particularly disheartening, matched by the song's closing lines: "I am trying/I am trying." The pretty blonde of '3 Speed' was replaced by a woman concerned about "skin is crawling off/ mopping the sweaty drops." It was a sliver of a story, but its despair was bottomless.

The first side — or "Part I" as it was labelled on the liner notes' "contents" page — ended with 'Efils' God', a track that featured E's falsetto and a mournful backwards cello. The title itself was backwards, the letters forming "dog's life" in reverse. But it wasn't simple cleverness: 'Dog's Life' was the name of a song E had written shortly after moving to California. "I was so lonely and, well... miserable," he explained in the liner notes to the *Useless Trinkets* B-sides collection that included the track. "[O]ne day I was running by this dog laying in his yard. I felt a wave of envy. I wanted his carefree life. I recorded the song on my four track cassette recorder in my closet that night." The song remained a leftover until E got the idea of flipping it backwards for 'Efils' God', which proved to be a wonderfully unfathomable tune.

Written from no clear perspective, the song sports a narrator who almost mockingly says goodbye to his or her loved ones who can't possibly imagine the experience of being dead. Two lines in particular stand out: "Now you can bring back my suitcase/but you can't bring me." Years later in his autobiography, he'd offer some insight into the words' meaning. Very shortly after Janet's death, he went over to Huxley's house and discovered that the deceased woman's suitcase had returned from the hospital, even though its owner had not. To E, the sight of the lonely suitcase made the loss of Janet even more depressing.

With 'Efils' God', though, E argued that at least the recently departed are free of the agony of mortal life. The slightly cocky narrator is happily letting go of the petty problems of the material world, specifically money. But the disorienting-yet-soothing backwards cello gives the song an ominous quality as well: is the narrator dying from natural causes or through suicide? Is the death a choice? E never lets on one way or the other, just another snapshot in the collection of *Electro-Shock Blues* that moves in and out of focus before forever vanishing.

Starting a tradition he would continue on some later albums, E began the album's second half with an instrumental, 'Going To Your Funeral Part II'. Jacobsen played clarinet on the gently soaring, orchestral 90-second track, which created a consoling counterpoint to the misery of the original song. Jacobsen was also credited, tongue in cheek, as the song's conductor. "It was a *huge* string orchestra," he says sarcastically, "in my right hand. That's all sampled strings — that's E's sense of humour."

Then there was 'Last Stop: This Town', which came about from a conversation E had with his landlady, Francis, after returning from Liz's funeral. In her eighties, Francis informed him that she could see spirits and that she had noticed that "a young woman" had entered his house while he had been away. (Francis had previously been Huxley's landlady, and when the two men talk on the phone now, they still take turns doing affectionate impressions of her nagging-grandmother voice.) And so 'Last Stop: This Town' could perhaps be interpreted as E's tardy response to his phantom guest. Almost an answer song to 'Efils' God', 'Last Stop: This Town' offered the survivor's side of the conversation, missing the newly departed, wishing to be reunited, but also astonished by the unknowable gulf between the dead and the living.

E's friendly, fantastical narrative was backed by a track dreamt up by Mike Simpson.

"Back in those days I would just make tracks," Simpson recalls. "In my spare time, I would just put things together and put them on the shelf until something came up, until I thought someone was right for it. That was a track that I really loved. I felt like it was a little weird, but I thought E would be the perfect guy for that."

In truth, it fits nicely with *Electro-Shock Blues'* approach of combining accessible melodies with occasionally jarring instrumentation. A trademark of the album, a heavenly choir, butted up against a chorus hook consisting of a record being scratched and then, later, a distorted guitar riff. Because at the time Beck had been the most commercially and critically successful in a scene that melded hip-hop culture with indie-rock purity, 'Last Stop: This Town' drew some comparisons with his work, but as Greg Collins, a producer and mixer who worked on *Electro-Shock Blues*, says, "knowing E and his processes and the way he works, he's a guy who does his thing. He takes great pride in not being influenced by anything in what you could call his 'genre'."

The next song was a wild card, a weird two-minute collage of toy instruments that sounded like the kind of rinky-dink lullaby one associates with a child's music box. The periodic rattle of metal or sampled spoken dialogue undercut the lullaby, though, leaving the listener on edge. It was called 'Baby Genius,' and its lyrics were spiteful, seemingly mocking somebody who had a high opinion of him or herself but who was really just a pain in the neck. Considering that the album was so much about his family, who could 'Baby Genius' be? His father was the most likely candidate because of the "genius" tag, but the lyrics matched nothing in his biography. Jim Lang, who put together the song with E, has little memory of its making, but he vaguely recalls its origins.

"I don't know if I'm telling tales out of school," Lang says, "but he was really angry with somebody that he had played with. It was him kind of working out his shit." Pressed further about the person's identity, Lang can only recall that "it was a bass player that was in his band at a certain point." You could see how the song could be a snotty kiss-off to Tommy Walter — nicknamed "The Professor", Walter was mocked for his music-education background. But even if Lang is mistaken in his memory, 'Baby Genius' was the one moment on *Electro-Shock Blues* where E deviated from his thematic through-line.

Getting back on message, 'Climbing To The Moon' was classic pop in the Silver Lake/Largo tradition. In fact, it featured several members of the scene, including T-Bone Burnett, Jon Brion, Grant-Lee Phillips and, of course, Butch. It was also a break from much of *Electro-Shock Blues* in that it was done in a traditional recording studio.

"E wanted to do a track that was kind of an all-star cast of his friends," says Greg Collins, who recorded and mixed the session. "That day was really fun, and it's a beautiful song. It was all done live — I'm not sure how many takes we did, but it quickly took on a really cool personality. Everyone was really kind of holding back, and Jon filled a lot of the space with his keyboards. You just go for a vibe and not fuss about it and trust all the people that are around. There's a lot of stuff that E does that's [made up of] two or three really sort of discrete sounds — a simple drumbeat or piano or guitar part. This was a much more woven sort of thing and a much looser kind of atmospheric thing. It just shows that he can go anywhere and be confident."

The track reflected that casual, warm rapport of friends playing together in a space. And on an album where songs could sometimes feel like suicide notes, 'Climbing To The Moon' might be interpreted as the most explicit, although the beauty of the arrangement was such that it made the idea of heading up into the sky seem inviting.

Electro-Shock Blues was a wonder at avoiding easy sermonising about its subject matter, and 'Climbing To The Moon' reflects that lack of judgment about suicide and mental illness. E was once asked if he felt any anger at Liz because she killed herself. "I might have felt that initially," he replied, "like the night I heard, but I've never felt that way since then. I've always understood, because of the way we grew up and because I'd had similar feelings at different times in my life. We were just so *lost*. I think she and I are two sides of the same coin. I just got lucky. She channelled all her lost energy into drugs and alcohol and crazy shit. I channelled it into music and that literally saved my life." His answer explains much about why *Electro-Shock Blues*, despite its occasionally volcanic surface, is ultimately an accepting and understanding record. E was able to forgive his sister because he knew where she had come from. Bravely, he didn't just try to tell her story on the album, but he also tried to sing it in her voice. Just as critically, E could relate to her despair — it required very little creative licence to make her pain feel like his own.

The vaguely country overtones of 'Climbing To The Moon' were more pronounced on the next track, 'Ant Farm', which any unsuspecting listener might assume was a love song. But highlighted by Lisa Germano's eloquently melancholy violin, 'Ant Farm' slowly revealed itself to be an edgy salute to Nancy. For the first time on *Electro-Shock Blues*, E was talking about his mother — and singing directly to her. It was a song about forgiveness, acknowledging that despite their differences in the past, he understood that she had done her best as a mother. At the same time, he recognised the fact that Nancy's death would leave him truly an orphan, and that no matter what their issues were she was all he had left.

The second side's post-'Baby Genius' songs were marked by a stripped-down aesthetic, and that continued on 'Dead Of Winter', which E referred to as "the saddest song I'd ever written". Anyone who's gleaned the song's lyrics could guess at its autobiographical nature: it was E's way of talking to his mother in a way he couldn't near the end of her life.

When he would go to visit her, he would find some solace by leaving the house after she went to bed. It would be the middle of the night, and E would be alone with his thoughts as he stood outside. From these quiet moments came the origins of 'Dead Of Winter.' E's acoustic guitar and John Leftwich's upright bass framed the spare composition, all the better to allow E's words to stand unadorned in the song's centre. Still early into his career, E had a tendency sometimes to indulge in simple but trivial wordplay, but when the moment required it, he could summon up exceptionally moving and artful lyrics. The title of 'Dead Of Winter' is itself a pun of sorts — the song is set during deepest winter, but it's also about the fact that his mother is near death — but it's a wonderfully apt choice for a song that's, in part, about the end of everything.

The song's three main verses are wonderfully constructed, the first finding E pondering what death must feel like. The second acknowledges his mom's inevitable passing, lamenting the cruelty of cancer but also the banality of medical care:

So I know you're going pretty soon
Radiation sore throat got your tongue
Magic markers tattoo you
And show it where to aim
And strangers break their promises
You won't feel any
You won't feel any pain

After a bridge in which he looks out at the rest of the world that never stops hurtling forward, he concludes with the realisation that being back home again — the place he couldn't wait to escape from — is fraught with memories:

Thought that I'd forget all about the past
But it doesn't let me run too fast
And I just wanna stand outside
And know that this is right
And this is true
And I will not
Fade into
Fade into the night

The song is inherently paradoxical: it's about the finality of death while at the same time hoping that something somehow lives on afterwards. Those who have religious faith at least have the comfort of believing that a spirit survives after the body dies. But for someone like E, there was no such comfort.

The album's final two tracks, respectively, posed a question and answered it. Working with producer Mickey Petralia and multi-instrumentalist Stuart Wylen, E pondered a life without his loved ones on 'The Medication Is Wearing Off'. Finding ironic comfort in a family heirloom — a simple watch that keeps working even though its past owner is dead — the song is pretty yet anxious, reflecting a sense of exhaustion about what the future might hold.

E's only answer? True love. The final song, 'P.S. You Rock My World', was a blast of rugged optimism and gorgeous strings. Tellingly, E is at a funeral at the beginning of the song when he realises that he wants to make a life with the mysterious lover he's addressing. But beyond its hopeful sentiment, 'P.S. You Rock My World' was also a bulletin of the here-and-now of E's life. Hanging out at the post office, going to a convenience store, heading over to the gas station, E was back in Los Angeles, trying to get back in touch with his normal life. Most indelibly, though, he was reconnecting to "the sirens and the shots" outside his bedroom window, another indication of the crime-heavy reality within spitting distance of his home. But even those urban dangers just provided more proof that he was still gloriously alive: "A careful man tries/to dodge the bullets/While a happy man takes a walk/ And maybe it's time to live."

The 16 songs that comprised *Electro-Shock Blues* had been born from a great deal of pain, but E was convinced it was the best record he'd made to that point. "I didn't really develop a strong vision until the *Electro-Shock Blues* album," he told a reporter seven years later. "That's when I feel like I started to really get focused and understand what I really wanted to do."

This was not the consensus within the Eels' ranks. The strongest dissenter was the man E most regularly spoke to about his songs.

"We'd sold a couple hundred-thousand records in America," Carter says about the band's standing after *Beautiful Freak*. "A hundred-thousand records in France. We were off and rolling. We've had five videos on MTV. We are a darling artistic entity — exactly where E wants to be, as far as I can tell. Could not be in a better situation — and [with] a more anticipated follow-up record. And E proceeds to start sending me the [*Electro-Shock Blues*] songs — every one of them is about suicide and cancer. And I'm saying, 'No one is gonna play a song about cancer over and over and over again, be that on the radio or maybe even at home'. Suicide, we all know about it, but 'Do I wanna hear that suicide song again this morning? Nah, I think I'll play my Prince record'."

Carter says he tried to reason with his client, telling him: "I understand that you are creatively expressing what's going on emotionally in your life. And I respect that, but it can't be your next record. It can't be your next record."

But according to Carter, E was insistent that this was the path he wanted to pursue. It was becoming clear to Carter that he and his client fundamentally disagreed on E's career plans. Specifically, E didn't want to be perceived as a pop artist in any shape or form.

"The hip factor was always *so* dominant," Carter says about E. "And as much as he could admit that some great pop stuff was hip — Paul Simon, Brian Wilson — he really struggled with it." Still, Carter persisted, telling E, "I'm sure that [there's] someone in your audience whose mom has just died of cancer, someone that's just killed themselves, but this is not your follow-up to *Beautiful Freak*. No, no, no, no, no, no."

The fact that *Electro-Shock Blues* was a concept album also raised red flags for Carter. "It was like he was excited about the fact that he was so capable of expressing this *huge* emotion in music. I'm like, 'Could you do this as an E record on the side and can we make another Eels record?' I mean, I tried and tried to work around it but, no, he was convinced that this is what his fan base wanted, that this is exactly the way it should go. And I've gotta say, he has followed his muse in that direction ever since."

Part of that following of his own instincts lead to what E has said was one of the hardest career decisions he's ever made. He decided to let Carter go.

Getting fired is simply an occupational hazard when you represent artists. So when he and E parted ways, Carter completely understood.

"I found as an A&R guy," Carter says by way of explanation, "that because I had to torture my artists with *better, better, better, better, better,* every time they'd pop through, I was the first guy off the list. And I always got it immediately: 'Oh, I changed your diapers. You've moved out of the house now, you're getting a lot of pussy. I'm like your mommy and your daddy — don't want to talk to me any more, because you didn't even have a car when you lived with me'. I get it."

Talking with Carter, it's impossible not to feel that the two men had equally valid world views that simply couldn't continue to coexist. "I did not see success as failure," Carter says. "The things that come with success would not necessarily have to be a bore or take your soul." To Carter's mind, E started out as ambitious but something changed in him along the way.

"I finally pinned him down one time," Carter recalls, "to ask him, 'What's your idea of success?' And he said — even the words are poetic — Big Star. And I was like, 'That's it? A hundred-thousand or eighty-thousand records and a regional audience of 800 a night — that's it, huh? That's where we're going here? I think bigger than that. Everyone around you thinks bigger than that. You think fucking DreamWorks is in this for Big Star? They wouldn't fucking sign Big Star. We're awfully committed here — you can't be the only one that doesn't have your eye on the prize. No one's saying compromise, but no one's asking you to lower the ceiling *that far*'." The depth of E's determination not to be a huge commercial success was encapsulated when Carter brought up the fact that Big Star frontman Alex Chilton had enjoyed an early chart triumph with his Sixties group The Box Tops and their hit 'The Letter'. "E would say, 'No, no, no, no'," Carter recalls. "It was like, 'Oh no, he made that mistake when he was a teenager'."

In 1997, E had somewhat acknowledged in an interview that his taste may not quite match up with the general public. "I've always thought that I was so normal," he said, "and it's not until I hear from other people that I realise I'm not. My problem is that I always use myself as a measuring stick for the rest of the world. 'Well, I like this so maybe the rest of the world will.' But the rest of the world is listening to Celine Dion."

E and Carter parted ways professionally but maintained a long-standing friendship. E gave him a copy of his memoir before it came out, and Carter was struck by a passage near the book's end when E admitted how much he hates going to a new doctor and having to fill out the

"In Case Of Emergency, Contact _____" section. ("I don't know who to put there, and it makes me really sad and embarrassed," E wrote.) "I read it and emailed [him]," Carter says. "'In case of emergency, call Carter'. I was sincere. I would do anything for him."

Even those who were turned off by his professional demeanour have acknowledged how instrumental Carter was to E. "My personal interactions with Carter were always fine," Jim Jacobsen says. "His business behaviour was obnoxiously aggressive... [But] Carter absolutely believed in him when everyone else was saying, 'His solo records didn't do anything: we don't give a fuck, go away'. And Carter never flagged in his support. He was a real champion for what E was doing. And he had the brilliant idea of making it into Eels."

"Carter's awesome," Huxley says. "And Carter's still a big fan [of E]. Always will be."

Having severed ties with Carter, E presented *Electro-Shock Blues* to his label. Whether or not because of the resistance he had received from Carter about the record, he explained to Waronker and the Ostins that *Electro-Shock Blues* was a different album from *Beautiful Freak*. Then they all sat down and listened to the record together.

"You realised the seriousness of the work," Lenny Waronker recalls about that first listen to the album. As for the sonic and tonal change of pace from *Beautiful Freak*, "it wasn't as surprising to us as it might have been to others — [we'd had] a group of artists who had changed up from time to time throughout their careers and surprised you. I mean, Neil Young, you *never* knew what he was going to do, which made it fun, sometimes frustrating, but mostly exciting and great. So we were used to it in a way. When we were sitting there, Michael Ostin was really taken by the record and spoke up immediately. Mo and myself, we just felt, 'This is a great record'."

The album's ambition carried over into its art design. The liner notes opened with a poem from E's grandmother Katharine Kennedy's book, *Music Of Morning*. When you removed the CD from the case, you saw a crude illustration of a boy literally crying at the sight of a spilled bottle of milk — E's father had drawn it at age 13 or 14. And throughout the liner notes, there was artwork done by different well-respected underground cartoonists, such as Adrian Tomine and the one-named artist Seth. "A lot of my friends are comic book artists," he told *Mojo* in 2010. "I seem to enjoy their company more than musicians." The combination of family art, hip illustrations and the childlike front cover painted by Fiona Hinckley Jr added to the album's mixture of artistic aspirations and wilful desire to return to the innocence of youth. "*Beautiful Freak* was kind of written to soothe the aching teenager inside of me," he told a reporter. "I kind of made a record that I would like as a teenager. This record, *Electro-Shock Blues*, is much more of a mature viewpoint, to the point where it's more like for a 30-year-old. I just skipped the twenties completely."

But no matter E's refusal to accept Carter's warnings about the album's commercial prospects, the fact remained that there wasn't a clear-cut single. "I think we all knew it was gonna be tougher," Waronker says. "We were hoping the quality of the record would give us a great start."

Released on October 20, 1998, *Electro-Shock Blues* got the sorts of reviews Waronker and the rest of DreamWorks were craving. One of the most ecstatic came from the newspaper of E's adopted hometown. Writing in the *Los Angeles Times*, Robert Hilburn opened his review thusly: "*Electro-Shock Blues* may be as close to a walk through the valley of the shadow of death as you'll find in pop music. It's a brilliant work that combines often conflicting emotions so skillfully that you are reminded at times of the childhood innocence of Brian Wilson, the wicked satire of Randy Newman and the soul-baring intensity of John Lennon." It's hard to imagine an opening paragraph that could have pleased E more, especially the part where Hilburn compared him with three of his biggest influences. *Billboard*, as is its nature, took time to focus on the record's commercial prospects but was nonetheless enthusiastic, calling it "[a]n album of subtle beauty that should not be overlooked despite its lack of obvious airplay candidates". Perhaps the clearest indication of *Electro-Shock Blues'* widespread critical acclaim was its appearance at number 30 in *The Village Voice*'s annual year-end Pazz & Jop music poll, the only Eels album to date to break the top 40 of the prestigious critics poll.

Not that everyone loved it. The poll's organiser, esteemed *Voice* music critic Robert Christgau, rejected the album's artsy trappings. "Mark Everett is a talented 31-year-old [in fact, he was 35] who bravely determined to deal with the dying he's seen in song," Christgau wrote. "But that didn't mean he had to make a concept album."

Others were unimpressed with what they considered the band's derivativeness. Chris Molanphy wrote: "If *Beautiful Freak* showed them as dilettantes, colliding toy pianos and found sounds against mangy guitars, the new album promotes them to full-fledged pillagers: E growls like Beck, and the band does Morphine-esque sax-and-bass as efficiently as it does Nick Drake-ian strings." (For what it's worth, it's rather amusing that when Beck later very consciously aped Drake's strings style on his 2002 break-up album, *Sea Change*, he was generally applauded for his excellent taste in influences. This is not meant to damn Beck but, rather, to suggest how derivative an artist is perceived to be by the critics can simply depend on how much we like how the artist has co-opted his sources.)

Writing in the *A.V. Club*, Nathan Rabin offered arguably the most well-reasoned assessment of the album's strengths and weaknesses. "At its best, *Electro-Shock Blues* deserves to be mentioned alongside such masterpieces as Big Star's *Third/Sister Lovers* and The Beach Boys' *Pet Sounds* as albums that capture the essence of deep, soul-crushing depression on an almost visceral level," Rabin declared. "At its worst, E's dour lyrics sound like the hopelessly self-involved, self-pitying diary excerpts of a moody teenager."

Whether or not one agrees with the latter assessment, the truth is that *Electro-Shock Blues* works as well as it does in part *because* it at times disregards self-reflection in the same way that moody teenagers do. For better or worse, the album felt very close to the bone, its snapshot songs very much of their moment. And if some of the more experimental tunes have not aged particularly well, they still pulsate with the anxious energy of their creator, who was clinging to making records as the only way to stay sane during extraordinarily trying times. For those who wanted a more considered and nuanced examination of what E was going through, *Things The Grandchildren Should Know* provided just such a perspective 10 years later — and, indeed, it's a wholly more articulate, eloquent, moving and sobering account of this time in E's life. But *Electro-Shock Blues* is raw and immediate and, therefore, just as valid and true — it feels constructed in pieces, its different songs arguing with one another about how "best" to cope with such tragedy as it's unfolding.

Rabin's review is also instructive because it backs up Carter's assertion that an album full of sober songs about cancer and suicide would be a commercial disaster. "For a society that doesn't often like to think about death or address its own mortality," he began his review, "Americans sure love songs about dead people. Few songwriting formulas are more commercial than those that transform the tortured, complex emotions associated with grief into self-pitying schmaltz in which the gory unpleasantness of death is ignored and the holy suffering of the living is glorified." Rabin used Puff Daddy's exceptionally syrupy number one hit 'I'll Be Missing You' — a lazy, nearly-wholesale cribbing of The Police's 'Every Breath You Take' — as an example, since it was a tribute to a murdered friend, rapper Notorious B.I.G. But the Nineties also had its fair share of artists who won praise by tackling mortality in starker terms. R.E.M'.s autumnal 1992 effort, *Automatic For The People*, was one of their most commercially successful, despite the fact that it was a record haunted by the dead. And in the wake of Kurt Cobain's suicide in 1994, critics and audiences embraced darker-themed artists like Nine Inch Nails. But those bands had found ways to make their pain palatable to audiences by marrying misery to pronounced commercial hooks. For *Electro-Shock Blues* to keep the fans Eels had snagged because of 'Novocaine For The Soul', it was going to need a comparable hit.

"We felt that we had enough ammunition for radio," Waronker says of *Electro-Shock Blues*. "I especially liked 'Last Stop'. But, you know, radio didn't. It made it difficult to market the record."

'Last Stop: This Town' peaked at number 23 in the UK, while the album lasted in the Top 40 for only two weeks. In the US, the showing was even grimmer. *Electro-Shock Blues* never cracked the Top 200, and the single never got higher than number 40 on the modern rock charts.

In the end, the irony was that both E and Carter were right. E had stuck to his guns and made an album that, for many, remains the quintessential Eels record. But Carter's warning that it was a difficult and momentum-crippling commercial follow-up was painfully accurate — indeed, it would take E five years and three records to return to the *Billboard* album chart.

Looking back, Waronker thinks that a shift in the musical landscape was also partly to blame for E's struggles to find a radio audience. "The real issue was, 'Could we go from modern rock radio to pop radio?'" he says. "Once you have a pop hit, then the world opens up in terms of sales. And we were on the brink of doing that, but I think pop radio at that time really had changed. Records like E's were looked at sort of [as] alternative records or modern rock records, and [radio] started to really lean towards playing pop music. It was very difficult for us. It was frustrating as hell." Looking at the number one Modern Rock hits of 1998 suggests that the format had cooled to the sort of lo-fi eclecticism that had been so popular just two years earlier. Poppy alt-rock from the likes of Semisonic, Goo Goo Dolls and Barenaked Ladies was the sound of the times, with only Cake's quirky 'Never There' bearing any sonic similarity (and even then not much) to Eels.

But in a cruel reprise of his experience with the release of *Beautiful Freak*, what was going on commercially and critically with *Electro-Shock Blues* meant little to E personally. More misfortune awaited.

The band had started touring Europe about a month before the record came out in the States, hitting the road with new bassist Adam Siegel, who had been featured in the 'Last Stop' and 'Cancer For The Cure' videos. While on the road, though, E's mother was getting worse. And by the time the band started their US dates, Nancy was in a bad enough way that E eventually had to cancel several tour stops to be by her side. She died at home on November 11 at the age of 68. In one of the bizarre cosmic twists that one either chooses to read a lot or nothing into, November 11 was also E's father's birthday.

Nancy's final moments still clearly unnerve E, so much so that he's said he has to chase away any thoughts of what she was like that last night — it's a horror he doesn't want in his head. But it could have been worse: E had the presence of mind not to be around when her body bag

Chapter Eight

was removed from the house. He had made that mistake with his father and would not let it happen again.

E was now the only person left alive in his immediate family, although he at least had the comfort of knowing that he'd been able to have a proper goodbye, something he was deprived of when both his sister and father died. "That's maybe the only good thing about someone who has a terminal illness," he said in 2008. "You have a chance to talk about anything that you think is important to talk about before it's too late. Whereas if someone dies like my father, you know, suddenly, you don't ever get a chance to do that. My mom and I spent a lot of time talking about stuff that we never got a chance to talk about."

One of those things, Hugh Everett III biographer Peter Byrne related, was E asking his mom if she had ever wanted to divorce his dad. "Oh, no," was her response. "Never. He was so unique and such an original thinker. There was something about him I knew I'd never find in anyone else."

Nancy's funeral was one of the last times many of E's childhood friends got to see him. "My brother and I went to the funeral," Toasters keyboardist Mike Kelley recalls. "It was at a little Episcopal church down the road here. We hadn't seen him in a while, and he was happy to see us." Kelley had wanted to catch up with his old pal, but "it wasn't the time or place. He was receiving a lot of people." And then E was off again.

Almost immediately following the funeral, E had to get back on the road to tour. The trio played the *Electro-Shock Blues* songs, E's primary instrument being the organ for much of the night. They tweaked 'My Beloved Monster', working the strutting riff of '(I Can't Get No) Satisfaction' into its musical DNA. In addition, Butch's persona as a comic foil to E was becoming further developed, heightened by the cowboy hat he often wore during shows that became his trademark chapeau. If all that wasn't enough, Butch even sang lead vocals on 'Efils' God' to superb effect.

"It's lucky that I found the Eels," Butch said during that tour, "because I can really explore and utilise all the sounds and voices I hear in my head. There are no limits to what I can do in this group. It's been a really great creative outlet for me."

An interviewer asked E if it was easier or harder to cope with his tragedies now that he'd made an album about it. "It's easier now, now that everyone in my family has died, I feel," he said. "Obviously it's a horrible thing to go through. Hopefully you get to the point where you start [to] feel like [you have] sort of a clean slate to work with. Try to accentuate the positive. It's like I look at what I have to hold on to. One of the things I have to hold on to is I can say whatever the hell and do whatever I want on stage and in the songs. And, you know, there's some freedom in that."

E would also get to experience an odd consequence of making art based on personal pain — that is, how do well-wishers applaud your achievement without seeming insensitive about the underlying messy emotions connected to the work? "People would say, 'Congratulations, I'm sorry'," E told an interviewer in 2000. "Which I think sums it up pretty well. It's not a good thing, it's not a bad thing — it's all life, you know?"

Only with the perspective of many years could E look back at the *Electro-Shock Blues* period and glean one of the ironic advantages of being an orphan. "When I made *Electro-Shock Blues*, my mom was dying and I kept it from her," he told *Spinner* in 2010. "I didn't want her to hear it because I thought it would be too much for her to deal with. And since then, I suppose, there were probably times when I've written a song that she probably would disapprove of because of the language or something like that. You don't have to worry about that any more. That's pretty much the only bright side."

You could argue that another bright side was giving the world *Electro-Shock Blues*, an album that continues to generate letters of thanks from fans who have clung to it during their own tough times. "I had a friend who recently had a mental breakdown," E told writer Bill Holdship in 2000. "He went into the hospital, and there was this girl there who had obviously slit her wrists. And the first thing he noticed about her was an Eels CD poking out of her purse. So I'm very proud and happy if we do indeed comfort people. It's not why I do it, but it's a great by-product. I would think someone going through a bad time might not want to hear more about the subject or deal with it, but some people, I guess, are willing to dive into it and ultimately find it to be a comforting and rewarding experience."

Another interesting by-product of making *Electro-Shock Blues* was it brought him to the attention of his beloved Neil Young, who invited the band to play the 1998 instalment of his annual Bridge School Benefit concerts. (Nervous about what to say to someone he so admired, E shrieked, "I like your beard!") After E fired Carter, Eels signed with Lookout Management and Elliot Roberts, who had been managing Young's career since 1967.

For most aspiring artists, being represented by the man who had guided Neil Young would have been a feather in their cap. And surely E was no doubt pleased. But this was a different world for E after the hands-on approach of the Carter years, when he had spent countless hours on the phone with his manager talking about every aspect of his career. Carter got to experience this change first hand in a later meeting attended by, among other people, Roberts, Carter and E.

"It was a big, intense situation," Carter says. "We're all kinda, 'No calls! No nothing! Big meeting!'" But once the meeting got started, Roberts' phone rang. Recognising who was calling, he quickly picked up. "He goes, 'Hi, Neil'," Carter recalls. "He proceeds to walk around the room, [talking about] frivolous shit. [It was] Neil Young." Clearly, not only was Young worthy of interrupting a "big, intense" meeting for, he was important enough to shoot the breeze with while everyone else in the room was waiting to get back to business.

Later in the meeting, the group took a break and E had a question for his new manager. "E turns to Elliot," Carter recalls, "and E says, 'If you were in a meeting and I called you, would you take my call?' Literally asked that in front of everybody. And the whole room cracks up. Because we all know the answer to that."

Chapter Nine

Ask Jim Jacobsen if he was ever seriously concerned about E's mental state, and his answer is very deliberately considered. "I worried a little during the time that his sister died," he says. "I just worried about him — it's not like I worried that he was going to kill himself or something. But, you know, sometimes you worry that someone is just going to be crushed by the intensity... [and] his mother died around the same time. It was just a really incredibly, incredibly heavy period."

That period had been exhaustively documented in *Electro-Shock Blues*, although Nancy had not yet died when he finished the record. Nonetheless, after that album's darkness, there was nowhere to go but up. E sensed it as well, which he signalled at the outset of his next record, starting off the lead cut, 'Grace Kelly Blues,' with 17 seconds of a New Orleans-style marching band blaring its brass horns and beating its drums.

"I think it's the perfect way to follow up how the last record ended," E told *Music Express* shortly after the release of *Daisies Of The Galaxy*. "The last record was more about mourning the death, and this record's more about celebrating the life. I think that the difference between a New Orleans funeral and the typical funeral is that you're concentrating more on the celebration."

A lively, self-conscious reaction to *Electro-Shock*'s despair, *Daisies* was surely meant to be a salute to life. The album gained an unlikely poignancy since it was made by someone who clearly thought that he was over the complicated emotions that had informed *Electro-Shock Blues*. As a result, *Daisies* is a bit of a hotchpotch, shifting from eccentric studio experimentation to cheery folk-pop concoctions to heartbreaking piano ballads. Adding to the album's misshapen structure, its biggest hit was buried almost as an afterthought at the end of the record — and it's not even included in the track listing.

By January 1999, E had moved into Beck's old Los Feliz house, which featured a much bigger basement than his previous Echo Park place. (Though he would get annoyed by Beck comparisons, he clearly didn't let it factor into his search for a better residence.) That sense of new beginnings continued with collaborators. Mike Simpson had a prior commitment and couldn't work on the album, so he suggested E hook up with Wally Gagel, an engineer and producer who had just moved to LA from Boston.

"I think that he knew of my work with The Folk Implosion and Sebadoh and bands like that," Gagel says about E's familiarity with him before working on *Daisies*. "And I also had done some work with Mike and The Dust Brothers. Mike wanted us to collaborate on something — he really thought highly of me, which was nice. He just said, 'I'd like you to kind of be involved in this', so that's how it started. I met up with E, and he really didn't have anything ready, as far as a big plan of how he was gonna do stuff. But we talked about how we were gonna record and then just started, just went right into it."

As with his earlier partnerships with Bobby Read and Parthenon Huxley, E impressed Gagel almost immediately with his speed for laying out ideas. But if E had intended *Daisies* to be a lighter or more hopeful record, that certainly wasn't something the two men discussed while making it.

"I think for E, he doesn't really relate the conceptual stuff that he wants to do when he's working," Gagel says. "I think for him it's just about getting the ideas down, and he wants people around him that can facilitate that, whether it's the players or the engineers or the producers involved. He has it all in his head, he just needs people to help him get it out for the stuff he doesn't do. Otherwise, he'd probably do everything himself, to be absolutely honest."

After listening to rough sketches that E had worked on at home, Gagel and E headed to the Bomb Factory for the initial recording, with Butch on drums and Grant-Lee Phillips handling bass.

"The plan was to have some stuff prepared, but they did play together live on a lot of the stuff," Gagel recalls. "I do remember it was a process of them jamming all those out. And in some cases we didn't have any ideas, but E wanted to have Butch play a bunch of beats, and some of those became song ideas later — we just took some of those beats and kind of wrote stuff over it or manipulated it."

One song that came together that way was 'Flyswatter', an intriguing mixture of childlike instrumentation and vaguely doom-laden imagery involving hungry field mice and a vengeful day of reckoning. "I got a thing about flowers and animals and bugs," he said at the time. "There's a lot of birds and spiders and tigers" on *Daisies*, he admitted. "I coulda called this album *More Songs About Flowers And Animals*."

Continuing that theme, another track from the Bomb Factory sessions turned into 'A Daisy Through Concrete', a jaunty, resilient keyboard number that finds its narrator (presumably E) walking down the street and discovering the little joys of life, such as babies in strollers, a skywriting airplane and the titular daisy pushing its way through the concrete.

"A daisy is a good symbol for what the whole record represents," E told Bill Holdship of *New Times Los Angeles*. "And a daisy through concrete is an image I like — a delicate but strong and beautiful thing trying to break through all the funk." Indeed, the album reflected that battle between a sensitive soul and the hard, cruel world around him. And while that struggle sometimes ended in defeat — epitomised by the album's gorgeous piano ballads 'It's A Motherfucker' and 'Selective Memory' — it also provoked one of E's most compassionate tales, the album's title track.

"['Daisies'] is based around a short story I wrote about a kid going to a movie theatre called the Galaxy," E explained to Holdship. "[T]here is a flower bed out front. These two young kids go to see *Terminator 2*, and it's way too apocalyptic for one of them. It really upsets him. So afterwards, his friend gives him a daisy out of the bed to try to cheer him up. So I just see a daisy as a symbol of something to cheer you up."

When the time came to put strings on the track, he turned to Lang, who immediately knew how to complement the song's lyrical ideas with an emotive accompaniment. "That particular track, I heard in my head this real dry... there's two viola parts that start that track out and there's no vibrato — they're just playing these long bows," Lang says. "I wanted to get it just as scratchy and rosiny as I could. I really had a picture in my head of what that movie theatre looked like [that was] really, really, really, really deeply ingrained in me when I was working on that track. I was really romanced by that track. I loved it — I still love it. It's one of my favourite things I've ever done."

But while the title track's meaning was overt, the hopeful tone of other *Daisies* tunes was less clear, particularly 'I Like Birds', a seemingly one-joke ditty about a guy who can't stand people and prefers the company of his fine feathered friends. Only when E started doing publicity for the album did listeners realise that the song was a tribute to his mother. When he had cleared out his parents' house after her death, he latched on to her bird feeders, setting one up in the backyard of his new home to have a little something of hers around.

"A lot of people would have their mother die and maybe want to write a tribute to her," E explained after *Daisies'* release. "And it would be 'Ohhh, momma's dead' or 'I miss you, momma'," he continued, imitating a pained country vocalist. "But I couldn't do that." In fact, E had initially wanted to relegate 'I Like Birds' to a B-side before deciding he liked the song enough to include it on the album.

The recording sessions went from March to May. "E works really fast, and he'd come up with ideas on the spot," Gagel says. "He likes to record fast, and I tended to be from the old school where I just got sounds quick, too. We'd start recording, and I think that allowed him just to throw these ideas down." There was so much material, in fact, that songs from the *Daisies* sessions eventually found their way onto future Eels albums, some that were released 10 years later. In his memoir, E would attribute that period's spirit of constant creativity to "a sense of urgency" after the deaths he'd had to endure. It was understandable: being surrounded by mortality helps one appreciate how precious our time on this planet really is.

Beyond being prolific, E was also challenging himself to write songs in unconventional ways. Speaking with *Sound On Sound*, a music recording magazine, he described how his process had evolved. "If I felt like writing a guitar song, I'd force myself to go over to a different instrument, like the auto-harp, or the Hammond B3, so I'd get something fresh," he said. "Or I'd try a lot of weird samples together on the keyboard or sounds on the Mellotron, which you would normally never think of trying to write a song with — like the choir samples, bells and distorted organs in 'Flyswatter' and 'The Sound Of Fear'."

And though E's ramped-up production was no doubt inspired by the personal pain he'd faced, one could also attribute it to that burgeoning Silver Lake scene in which Beck was being hailed as the leading light.

"I think [E] would like to have every one feel like he didn't think about it, but I'm sure he did," Gagel says when asked about E feeling competitive with others in the same scene. "He knows Beck, and there was this mutual respect, obviously. So working on the Eels record, it was not at all sonically [similar], but it was that same atheistic: 'Let's make a record this cool and this good that can still be a pop record.' Now the problem, I think, was E wasn't wanting to make a pop record at the time. And I think DreamWorks was a little kind of 'We want to [capitalise on] something that Beck has done in the sense of a talented artist doing his songwriting from the heart, and let's get a commercial record out of it'."

But while *Daisies* may have been an album that embraced optimism, E made it quite clear on the record's second half that he was increasingly uncomfortable with both commercial pop and the indie-friendly environment that had made 'Novocaine' a hit. The quirky keyboard-and-horns 'Tiger In My Tank', E wrote in his memoir, was "an anticommercial 'jingle'" that looked dimly at the faddishness surrounding alternative rock. The dreamy acoustic lament 'Wooden Nickels' continued the theme of "selling your soul" and was followed by 'Something Is Sacred', which was also highlighted by an acoustic guitar but featured a starker sound and returned to the apocalyptic imagery of 'Flyswatter'. "It's kinda about how irony is a big thing now," E told *Music Express* about 'Something Is Sacred'. "Nobody says anything direct any more or how they genuinely feel — it's very uncool to do that. By definition, I think the word 'cool' means to not reveal and to hide behind sunglasses or whatever. So it's very uncool to put yourself on the line and say, 'Here's how I really feel'. There's not much room for that nowadays. I wanted to be brave enough to write a song that said, 'Well, some things still are sacred and you gotta believe [in] something'. That is putting yourself on the line to try and get to a bigger place, a greater place. But in the process you're risking being humiliated."

If he was displeased with the state of alternative culture, he drew strength from his heroes, in particular Neil Young, whose piano from *After The Gold Rush* was used during the sessions for 'Motherfucker' and 'Selective Memory'. It was a perk of being managed by the same man as Young, Elliot Roberts, which enabled the piano to come into E's possession.

"It was in Elliot's office," Gagel recalls, "and Elliot let E have it. That piano... that sound is pretty much undeniable. It's got this vibe, it just had this out-of-tune character. It's not good for 'beautiful' pieces, it's more for these. I remember recording 'It's A Motherfucker', and I think we were just literally using one ribbon mic. It was a very mono, old-school recording process on it. And it just has that tone and the gentleness. Like, a beautiful huge grand piano, it just would not fit what E is about. He's got a real good sense of what he's about. He has a strong sense of his aesthetic — slightly quirky, nothing's-too-perfect-sounding. So the fact that it's slightly out of tune, it wobbles a little bit, it's got almost like a chorus effect on it just naturally. [Everything's] just a little bit off, and that's what's so beautiful about all that stuff." But although the piano gave the songs their haunting, fragile quality, the old instrument creaked considerably during takes, prompting E to tell *Sound On Sound*, "I was smashing my fists on it in frustration."

The sessions quickly fell into an orderly, almost nine-to-five routine, with Gagel coming by E's house in the morning, occasionally seeing the woman E was living with at the time. But soon the two men headed to the basement to pick up where they'd left off the day before. And in the flurry of ideas, there was little time to talk about the lyrical content of the songs.

"It was a working relationship, and at the same time somewhat oddly intimate," Gagel says, "because here's this personal stuff coming out of him. I'm with him, by ourselves, 90 percent of the time in the basement everyday for eight to 10 hours a day. You just kind of grow together in this weird space. But at the same time, there had to be this certain distance, because it was about getting the songs done. But 'It's A Motherfucker', I do remember while we worked on the record we went to Largo on a Jon Brion night and he played that. Just even hearing him play it live and just the power of that one — that's amazing."

"That's another song that's really near and dear to my heart," Lang says. "'Motherfucker' was just a beautiful, beautiful piece of music." When E asked him to come up with strings for the song, Lang didn't need any guidance: "It was just, 'Write some shit that sticks to this'. Writing it was delightful, and hearing the string players play it in the room was breathtaking. I cry at the drop of a hat, and I'm pretty sure when they started playing the first run-through of that I had tears in my eyes. Such a really poignant song, for starters, and it was a really good performance — a fantastic performance."

In his memoir, E talks about the experience of working on *Daisies* with an engineer who was fond of imitating Eddie Murphy's *Saturday Night Live* parody of the *Little Rascals* character Buckwheat. Though E doesn't name the individual, Gagel's pretty sure it's him. "That sounds like me," he says, smiling, "because I used to do that stuff. The funny thing is he's got a really dark sense of humour sometimes, and I don't take things too seriously — I tend to try to lighten up the mood. And there would be days where it would be a little heavy, to be absolutely honest with you. So, yeah, it sounds like something I might have [done]."

Gagel worked the closest with E on the record, but Lang's contribution should not be diminished. Lang had come to Los Angeles in the early Seventies and then moved there permanently in 1978, eventually becoming a studio musician and composer for films and animated kids' shows. He and E had worked together on *A Man Called E* and *Electro-Shock Blues*. And he made a crucial impact on *Daisies*, arranging and conducting the album's prominent horns and strings.

"E had a pretty good idea of which songs he wanted strings on and which he wanted brass on," Lang told *Sound On Sound*. "We also talked about styles. He's a big Randy Newman fan, as am I, so we used him as a reference point. Randy is the perfect example of somebody who writes like that; his harmony is always very clear and his voicings are just beautiful."

"His arrangements are quite different," Gagel says about Lang. "They are really in their unique place, and he seems to work well with E. He definitely came from a different perspective than a lot of arrangers would. There are certain arrangers who work in the pop field, I think, who know how to use strings that are kinda typical and they kinda do a certain thing. He comes from, I would say, a little bit more of an experimental place." To Gagel's mind, Lang's film and TV work lent his arrangements a kinetic, cinematic quality. "A lot of his arrangements, they don't quite stay the same — they kinda move."

"I would attribute it to being self-taught as an orchestrator," Lang says of his "different perspective" on scoring strings. "I didn't go to music school, and most people that are arrangers are people that are schooled. My approach is just different. My tools are different. I don't write on paper, I write at a computer. I mock things up. I play with the sounds in the computer and use that as a model."

Gagel's description of Lang's fluid arrangements deftly articulates the lulling strings that buttress the melancholy of 'Selective Memory' or add grandeur and gravitas to the otherwise lightweight 'Wooden Nickels'. And it was Lang who came up with the brass band intro that gave 'Grace Kelly Blues' (not to mention the whole album) its initial ear-catching boost.

"No one uses Jim for what I use him for," E told *Sound On Sound*. "They might start to, though, if word gets around. A guy who does the music for kids' TV shows is a smart choice. People like him have to work so fast on cartoons, they can do *anything* you can dream up, and *real* quick."

By this point, Butch was already becoming just another sideman assisting E with his vision, laying down drums and taking part in the afternoon croquet matches that went on in E's backyard as a way to break up the monotony of the studio work. And then there would be days when random musicians would stop by, like R.E.M. guitarist Peter Buck.

"A lot of musicians have a lot of respect for E," Gagel says, "so there's always people who would say, 'Oh yeah, I'll work with him. I just remember one day [E] mentioned it, and then Peter showed up. We set some mics up and got things down. And it wasn't just one quick thing — we worked on a bunch of material."

The only Buck collaboration that ended up appearing on *Daisies* was the palette-cleansing, 97-second instrumental 'Estate Sale' that E intended to symbolise the difficulty of having to pack up all the belongings out of his parents' house. After his mother's death, he put everything from the house in boxes, sold the property and dumped all the memories into his LA basement's crawl space, wanting nothing more to do with them. Explaining the song's genesis, E said: "Peter played some piano and I played a few old records of mine. I thought it was nice — a minute and a half of collage that I think says more than I could say with lyrics. I like little vignettes like that. I always think of albums, even on CD, as being made up of a part one and a part two, and 'Estate Sale' is the little divider."

As with *Electro-Shock Blues*, E got a tremendous response from Lenny Waronker when he played him *Daisies*. But as Gagel had suspected, DreamWorks was looking for something that could be a radio hit. For E, who had chosen DreamWorks specifically because they offered him a creative freedom he assumed wouldn't be forthcoming with a bigger label, it was a crushing blow. He fell into what he called "a deep depression". Who could blame him: *Daisies* had been his way of trying to fly clear of the dark clouds. When it wasn't embraced, it was tantamount to E being told he couldn't put the last few painful years behind him.

"It was difficult for me because I had to play both sides," says Mike Simpson, who was still doing A&R for DreamWorks at that time. "But

I am pragmatic and I do understand that, yeah, when you make a deal with a major record label, no matter what they promise you and no matter how artist-friendly they are, there's certain unstated expectations that if they're going to give you half-a-million dollars to make a record then you are going to deliver a half-a-million dollar record. E makes *albums*, which is really a lost art — all the songs may not be singles, but they're all important and integral to the theme of the record, and the whole record tells a story. E is really good at that. So I understand his frustration with being told, 'OK, you need to tack something on there that we can use as bait to get people to buy this'. He was definitely not happy about being forced to put another song on that record."

Simpson agreed that, despite the quality of *Daisies*, there weren't any marketable singles. "I didn't think there was anything that they could sell," Simpson says. E may have been irritated that his artistry wasn't being supported, but he may also not have fully grasped how much his label had morphed in just a few short years. "By that point, DreamWorks had grown to a huge record company with a giant building full of people and all the different departments," Simpson says. "They were putting out tons of records, and so basically what would happen is the record would get shot over to the radio guy. He'd listen to the record, and then he'd report back to Lenny and Michael and Mo and say, 'I've got nothing here'."

Frustrated, E approached Simpson to work on one more track. Incorporating a sample of Simpson's pager and a looped blues guitar figure, 'Mr E's Beautiful Blues' reflected the conflicting emotions of the entire album. The music was buoyant and resilient, and the chorus *seemed* breezy, but the way E bit down hard on the refrain ("Goddamn right, it's a beautiful day") underlined the unhappiness of the song's characters, which included an elephant trapped in a cage and a circus ringmaster performing to empty seats. Despite E's discontent about having to essentially "write a hit" to make the label happy, he had done just that. But in typical E fashion, he had done it in a way that expressed his loathing for such commercial concessions, ostensibly writing a pop song that really wasn't sunny at all. ("When I told Lenny Waronker the title he made a gesture of shooting a pistol at my face," E later wrote in the liner notes for the band's greatest-hits collection, *Meet The Eels*. "I guess he wanted it to be called 'Beautiful Day', but I knew U2 would be needing that title in a few years.")

"That was actually a track that I had written for Hanson," Mike Simpson remembers. "I wasn't hired to write it [for Hanson], but when I came up with the track I thought, 'Oh my god, this would be a great follow up to 'MMMBop'," the 1997 hit from the Oklahoma teenaged trio, which had been produced by The Dust Brothers. "It just kind of had that sound [but] I never actually presented it to those guys — I never had the opportunity to." Simpson's memory is that Lenny Waronker asked him to help E come up with a single for *Daisies*. "I don't think E wanted to do it," Simpson says. "I played the track for him, and he actually really liked it. He had some ideas, and he wrote the lyrics."

Gagel had already moved on to producing the next Folk Implosion record when he heard 'Beautiful Blues'. "I was like, '*Damn*, I wish I had done that one'," he says. "It was so good. You know, *that's* the single. That's obvious to me."

But E's problems with DreamWorks weren't over. E couldn't figure out where to put the song on the album without ruining the flow of what he'd painstakingly conceived. Finally, he came up with a solution, although it didn't thrill him. Leaning on a popular trend of the time, E made the song a so-called "bonus track", which meant that it appeared at the very end, almost as an afterthought. It wasn't listed anywhere in the packaging, and E even made sure there was 20 seconds of silence between *Daisies*' final track, 'Selective Memory', and 'Beautiful Blues'. It was E's way of saying that the record's first (and biggest) single wasn't really part of the album.

"It's true," Gagel acknowledges, "it doesn't fit into the rest of the record as far as the whole tonality of it and what it was about. It's more of a fun, cool pop song — but, of course, an Eels pop song, which is a very different one than the traditional stuff. I think he was a little annoyed that he had to kind of... I don't think he gave in to the label 'cause I think he liked working on that song, and it was a good song. But it's hard when he obviously did in his head have this concept of where that record was supposed to be and what it was about. It was really heartfelt — I mean, my god, it's all about this stuff with his family but in a way that was a little more uplifting and spiritual. It makes sense why that song wasn't in there."

But E's refusal to "properly" place 'Beautiful Blues' on the record caused headaches for Simpson on the A&R side. "He made it a hidden song on the record and it's not even credited," Simpson remembers. "So if you heard the song on the radio and went into the record store, you'd be really hard-pressed to find it. No one even knew that this song existed."

Released in the spring of 2000, *Daisies* was, not surprisingly, compared to *Electro-Shock Blues*, with most reviews noting the new record's lighter, more hopeful sound. And some of the most positive reviews commented on how out of step E was from the current music scene. In *Entertainment Weekly*, David Browne wrote, "Not too long ago, rock stars were neither wrestlers nor keg tippers" — a reference to the meathead nu-metal movement (anchored by groups like Korn and Limp Bizkit) that had become popular in the late Nineties — "but bespectacled nerds who crafted sonic splendour in the solitude of their garages or bedrooms. Mark Everett — or E, as he has been calling himself for a decade — is one of these endangered species." Praising E for "[i]gnoring the slightest whiff of trendiness", Browne approved of the album's "old-school instrumentation" and "genuinely sublime pop". *CMJ* critic Gary Susman commented on the album's "heartbreaking beauty" and enjoyed "the homespun awkwardness of E's yearning lyrics, plinkety-plink arrangements, hoarse falsetto, and anxious harmonies." *NME* cut to the chase, calling *Daisies* a "masterpiece in almost every way."

But the reviews weren't universally rosy, with some of the least kind indicating the resistance that E's sonic tendencies were starting to provoke from the unsympathetic. In *The Village Voice*, Alex Pappademas dissected his dissatisfaction with the album. Although he acknowledged that E "writes the kinds of songs you want to root for, darkly empathetic, conscious of both gallows humour's usefulness and its limits, full of characters who obsess on whether or not they've got a wire crossed upstairs until they actually go nuts and don't notice", Pappademas couldn't get past E's "drag-ass voice" that made Beck "sound like the owner of a golden throat by comparison." Dismissing him as a second-rate Randy Newman, Pappademas groaned about the "sadly thwackless drums, tentative jazz-funk... and observational songwriting that slips way too easily into pat ain't-life-strange shtick." The reviewer also took issue near the end of his piece with *Daisies'* recurring lyrical motif of selling your soul, but his harshest assessment came earlier: "Even when his characters enthrallingly map the tubes they're going down... E's effect stays landscaped-flat, a liability that makes you want to go, 'Dude, write a book' — or just tune out till somebody fetes E's band with a tribute album."

While *The Village Voice*'s assessment was far too harsh, it did point to a nagging problem with the record: despite the number of excellent songs *Daisies* contained, it lacked the thematic force or musical urgency of *Electro-Shock Blues*. The result was an album that felt more like a collection of fun bits and pieces than a coherent whole. And yet, those "plinkety-plink arrangements" and "old-school instrumentation" radiated a charm that suggested a young man trying to regain his equilibrium after the hardships he's seen.

"I can understand why people might not want to put on *Electro-Shock Blues*," E admitted after *Daisies* was released, "'cause there's times when I think about it and I just feel like, 'Mm, not in the mood for that — I don't want to deal with that right now'. So I'm glad to have a record now that I actually do want to listen to." And that remains *Daisies'* chief asset: It's a marvellous *sounding* record, full of lush strings and off-kilter compositions.

But lyrically, it's more of a muddle, with E inventing fictional characters in several songs that don't always evolve beyond narrative constructs. After bands become successful, their follow-up albums usually contain a song or two about the limits of fame or the hazards of the road, and it's interesting how *Daisies* is in a way E's version of that record. The commercial breakthrough of 'Novocaine' and the critical success of *Electro-Shock Blues* had been tempered by the suicide of his sister and the death of his mother. Now, he was finally able to lash out at the music industry, while at the same time trying to figure out how to cope with the very public grieving he'd done for his family. (This was no more apparent than on 'It's A Motherfucker', which he repeatedly had to explain *wasn't* about a dead relative but, in fact, an ode to an ex-girlfriend he was missing terribly.) Feigning contentment and failing, *Daisies* could very well have emanated from the narrator of 'Electro-Shock Blues', who keeps writing down on that pad "I am OK" over and over again, eventually conceding that she's not OK.

If something felt off about *Daisies*, that sense would continue through its release. 'Mr E's Beautiful Blues' just missed the Top 10 in the UK, but it failed to have much of an impact in the States. The reason was obvious: American radio wouldn't play songs with *goddamn* in the lyrics. The band couldn't perform it on *Late Show With David Letterman* for the same reason, although, in an example of how restrictions ease over time, Letterman used the term a little more than a year later when he addressed his audience on his first show after the 9/11 terror attacks.

In addition, E found himself an unlikely talking point during the 2000 presidential campaign when George W Bush's strategists condemned Democrats for giving out the album in a gift bag during the Democratic National Convention, alleging that *Daisies* was targeting children because of its storybook-like artwork. Bush spokesman Dan Bartlett took the opportunity to blast then-Vice President Al Gore: "America's parents can't count on Al Gore to protect their kids from Hollywood's inappropriate marketing practices. If the Democrats didn't stop DreamWorks from handing out a CD with explicit lyrics at a convention under their control, why will they stop Hollywood from marketing the same material to children at other venues?"

Years later, E said: "The funny thing is our idiotic management at the time — this might have been the last straw, too — they wanted to cover it up. They were like, 'This is kinda negative'. And we were so excited. We thought, 'This is our big break!'" (E invited President Bush and First Lady Laura Bush to his 2008 concert in Washington, DC, writing them personally to say, "Mr President, I know that you're a Christian, and Christ taught forgiveness. So in the spirit of forgiveness and fence-mending, I'd like to let bygones be bygones..." The White House Presidential scheduling office called to politely decline, citing the invitation's short notice.)

The controversy didn't boost sales significantly, nor did the decision on what the second single should be. E went with 'Flyswatter' as opposed to something more melodic and accessible, like the bittersweet 'Jeannie's Diary', which had been inspired by a crush E had on a girl who worked at the post office. The standout track was one that E originally wrote in the late Eighties, presumably during his time toiling away at dead-end jobs in the Valley while looking for some interest in his songs. But for E, the challenging 'Flyswatter' probably seemed akin to putting out the *Bone Machine*-like 'Cancer For The Cure' as *Electro-Shock*'s second single: a bold curveball that wouldn't fit neatly with commercial radio.

E's wilfully antagonistic streak also manifested itself elsewhere, particularly in the way that he would slag off his (more successful) peers in interviews. He had a low opinion of the bands playing on LA's popular alternative station KROQ, which had helped launch 'Novocaine'. "I imagine a kid who listens to KROQ would be bewildered by *Daisies*," he said. "Imagine one of those children of the Korn — and that's Korn with a K, of course — the second they put this on and heard the horns, they'd be like: 'What the fuck is this? Get it out of my CD player!' But young, white teenage boys are full of rage these days, and they need to get it out." His most visible moment of acting out occurred during the aforementioned appearance on *David Letterman*. E kicked off the performance by announcing, "I am the real Slim Shady!" and then launched into a 'Flyswatter' that was decked out in full Waits-ian garb. (He ended the performance splayed on the floor underneath his keyboard.)

But that's not to say there wasn't a lot of joy on that tour. In fact, it was exactly what E had in mind. Inspired by a dream of Butch's in which the band played with horn and string players, Eels went out as the Eels Orchestra.

During the tour, a medley of earlier Eels songs kicked off each night's performance, done in the style of an orchestral chamber piece. 'Last Stop: This Town', 'Beautiful Freak', 'My Descent Into Madness' and 'Novocaine For The Soul': the melancholy and agony of these songs were transformed into soothing, slightly jazzy dinner music, scrubbing away their prickly edges until only their redoubtable melodies remained.

Multi-instrumentalist Probyn Gregory, who has been part of Brian Wilson's band since 1999, was involved in the first group of orchestra shows. He still remembers working out the overture during the weeks of rehearsals before the tour. And while E directed its development, "we all sort of threw in [ideas]," Gregory says. "Once in a while, one of us would just quote from another song and see if someone picked up [from] there and said, 'Oh yeah, let's go into that'."

If the *Electro-Shock Blues* tour was an unflinching examination of death, this new tour was many shades lighter in tone. E aimed for something that was theatrical and festive. It was a daring undertaking, which sometimes meant radically reinventing the songs, such as the gorgeous folk-pop-with-horns rendition of 'Not Ready Yet' that was a tour highlight. This required players who could bounce around from different instruments.

"My main role in the band was on trumpet and valve trombone," Gregory said, who modestly refers to himself as "an OK horn player". ("I'm a pop guy," he says, "and I can do little solos if I work 'em out ahead of time.") But during Eels rehearsals, Gregory started adding more instruments to the set: electric guitar, banjo and melodica. Butch played a timpani. E session player (and recording artist in her own right) Lisa Germano went from violin to keyboards to guitar during shows. It was an ambitious tour, one that demonstrated E's willingness to evolve.

"We used to rehearse a lot," Gregory remembers, "and we'd work out various versions of the tunes. We'd come to something and then for some reason it would be abandoned, or there would be a change of approach — like, 'Let's try to put a hip-hop section in the middle'. It was fairly creative from both [the players] and from the helm."

The tour also allowed Butch to become more of a breakout star among E's cast of characters, providing a humorous intermission during the shows.

Orest Balaban, who played bass during the tour, recalls that at one point during each performance, "E would leave the stage and Butch would do his thing for a few minutes. It would be the same basic idea — he might change it slightly every time, depending if something happened or if he thought of something. It was like rambling poetry with comic elements in it. It was pretty funny."

This nightly bit was best captured on the live album *Oh What A Beautiful Morning* with a track called 'Hot And Cold', in which Butch delivered a seemingly improvised rant to the band's Glasgow audience about his unhappiness with Europeans' use of separate faucets (or taps for the European audience) for hot and cold water.

In addition, during the shows "there was a section where [E and Butch] were going back and forth and it sounded like a real conversation," says Balaban. "E would be telling Butch to not do something and admonishing him, and they would be going back and forth. A couple times, the rest of the band would start looking at each other like, 'Are they for real?' But it always would wrap up and then it would go directly into the next tune." While it was all a joke, Balaban wondered if there was more to it than that. "There was a certain underlining tension that was feeding them," he says.

"People like to think of it as the E show," Gregory says. "But when I was in the band, it seemed like both E and Butch were sort of at the helm, both throwing out ideas and listening to each other and having the same amount of authority. And maybe if E and Butch were here they'd say, 'Well, that was actually a mistaken perception'. But that was my perception. They generally were in agreement — if Butch had an idea, usually E would say, 'That's great'. Or vice versa. It was always cordial; it was always fun."

But the tour also spoke to the fact that Eels were more beloved in Europe than they were in America. The band did two European legs, while E had to perform solo as an opening act in the US. Rumoured budgetary concerns forced the cancellation of several Eels Orchestra shows in the States, but in Europe the group were treated like heroes.

"*I* was signing autographs," Balaban says, amazed. "After the shows, whoever stayed on stage, people would ask them for their autographs. Nobody ever heard of me, I didn't record with them or anything. It was fun — I enjoyed being a rock star for a few months."

"I remember one show we played in France," Gregory says. "We played in an old converted movie theatre and the place was packed —

1,500, 2,000 people and they're all crowding up, a lot of them calling for *Electro-Shock Blues*. He went out to the bus afterward, and we couldn't even move. The bus couldn't go because the people were standing outside." Before Gregory had toured with Eels, he assumed their fan base would consist of adults, but the bus incident proved to him that in Europe that wasn't the case. "These teenagers just *adored* him," he says. "They had signs up saying, 'We Love You, Eels!' I've never seen that for Brian Wilson — people don't keep the bus from leaving."

That ongoing disparity between Eels' popularity in the US and Europe doesn't shock Jim Jacobsen, who has an unflattering (but rather accurate) view of the American listening public. "In the United States, people have to be told what they like," he says. "They will like anything that they're told to like. And I think it's a little bit different in Europe. I mean, I'm not going to say that Europeans are universally better people than we are, but just in general, I think they're just a little more evolved across the board politically and culturally. I don't know why it is that way, but in terms of America we sort of have to be told what to listen to — it's the whole publicity machine. In this country, popular music is essentially toilet paper — it has the same kind of longevity. People use it for whatever they're [doing], so that they can bob their head around in their car, or dance, or whatever it is that they're doing."

E had wanted the *Daisies* tour to celebrate life after what he termed the "death-rock" of the *Electro-Shock Blues* concerts. And despite the abbreviated US dates, it succeeded in that mission. And then they got to Australia in July 2000.

The band had just wrapped up shows in Brisbane, Sydney and Melbourne and now had a few days off. This allowed everyone to wind down and do their own thing, including Eels roadie Paul Hanson. Nicknamed Spider, he had come into their orbit at the start of the *Beautiful Freak* tour through an introduction by Aimee Mann.

"He and I got along pretty well," Balaban says. "I liked him. He was from North Hollywood. I think he was into the punk scene when he was a kid, and he had a real different personality and style than [the rest of the band]. He was kind of more grungy and more of a 'downtown' kind of guy — he wasn't really a tough guy, but he was a from-the-streets kind of guy. He would always wear camouflage fatigues and stuff. But he was totally dedicated to the band. He'd been with them for a long time — he loved the music."

"I loved Spider," Gregory says. "He was such a great guy. He used to bring out his guitar and play." In fact, Spider for a short while was the Eels' opening act. "I can't say he was an artist in his own right, but he was a musician."

But despite Spider's outward appearance, his songs, according to Balaban, were "folk-rock kind of love things."

"He was like this punk kid that never really quite grew up but got old," Balaban recalls. "I don't think he had that energy [to write more aggressive material] — it was more appropriate to do that more reflective kind of music."

But although Spider had established a reputation for being a go-to guy on the road, he could also be a handful, especially when he drank.

"I remember when we went to London, I was talking to him about all the pubs 'cause I really wanted to drink English beer," Balaban says. "The first thing he'd do is, we got into the hotel and he's like, 'You're coming with me.' And we went to a pub, we had a Guinness, and I didn't quite notice at the time but it didn't take long before I realised that he got drunk really fast."

There was also a situation before the *Daisies* tour when Spider had been on a commercial flight from Europe heading back to the States with the band. Balaban wasn't on the flight, but he had heard details about the incident in which Spider "got pretty hammered and fell down or knocked some stuff down or something. He kind of like embarrassed himself." According to Balaban, his drunken behaviour had gotten him kicked out of the band, which prompted Spider to go into AA. Eventually, E let him rejoin them on tour.

And while it was clear that Spider was grateful for the second chance and thrilled to be touring with Eels again, Balaban recalled some despondent conversations the roadie had with him during the *Daisies* tour. "There was once or twice that we talked where he was just kind of reflecting on his life," Balaban says. "You know, 'What am I doing

153

here?' I think maybe he would look at E's success or Butch's ability as a musician and then he'd think about himself — an aging stagehand who doesn't know if he has a retirement or not."

When the Australian leg of the *Daisies* tour ended at the beginning of August, the band had a little downtime in Melbourne before heading to Japan — the first time Eels would play there. During one of those days off, Butch was hanging out in his room when someone from the hotel paid him a visit.

"I heard a knock at the door and it was the hotel security guy with a local policeman," Butch recalled years later to *Drumhead*. "He asked if I knew a Paul Hanson. I immediately cringed and asked what he had done. The policeman said, 'Mr Hanson is dead, and we need you to come to his room and identify his body'."

E was doing press, which left Butch the job of sorting out what had happened to Spider. "It seems that Spider had gone out on a bender the night before with an old roadie buddy from Australia, and he imbibed many different substances, which resulted in a massive coronary," Butch said. "His 'buddy' freaked out and left him there, dead."

After digesting this information, Butch was given more bad news: "I had to call Spider's mom in Boston to tell her that her 45-year-old son was dead."

Butch has said that Spider's death is his worst memory of his time with Eels.

Oblivious to what had happened with Spider, E had been asked by a TV reporter about his impressions of Australia. Drawing on Melbourne's reputation as a heroin mecca, E displayed his dark sense of humour, and joked that he liked the weather and the heroin.

E returned to the hotel late that evening, still completely unaware of Spider's death. Only when he got back to the hotel and found Butch in the lobby did he learn the awful truth.

Balaban had used the day off to travel down the coast. When he returned to the hotel in the afternoon, "there was a police car out front — I immediately thought of Spider. I was thinking there was some trouble or something — maybe he'd had some drinks and got into a fight or something. It was like, if there was any trouble then Spider was probably involved. It's not because he was a troublesome person, but he had this unpredictable chaotic side to his life."

Instead of going to Japan, the band returned to the US and threw a memorial for Spider.

Gregory, who was no longer on the *Daisies* tour by the time Eels hit Australia, says, "I think the reason E liked him was that he was a bit of a curmudgeon too — he was very opinionated about music and the things he liked and didn't like. It felt like they went way back, like they had been friends for a long time. And whenever Spider was free E was going to call him, and he was going to be there."

That bond between E and Spider had been cemented when the artist had asked him to drive all of his family's boxed-up possessions from Virginia to Los Angeles after his mother's death. Unable to sleep in his parents' empty house because of the memories, E had stayed with a friend's family, leaning on Spider for support during that truly difficult period. Now less than two years after his mom's passing, yet another person close to E had died.

After Spider's death, Balaban asked E how he was coping. "He's like, 'Well, it's just a normal day,'" Balaban says. "'Just collecting the belongings of another person that I loved that died.' It was something to that effect — I don't remember exactly what he said. It wasn't [said] like cold or heartless. It was like, you know, 'Here I go again.'"

In a post on the Eels website entitled "My Beloved Spider", E said farewell to his friend. "I really can't imagine going on without him," he wrote. "My guess is we will, but it will never be the same, or as good. We just have to accept that, I guess."

Daisies Of The Galaxy had started out as an album in which E tried to embrace life in all its messy glory, and life had once again proved to be messier and more unpredictable than he could have scripted. The *Daisies* tour, mostly a success, had ended in sadness, in its own way an apt illustration of what Lenny Waronker had said about the album, describing it as "a nice walk in the park, where you're occasionally bitten by a snake."

But the amazing period of productivity that had resulted in *Daisies* had also led to another group of songs, one very different in tone.

"I didn't set out to make two different records," E told *Music Express* after *Daisies'* release, "but I realised that that was what was happening — some material was really dark and loud and full of feedback and kinda scary-sounding. And the other stuff was the opposite — very pretty and simple and sweet and positive. I realised for my own sanity that I really wanted to focus on *that* stuff — on the simple and sweet stuff more than the other stuff. The other stuff I felt like I needed to get out of my system some more, but I didn't feel the need to inflict that on the world right now."

He'd be ready to do that on the next Eels album.

Chapter Ten

Weeks before Eels released *Souljacker*, the band's fourth studio album, in Europe, E was speaking with a Dutch reporter, who was asking what the artwork would look like and if it would resemble the earlier albums, which the interviewer very much liked. E was in a feisty mood — he had previously told his inquisitor that he enjoyed entertaining himself during interviews by telling lies — and he seemed to relish this particular question.

"If you loved the previous ones then you'll *hate* the artwork for this album," E replied, "because it really is very different than the other ones. It's very scary. Someone described it as like a punch in the face... It's so disturbing." His warning didn't end with the artwork, though, but extended to the album's sound. "If you like the last one, you might not like this one," he offered. "But if you never heard any of 'em, you might really like this one."

Easily the most sonically unique album in the Eels canon at that point, *Souljacker* came together thanks to a series of unlikely pairings that helped shape its creation. Specifically, it was the influence of three new individuals into the Eels universe that gave the album its precise shape and tone.

The first was a man E never met but whose impact visited him in a most unlikely setting. During the making of *Electro-Shock Blues*, presumably around January 1998, E had decided to go to a meditation

157

retreat in central California. Susan, his old girlfriend, had recommended the retreat to him, which consisted of 10 days in which the participant can't read, write or speak.

While E has not specified the name of the retreat he attended, it very likely could have been the California Vipassana Center in North Fork, approximately four-and-a-half hours north of Los Angeles. Vipassana meditation, according to the centre's website, "is a way of self-transformation through self-observation. It focuses on the deep interconnection between mind and body, which can be experienced directly by disciplined attention to the physical sensations that form the life of the body, and that continuously interconnect and condition the life of the mind. It is this observation-based, self-exploratory journey to the common root of mind and body that dissolves mental impurity, resulting in a balanced mind full of love and compassion." That sounds pretty wonderful, but for E during the first days of the retreat, it was anything but love and compassion. While E had preferred menial jobs in his youth because they allowed him time to think, the meditation retreat proved to be *too* reflective. Indeed, he felt like he was going crazy amid the silence: "I would have these passionate dreams about checking my phone messages or something — stuff that you don't even think about in everyday life," he later told MTV News.

But inspiration soon found its way into his meditations. His friend Sean Coleman had told him about an alleged San Francisco serial killer who had been arrested in 1996. He dubbed himself The Soul Jacker because, as E related later in the press release for *Souljacker*, he "claimed to not only kill, but also steal the souls of his victims."

What happened next was a story E repeated so much during the promotion of the *Souljacker* album that most fans should already know it. Early one morning, he snuck away from the rest of the campers, grabbed a pencil from a clipboard in the bathroom, and wrote down some lyrics about how a souljacker couldn't get his soul. (One has to wonder if the extreme isolation and forced silence instilled at the centre in some ways provoked the self-affirming, almost defiant tone of those lyrics. If you feel like you're going crazy, the last thing you want to think about is the possibility of some psychopath coming and taking your soul.) Regardless, the lyrics, which would eventually become 'Souljacker Part II', suggested a theme for an album. "I started thinking about it in a bigger sense and a broader sense," E would later tell a Helsinki writer about the concept of a souljacker. "Seems like people are losing their souls every day in the world we live in just by forgetting they have it. We don't need a serial killer to take it away."

It's impossible to know just how much information E had about this so-called Soul Jacker. And considering that E would happily invent fictional characters to further his creative efforts, it's understandable that some might assume that the serial-killer conceit was wholly bogus. But in fact, there was a man at the time in San Francisco who went by that name. However, he wasn't a serial killer, per se.

Bernard Temple was, in actuality, an African-American who had been standing trial in San Francisco on two counts of murder in the first degree. George Cothran, who followed the trial for *SF Weekly*, reported that Temple, who was then 28, "calls himself the Soul-Jacker because he believes that when he kills someone he acquires the soul of the victim and thereby makes himself stronger." Born into one of San Francisco's poorest, most crime-infested areas, Bayview-Hunters Point, Temple had aspirations of becoming a boxer but soon acquired a rap sheet. Cothran noted that during his final year of high school, "Temple was arrested for locking a girl in a schoolroom and sexually assaulting her." The case was later dismissed, but a year later he was convicted for the rape of a 14-year-old girl.

(For the record, Temple was acquitted of the murder charges, and in a twist that would have been deemed too wonderfully ironic for fiction, he eventually was hired for the city's gang prevention programme.)

Back from the meditation retreat, E had 'Souljacker Part II'; a 'Part I' would present itself soon after when the band — at that point, him, Butch and bassist Adam Siegel — were jamming during rehearsals for the *Electro-Shock Blues* tour. For the lyrics of 'Souljacker Part I', E detailed the saga of teen lovers Johnny and Sally — outcasts in a world of incest and trailer parks — with unnamed but unsettling thoughts bouncing in their brains. (The band actually played the song during the *Electro-Shock* shows, which were documented later on the *Electro-Shock Blues*

Show live album that was released in 2002. It's interesting how the live version isn't terribly different from the one that ended up on *Souljacker*, save for the fact that the young woman is called Mary rather than Sally. E made the change later so as not to confuse listeners with another song he was working on called 'Mother Mary'.)

'Souljacker Part I' was recorded by Wally Gagel during the *Daisies* sessions, as was the funky 'Jungle Telegraph', a tale of an unloved young man who flees society, perhaps because of a murder he's committed, only to wind up living in the jungle like a wild animal. This particular batch of material was shaping up to be a parade of loners struggling to find their place. It's little wonder that E decided to keep them off the sunnier *Daisies*.

But now the second integral *Souljacker* participant was about to emerge. As Eels began touring to promote *Electro-Shock Blues*, they appeared on *Top Of The Pops*, a British TV programme devoted to the week's hit records, in London on September 24, 1998. At the show, E met John Parish, a British songwriter and musician perhaps best known for working on PJ Harvey albums like *To Bring You My Love*. "It was kind of remarkable," Parish recalls, "because neither of us are typical candidates to be on that programme. It was very fortuitous."

Strangely, if things had worked out differently, they would have met much earlier. "We shared a publisher," Parish explains, "and they previously tried to put us together to write something when I'd been in LA working with some other people. I kind of turned down the opportunity because, in my experience with publishers, they often put two people together because they think it's a good idea, whereas the people may not be aware of each other's work at all. And I already had been in a couple of slightly uncomfortable writing situations with people. I really did like E's work — I liked Eels — and I didn't want to be stuck in a room with somebody that didn't know who the hell I was or wasn't familiar with my work. So I actually said, 'I don't want to do it'."

For E's part, in a 2002 interview he mentioned his own misgivings about the proposed pairing: "Someone had talked about us working together several years ago and at the time, whatever I was working on, it didn't seem like the right idea to me and I didn't think a lot about it."

But when the two men ran into one another at *Top Of The Pops*, they started talking. "He sort of questioned me about [the potential pairing]", Parish recalls. "He said, 'Hey, why did you blow off that writing thing? I was looking forward to it'. And so my response was, if I had known that he knew who I was and that he liked my work, then I would have definitely been there."

E's version of the events was slightly different: "We met and he really liked *Electro-Shock Blues* and I'm always willing to talk to someone who's gonna be nice about one [of] my records."

They talked about possibly collaborating, but Parish didn't think anything would come of it. Then came another fortuitous run-in — this time in Boston on November 2, 1998. Eels were playing Bill's Bar & Lounge that night, while PJ Harvey (backed by Parish) was playing nearby at Avalon. "They were playing kinda quite late," Parish says. "So after our set, I just went down to the club and caught the very end of the Eels set. We had a chat afterwards and said, 'OK, let's definitely try and write something together'. And that was really how it all got set up."

Almost a year later, Parish heard from E, who had already recorded what would become *Daisies*. He sent Parish a CD which included versions of 'Souljacker Part I' and 'Mother Mary', a song that wouldn't see the light of day until *Blinking Lights And Other Revelations*. And he also shared with Parish his sonic ideas for what would become *Souljacker*.

"He said, 'I'm working on an album that's a little bit more hard-edged, kind of swampy and bluesy'," Parish recalls. "'I think you would be a really good person to collaborate on it — see what you think'. And so he sent me the tracks, which I liked very much." The plan was then for Parish to fly from his home in Bristol to Los Feliz to work on ideas. "I thought that I should take some things with me in case — you don't wanna show up to the table with absolutely nothing," Parish says. "So I thought, 'I'll bring a couple of things that I've been working on that seem to be in the right kind of ballpark for what he's thinking about'." On the day he arrived, Parish told E: "Hey, I got this song — maybe this might be the right sort of thing for you." It was 'Dog Faced Boy', the thick, strutting rocker that would open *Souljacker* and announce its bruising, nasty personality. "What was really great about working with E is how quickly he'll run with an idea if he likes something," Parish says. "I gave him the track that day, and he said, 'This is great. I really like it'. Then I showed up the next morning, and the song is written. The words were all done, and the track was complete after one day of being together, which was a really good start."

Encouraged, Parish went back home to work on more material. As someone who was comfortable collaborating after his experience with PJ Harvey, he didn't worry about what type of song would be right for *Souljacker*. Knowing that 'Souljacker Part I' and 'Part II' were radically different-sounding tunes, he says, "I was aware that it wasn't going to be an album with 12 rock'n'roll songs or anything like that. There was space to try out different things. But, you know, I would work like that anyway... When I'm writing, I like to have some kind of parameter that I'm working within, but I wouldn't necessarily shut off an idea because I didn't think it was fitting some idea of what somebody else had. As a writer I work quite instinctively — I kind of build things up, and I find a sound that I like or a chord progression or a melody. I just work around it until I feel like it's doing something that's interesting me." Soon, he had the basic tracks for 'That's Not Really Funny', 'What Is This Note?' and 'World Of Shit', three moody, musically aggressive tunes that reinforced the album's snarling spirit. E instantly loved them. "He gets some amazing sounds," E told the *Los Angeles Times* in 2002. "We both have a love for the kind of sounds that make people get up to check their stereo to see if something's gone wrong." Parish returned to Los Angeles in January 2001, living in E's backyard cabin for three weeks to make the album.

Also coming on board around this time was engineer Ryan Boesch. He officially began his partnership with E on *Souljacker* and earnt the nickname "beat specialist" from the songwriter, although he had taken part in some *Daisies* sessions. In 2002, he talked about what his initial *Daisies* session was like. "The first day, the guitar player from R.E.M. [Peter Buck] and another guy, Grant-Lee Phillips, were there," he recalled. "That was pretty amazing. I thought, 'Wow, the guitar player from R.E.M. — this is going to be fun!' We picked up on a song that E had already started doing vocals on and I did a couple of programming things. Then E said, 'Okay, let's mix it'. I said, 'Oh, okay'. I wasn't questioning it, but I was thinking in my mind, 'We're mixing already?' By eight o'clock, the song was done and he said, 'Okay, we'll work tomorrow and do the same thing'. Once we got used to each other, it became a natural flow. E's always got something to record."

That quick process continued with Parish part of the Los Feliz team. "He had a lot of production ideas and added guitar parts," Boesch said of Parish at the time. "He could play just about anything he picks up. Often he'd be listening to what was tracked and grab an instrument and just start playing stuff. E would be on his laptop in the other room and would run in and say, 'That's cool! Yeah, lay that down'. And we'd keep going with it. A lot of *Souljacker* was really spontaneous."

At the end of 2001, Parish reminisced about his time in LA: "Our working day had to contain at least an hour's croquet, which either myself or Butch would win." (Not bad for a bloke who had never played before joining the Eels camp.) Another memory of his time doing *Souljacker*: "We took a day off to attend Jennifer Jason Leigh's surprise birthday party. I knocked a full glass of wine into her bowl of ornamental wooden carved plantains."

But while the album was taking on a more hostile tone, not all the songs fit that mode. One of its strongest, and most enigmatic, tunes was stumbled upon almost as an afterthought. 'Woman Driving, Man Sleeping' is a seemingly simple tale of a couple driving at night on the open road. On its surface, 'Woman Driving' could seem benign, but on an album filled with unhappy, potentially dangerous characters, the song took on a sinister bent — particularly because nothing about the couple's relationship is explained. She's driving, he's sleeping, there's a suitcase tied to the top of the car, the radio doesn't work, the map is in her lap, she's looking for toll money, he's dreaming of walking through an apartment complex, and she's never looking behind her as she drives through the starry night. Each innocent detail of the story, laid out with a noncommittal tone through E's subdued vocals, added up to... well, what exactly? It's an intimate portrait of a relationship, but the strummed acoustic guitar and gentle, insistent drum track reveal nothing about the state of that relationship. It's an especially tense song despite the fact that there's really nothing tense about its set-up.

"I think that it is open to interpretation," Parish says of the song. "But I think that's the mark of a good writer, and that's what I like about E's lyrics — [he's] able to write a very big story with very few words. I think that's a real skill."

The song was also a testament to E's ability to work quickly when an idea struck him — even pulling out a rejected piece of music if it served his purposes. The song's chord sequence was something Parish had crafted in Bristol, although initially E hadn't shown much interest in it. But then, when they were hanging out at E's place early one morning, "we were just kicking ideas around and E had come up with that line, 'woman driving, man sleeping', which, I seem to remember, was a phrase that Natasha came up with — she just said it in passing while they were driving. And I think that E recognised, 'Oh, that's a really nice line for a song'." The rejected chords were dug up and by that evening 'Woman Driving, Man Sleeping' was complete.

Which brings us to the third essential figure in the shaping of *Souljacker*.

Understandably, E has been intensely guarded about the woman he married before the making of *Souljacker*, going so far as to call her Anna in his memoir. But what is known is that her name was Natasha. And just as the idea of a souljacker came to him at a time when he actually allowed himself to take a break from working, Natasha entered his world during a rare musical sabbatical.

On Tuesday, February 15, 2000, Eels had finished a show in Paris, wrapping a week of European promotion for *Daisies Of The Galaxy*. But the band had a brief break, not having another appearance until March. So everybody returned to the States — everybody but E, that is. He journeyed to Germany, to meet with, as he described him later to *LA Weekly*, "this kooky doctor just outside of Hamburg who helps you recharge your batteries." Concerned that he was suffering from Epstein-Barr or chronic fatigue syndrome — his friends and colleagues have heard him mention both ailments — it would be understandable that E might have sought a rather radical kind of treatment.

When E arrived at the facility, there was only one other patient: a Russian woman named Natasha. He instantly fell in love with her. When the band got back together to tour *Daisies*, Natasha was very much part of E's life.

"She was around a lot," says Orest Balaban, who played bass on the *Daisies* tour. "E wanted to have her around, so before and after the shows they would be together and hang out. She was kind of a quiet, mellow person. She was there for E and wasn't into the whole scene."

Those who worked or played with E tend to clam up when Natasha's name gets mentioned, wanting to respect the privacy of their friend and colleague. "She was friends with someone in Brooklyn who was best friends with someone that ended up being my girlfriend for quite a while," guitarist Shon Sullivan offers. "You think about it and [you think], 'Oh boy, now I kinda know some things I don't really [want to know]'."

But even though E's colleagues don't want to discuss many specifics about Natasha, it's apparent that their relationship became serious pretty fast. "E always struck me as someone who knew what he wanted," Balaban says. "So it was easy to sense that if he's with somebody then it's because the chemistry's right. They were very comfortable together — neither one was, like, overly romantic or into [showing] physical displays of affection. But they seemed solid." In November of that year, with chances of her getting a visa looking unlikely unless she and E married, she arrived in the States. And then, as E remembered in *Things The Grandchildren Should Know*: "One Saturday morning we went to the courthouse and stood in line with eight or nine unhappy-looking pregnant couples to get married." For the occasion, he brought an old gramophone and a 78 of Felix Mendelssohn's 'Wedding March' that belonged to his grandparents. It's a touching moment in his memoir and one that's very indicative of his personality — using charmingly lo-fi sounds to express genuine emotions from a safe distance. (Reflecting on their first meeting, E told *LA Weekly*: "I lived in this boarding house for two weeks. It was just me, my future wife and the doctor's mother-in-law, who ran it. The doctor didn't make me feel any better, but I got a wife out of it. So it was a pretty good deal." He laughed. "It was really a great, romantic thing — if you go in for that sort of thing.")

That feeling of love is profoundly felt on *Souljacker*, ironic for an album best known for its gruesome protagonists and ostensibly ugly-sounding songs. While the record opens with two broadsides — the lumbering riff of 'Dog Faced Boy' and the antagonistic 'That's Not Really Funny' — *Souljacker* then segues to 'Fresh Feeling', a lovely, unabashedly romantic song about the buoyancy of new love. It couldn't have been prompted by a more unromantic mind-set.

"I'm always trying to get inspiration from unlikely sources and I was inspired by feminine hygiene products," he told writer Rob Kallick in early 2002. "I remember the day I wrote 'Fresh Feeling' I was really sick, I was in my pajamas and I felt really shitty, and I was like, 'I want to write something really fresh'. And I started thinking, 'Well, isn't there a saying for those not so fresh feelings', and I just thought, 'Well, what about those fresh feelings?'" With help from bassist Koool G Murder, he sampled the strings from *Daisies*' 'Selective Memory' for the track, which could perhaps be seen to have a deeper meaning. 'Selective Memory' was E's choice for *Daisies*' finale, concluding that album on a brilliantly bittersweet note, presumably about his dead mother or sister. Resurrected for 'Fresh Feeling', those strings were no longer haunted but instead hopeful, suggesting that, deep down, maybe love could indeed cure all ills.

But if the loving sentiments on 'Fresh Feeling' were overt, other *Souljacker* tracks buried their beating heart. E would juxtapose sappy love lyrics with combative musical arrangements so that they would feel cathartic and liberating rather than sentimental. This tactic worked to great effect on the album-closing 'What Is This Note?', in which manic guitars, maracas and over-amplified vocals work together in service of lyrics about gentle kisses and serenading birds. "I love the song," Parish says. "It's such a punk-rock, fast, heavy thing with this very, very sweet set of words but sung in a really distorted way and buried in the mix — you can't really hear them." During his time in LA, Parish had taken a couple of days off from recording to visit friends in Tucson, and when he returned E had come up with the words for the track that they'd already written. "I was just over the moon when I heard that," Parish remembers. "I thought it was so exciting and such an interesting mishmash of sounds. You would never expect a lyric like that to work over a piece of music like that, but I thought it works fantastically. I love it when you get a really unexpected clash of things."

The approach was not that different on 'World Of Shit', in which E lays out his case for domestic bliss, looking to a future that for once might actually be bright. But even here, he keeps his guard up: he acknowledges that misery is never far from his door and recognises what a handful he can be. But it's clear that the song's moody, tense textures are really a way for him to hide his deeper feelings; indeed, E, who had never expressed much interest in settling down previously, allows himself to imagine a life with a wife and children. He was more upfront with his feelings in a 2002 interview with *LA Weekly*. "I gotta tell ya, it's the best thing I ever did," he said, referring to getting married. "Two things have saved my life: one was Lenny Waronker at DreamWorks and the other was my wife. The two things that kept me from blowing my brains out."

When E wasn't wearing his heart on his sleeve, *Souljacker* drew from childhood traumas of people he knew: a woman who was mocked for her hairy arms became 'Dog Faced Boy'; and an engineer whose father encouraged him to fight other kids became 'Bus Stop Boxer'. But these fictional characters could also be a way for E to articulate personal agony without feeling like he was expressing personal agony. "When anyone writes in character," he told me in 2003, "you always have to have some emotional connection to your own state of mind at the time of the writing. Quite often, guys like Randy Newman are probably exposing a lot more of themselves than they think they are when they're writing in character. You feel more fearless to really get down to the nitty-gritty when you feel like you have the mask to hide behind."

No more prominent mask was apparent than on the album's artwork, which was the first time E's countenance adorned the cover of an Eels record. And yet it looked nothing like the artist that audiences knew. Wearing a nondescript sweatshirt with the hood covering the top of his head, he further hid behind dark sunglasses and a long beard. (It was both funny and slightly creepy that the adorable dog he held in his arms seemed freaked out.) The cover was consciously antagonistic, and yet the artwork could also be interpreted as a critical commentary (much like *Daisies'* 'Something Is Sacred') on the self-conscious cult of coolness, whose practitioners hid behind sunglasses. E likes to take the piss out of journalists, but when he warned that Dutch reporter that he probably wouldn't like the *Souljacker* artwork if he had liked the previous records, he wasn't entirely kidding.

And he also wasn't exaggerating when he predicted some people's negative response to the record. In fact, even those who have worked with him or know him personally have misgivings about *Souljacker*. "My wife, who's not a rock critic remotely, just loves E," David Wild says. "I think she has five CDs in her car, and two or three are E. But she didn't like *Souljacker*. She didn't like seeing him look disturbed or upset or [see] that sort of tortured side of him." Along those same lines, Probyn Gregory, while talking about E's "lovable curmudgeon" persona, mentions: "When I first saw the *Souljacker* LP cover and that whole concept, it was like, 'Whoa!' It seemed pretty not him."

DreamWorks agreed with Gregory's assessment and, according to E, didn't like his new musical direction or the lack of clear-cut singles. Without a last-minute 'Beautiful Blues' to rescue the album, *Souljacker* didn't get released internationally until September 2001. (The record didn't come out in E's home country until March of the following year.)

Parish is more philosophical about its standing in the Eels canon. "We kinda did that record really fast without too much thought," he says. "Everybody was really working quite instinctively, working quickly and making quick decisions. And hearing the record back, almost 10 years later, it really stands up remarkably well. And it's a record that, if anything, I've kind of grown more and more fond of over the years. I'm very, very proud of that record. I'm very proud to have been involved in it. I think it's really stood the test of time well. You know, it's not like I'm saying we bashed it out without a thought — it just happened very, very quickly. Sometimes the best work does like that — it almost kind of makes itself. And you just have to be there for the ride."

Souljacker was the third straight Eels album not to chart in the US. It did, however, score high on charts elsewhere, from the UK to Belgium to Australia. And whatever reticence DreamWorks may have felt about the album's new direction, Parish took note at how receptive UK critics were. "When the reviews for *Souljacker* came out over here, they were pretty much uniformly very, very good," he says. "Nobody seemed to be that surprised that it was a hard, rock-oriented record after he'd done an acoustic one before. People weren't worried that there weren't sweet melodies. I think people said, 'Well, it's really an exciting record, it's full of really interesting characters, it's got E's wit, it's got a really powerful sound'. And people liked it."

"E from Eels has the potential to be among the best rock stars in the world," *NME* declared. And while the review faulted *Souljacker* for trying to duplicate the success of 'Novocaine' in some of its songs — how happy E's label would have been if that were really true — writer Andre Paine concluded that "Scarier than Suge Knight's board meetings, *Souljacker*'s songs rock harder than most of E's nu-metal enemies."

The Sunday Times positively gushed: "The conventional wisdom that *Electro-Shock Blues* was E's masterpiece will have to be reassessed. It was clearly just one of his masterpieces." The paper's critics poll picked it as 2001's album of the year.

Asked what it is about E that Brits so fancy, Parish gave the question careful thought. "Obviously there's a certain readiness to appreciate kind of odd, left-of-centre characters," he replies. "And E's sense of humour, I think, is very understandable to a British sensibility. That kind of bittersweet humour of E's, kind of like a 'beautiful loser' sort of character, I think is quite appreciated in Britain." Then he chuckles. "I dunno, I can't speak for the British public really because we're quite able to champion the biggest load of rubbish as well as picking up on some good things. It's not like we have some blessed good taste or anything like that."

Nonetheless, by the time E was doing promotion before *Souljacker*'s release, he could sense an increasingly chilly relationship with DreamWorks. Asked by a journalist if he could imagine putting out his records in the future without a label, he responded: "I think I'd better start imagining it, the way things are going. We haven't been a financial success to the record company. You never know when you're gonna be moving on to something else."

Whereas when he made *Beautiful Freak* the label heads stayed away, now he was beginning to notice their interference. "They're starting to get a little nosy about what I do," he said, "which I of course don't appreciate. But that's the way it is these days. It's really a sad time — it's just about the bottom line. They just want to make money now." And when music is the only family you have left, it can be hard for an artist to understand a label's mind-set.

Undaunted, the band (with Butch on drums, Koool G Murder on bass and John Parish on guitar) started a European tour in August 2001 that would emphasise *Souljacker*'s hard-rock aesthetic. But E was quickly going to discover the one thing that was harder than touring an album that was radically different from your earlier efforts — touring an album that's radically different and which no one in the audience has yet heard.

But the hardships of facing lukewarm audiences were nothing in comparison to the events of a few weeks later. On the second Tuesday in September, Eels were in London doing radio promotion. Butch was keeping a diary at the time that was published on the band's website, and he chronicled what turned out to be a terrifyingly unforgettable day. "At 2:30pm I leave to go to a coffee shop and order my usual," he wrote. "A customer sees my cowboy hat and asks if I'm an American. I say 'yes' and he turns a pale colour and says 'It sure is a bad day to be an American'. Flustered, I say, 'have a nice day', and leave, assuming that Bush or some arrogant American has shamed us once again. I quickly head back to my hotel room where I switch on CNN and then I'm lost in a surreal reality. The towers are just about to collapse and that's where I come in to the tragedy. Phone calls are placed to all different parts of the US to see what's going on and who's involved in our EELS family."

The terrorist attacks of September 11 hit particularly close to home for E: his cousin, Jennifer Lewis, was a flight attendant on American Airlines Flight 77, which struck the Pentagon 34 minutes after the second tower, the south tower, of the World Trade Center was hit. Even more terrible, her husband, Kenneth, who was also a flight attendant, was aboard as well. She was 38, the same age as E. Jennifer was E's cousin on his mother's side and lived with her husband in Culpeper, about 65 miles away from McLean. An obituary that ran in the *Chicago Tribune* reported that Jennifer and Kenneth's friends thought they "were such a good match that they collectively referred to them as 'Kennifer'." Jennifer was described as someone who "loved a good practical joke, shoes, horseback riding and her horse, which she named Poet." She met her husband at a party — a fellow flight attendant did the introductions. In his memoir, E referred to her as his "hot, blonde cousin" who sold him her 1971 Chevy Nova back in 1982, which allowed him time to drive around and think about how to escape his awful life in McLean. (Three years after the 9/11 attacks, Jennifer's parents and brother would be part of a group of victims' families to sign an open letter endorsing Bush's 2004 re-election, citing his "strong leadership in the war on terror.")

For bands on tour around 9/11, it was a period of uncertainty as artists postponed or cancelled shows. But for Eels, that wasn't an option. "We considered cancelling the remaining shows but quickly realised that we can't go home even if we want to," Butch wrote in his online diary on September 12. "And, as E has learned in the past, it's better to try and make some good energy in the world at a time like this, so we forge on."

Despite his resilience, E was facing a world that was dumbstruck by the terror attacks. And at a time when emotions were polarised — some adopting a kill-'em-all attitude while others retreated to the comforting familiarities of family and religion — E was going around in a big bushy beard that only caused him endless grief at airport security, which was now erring on the side of extreme caution with any unusual-looking characters. But even disregarding the social climate, E's beard-and-sunglasses look — backed by aggressive rock songs about angry, vindictive characters — flew in the face of everything Eels had represented to a lot of his fans. It would have always been a daring artistic choice, but in the wake of 9/11 it seemed just plain foolish, not that E could have possibly known how profoundly the world would change between the time he made the album and the time it was released.

The band finished their European tour and headed back home for some US dates that corresponded with the album's release there in early March. Parish had stopped touring so he could be in Bristol for the birth of his second child, a daughter named Hope, and was replaced by Joe Gore. When the group appeared on KCRW's *Morning Becomes Eclectic* on March 14, it was apparent just how long they'd been touring the record since the songs sounded so radically different. 'Souljacker Part I' was now a slow, ugly blues; 'Dog Faced Boy' was almost Beats-style jazz. "It's kind of a dreadful proposition to have to play the same songs night after night," E explained to host Nic Harcourt about the redecorated tunes. "You start to experiment around and see if they can keep you interested."

Daisies had been a struggle because of the label's tepid reaction and the nonsense that greeted the 'Beautiful Blues' single from radio stations. But if anything *Souljacker* proved even more challenging, sounding nothing like what E had done before. If that wasn't enough, the worldwide and personal tragedy of 9/11 added its own foul aftertaste. Perhaps, then, it was no surprise that even years after the fact, E still felt a little sore about the fight it took to get *Souljacker* out. In particular, he seemed irked at fans who were thrown by *Souljacker*'s sonic experimentation. "Every record I've ever put out has been met with some torrent of angry fan mail because it wasn't what they *expected*", he said in his memoir. "If you want what you expect, why not make your own album, then?" It was a rare example of E actively lashing out in such an obvious, public way, but you couldn't blame him, especially since the accusation that he obstinately switches styles on each new album has long dogged him.

Asked about the impression that E somehow doesn't respect his audience because he experiments with different sounds, Jim Jacobsen says: "I think it's the opposite — I think that he's trying to not insult his audience by doing the same thing over and over again. He's trying to do something genuinely new. And he might pick something that might not be what people are expecting now or what people are wanting, but it's not deliberate — he's trying to keep doing something interesting."

Despite the misconceptions people might have had about his new style, E could at least take comfort knowing that he had a rather powerful figure on his side. Granted, it was a green cartoon ogre, but beggars can't be choosers.

In May 2001, DreamWorks Animation released *Shrek*, a film version of a children's book by William Steig about a grumpy green monster named Shrek. Featuring the voice talents of Mike Myers, Cameron Diaz and Eddie Murphy, *Shrek* grossed over $484m worldwide and birthed a franchise for the studio. For E, whose 'My Beloved Monster' was on the soundtrack, the film helped expose his music to a family audience that otherwise would probably not have heard him. And that relationship continued on the film's first two sequels, which also featured Eels songs.

"Shrek and E have a lot in common," Chris Douridas observes, having come aboard on *Shrek 2* as music supervisor. "There's a very kid-friendly, mainstream-viable aspect to what Shrek is about. He's a cartoon, he's funny, he's lovable, he's very direct. And the other thing about Shrek is he's very unpleasant and a stick-in-the-mud — he's got this dark cloud." Douridas laughs. "Those same descriptions could apply to E. I mean, he's got this very dark and brooding sensibility that's wrapped in this pop confection. His music has become synonymous with the *Shrek* sound."

Shrek wasn't the first time E had allowed his music to be used in a film or TV show, but it was certainly the biggest — and, considering how insanely popular the *Shrek* series has been, probably his most lucrative. It brings to light another aspect of E's career — licensing.

Artists of all different stripes have discovered that they need to find new ways to make money, especially as record sales have dipped since Napster came of age at the turn of the century. As other revenue streams have presented themselves — films, TV shows, commercials — individual artists have had to decide how comfortable they are in letting their music be used in other media.

E's philosophy on this point has been pretty clear, absolutely refusing to give his songs to commercials. For instance, Volkswagen approached him to use 'Beautiful Freak' in a spot, which he declined because he didn't want to cheapen a song written about someone special to him. In a 2003 interview, he explained his stance on refusing to license his songs for commercials while at the same time allowing it for movies. "I can afford to throw stones," he said, "I don't have any kids in college. And everyone seems to be doing it now. But that doesn't make it right. I will let a song be in a movie sometimes, because at least that's *somebody's* idea of art. And I don't mind advertising myself. A video is basically a commercial for a song. But I don't want to be singing for some product. It doesn't seem right. Every big company you can name wants to use my songs. It's funny. In the music business I can't get arrested. But in advertising I'm a hot, but unwilling, commodity."

Nic Harcourt, the *Morning Becomes Eclectic* host who has also done a fair share of music supervising, understands where E is coming from. "Any artist who says that they don't wanna push a product with their song, I have the ultimate respect for," he says. "If that's where they're coming from, that's where they're coming from. I also understand why some bands do. I mean, there are some artists who can license a song into a commercial for 50 grand or 100 grand, and that's a big deal — that can keep an indie band on the road who's not making any money selling records. So I can also understand the trade-off, you know?"

Jim Jacobsen remembers talking about it with E, who told him, "It's like a deal I have with my fans — if they will listen to what I do, I promise I won't be a whore." (No doubt that's exactly how E felt when in 2000 he was forced to appear in the video for 'Mr E's Beautiful Blues' with the cast of the DreamWorks teen comedy *Road Trip*, which featured the song.) "He makes a good living," Jacobsen says, "but I'm sure he's passed up millions of dollars."

But as The Beatles once advised, money can't buy you love. And love was something E had in abundance at the moment. Natasha had been a guiding influence on *Souljacker* and would continue to make her presence felt on his work in subsequent years. When E was wrapping up his 2002 appearance on *Morning Becomes Eclectic*, Harcourt asked if he was going to play anything off his next record, alluding to their earlier conversation when E had mentioned that there wasn't room for break-up songs on *Daisies* or *Souljacker*. So maybe the next album would be filled with such tracks?

"No, it's not a break-up record," E replied. "It's the happy marriage record."

For a guy who likes to keep his true feelings close to the vest in interviews, E was actually being pretty honest about his next record — perhaps even more than he could have known at that moment.

Chapter Eleven

During an interview with E, *Q* writer Mischa Pearlman asked how he collaborates with his fellow musicians while making a record. "Well, I'm smart enough to always keep an open floor," the songwriter replied. "Everybody in the room, I want to hear all of their ideas all of the time, but the buck stops here. I've got to be the one who filters the 99 shitty ideas for that one good idea, but that I wouldn't have thought of on my own."

As most of E's collaborators can attest, he's an artist who tends to have a very strong idea of what he wants from the start — any sort of songwriting partnership would happen only if the other party brings in ideas that complement a concept already floating through E's brain.

But there was one instance in which he ceded some control to his collaborators, resulting in one of the funniest, funkiest, oddest albums in the Eels catalogue, although it's not even an official Eels album. In fact, to this day E would probably insist it's not even his album.

When *Sound On Sound* published its feature on *Daisies Of The Galaxy* in September 2000, the piece ended with a look at E's musical future. Writer Matt Bell mentioned that beyond leftover tracks from the *Daisies* sessions, "[E is] now putting together a predominantly sample-based album which may or may not end up as the next Eels album." Turned out that it did not — but it surfaced a few years later as the début of MC Honky.

Before the world had first heard of the reclusive 50-something DJ and remixer, the seeds of an MC Honky record were sown by 'Mr E's Beautiful Blues', the late addition to *Daisies* that E and Mike Simpson pounded out at the last minute to give the album its required "hit."

Butch had wanted to do a remix of the track and decided to collaborate with Joey Waronker, Lenny's son who had made a name for himself drumming for R.E.M. and Beck. Joey Waronker had first seen Eels play around the *Beautiful Freak* period and had become friends with Butch, working with him on side projects. "We had mutual admiration for each other's musicianship," Joey says. "We didn't actually have the same kind of taste and musical backgrounds, but we definitely had a lot of the same ideas and approaches about what we were doing as musicians. It was like, 'How could we as musicians push what we're [doing]?'" Wanting to get into production, Joey Waronker jumped at the idea of putting together a remix, although he admits that, as a novice, "I was just winging it". But as he searched for an angle on how to approach the 'Beautiful Blues' remix, a light blub went off.

"Those were the days when people were still relying heavily on loops that you would have to get licensed," he says. "And I thought, 'Whoa, wouldn't it be a novel concept to create stuff yourself and use that instead of records?'" Playing in Beck's band and on other people's records helped open the doors for him to meet possible instrumentalists. "I had a friend come over and play guitar stuff," he says, which inspired the remix's prominent hangdog blues riff. "And then I was trying to build something around that and I came up with a percussion idea and how to layer it. It was pretty primitive and bedroom-style."

Bedroom-style or not, the redesigned track impressed E. And it gave the songwriter an idea.

"I got a call from someone in the A&R department of DreamWorks," Waronker remembers. "They said, 'Hey, we love your remix and we got your number from Butch — E's gonna give you a call'." Waronker knew E socially but still it was a surprise when the songwriter approached him with a proposition. "He called me," Waronker says, "and he was saying, 'Man, that [remix] is amazing. We're gonna make the next Eels record together and you're gonna produce it and I'm really excited.

But before we do that, I really wanna do [another] project. I want to do a Fatboy Slim kind of thing'." Fatboy Slim, the DJ moniker for English musician Norman Cook, had become an international sensation near the end of the 20th century thanks to his big-beat anthems, 'The Rockafeller Skank' and 'Praise You'. "Knowing E, his tongue was in his cheek," Waronker says. "E was like, 'Oh, we can do that better than anybody. I want to dive in to this and do it. So maybe the first thing to do is for you to pick out some loops, pick out some ideas and some beats, and we'll get going'." Waronker was keen on creating organic beats, but E insisted on also incorporating breakbeats for the record.

Waronker took a trip to Fat Beats Records on Melrose Avenue. "I bought probably the most typical breakbeat records," he says, "because they were like public domain." E then ventured over to Waronker's new home studio, which was still getting set up. They worked for a few days at Waronker's place from tracks Waronker and Butch had put together before E decided that he wanted to move the base of operations back to his own home studio. For three weeks, E, Waronker, Butch, Koool G Murder and Ryan Boesch worked on the project together.

These weren't E's only collaborators on the album, though. "I think it was toward the end of recording all the [*Daisies*] stuff," Wally Gagel says, "and he just said, 'You want to come over and work on some stuff? I got some ideas'. And it was literally him throwing on all these bizarre old-school, obscure records." Using the records for inspiration, Gagel would play guitar and bass, as well as programme drums and loops. "Obviously, there's no vocals, quote unquote, on it," he says. "It's all these samples and loops... I think it's probably a publisher's nightmare, that record," he adds with a laugh.

As per norm, E worked quickly, forcing Gagel to keep up with his speedy pace. "Half the time I'm just putting down guitar parts or bass stuff," he says, "and then [E would say], 'OK, that's it'. I would wanna go back and work on it more, but there was no time — it was just getting things down. But there's something cool and rough about that." From this quick working process, the two came up with 'The Devil Went Down To Silverlake' — a mix of cheap keyboard, sampled blues vocal and distorted guitar — and 'Baby Elephant Rock-A-Bye', which combined a soothing keyboard melody with funk guitar. And as with E's other musical partners, Gagel loved the experience of contributing more to E's sonic ideas. "Maybe it was fun for him," Gagel muses, "since he wasn't singing and he didn't have this preciousness of it having to be an 'Eels thing'. It was a little bit more freeing, and he let go of the reins a little bit, so I was able to kinda contribute, which was fun. I wish we could have done more."

The sessions were put on the back burner for years as Eels focused on the *Daisies* tour and then the *Souljacker* album, but the series of off-the-cuff collaborations finally surfaced on November 2, 2002, when a record credited to MC Honky called *I Am The Messiah* hit stores in Australia through Liberation Records. Its release was a surprise to even those who worked on it. "We unfortunately hadn't talked in a while," Gagel says. Then out of the blue, "I got these random messages from his management company: 'Where can we send copies of the MC Honky record?' I'm like, 'What the hell's that?'"

Released in Europe at the end of March of the following year and then the States in early April on indie labels, *I Am The Messiah* was draped in mystery, a press release explaining that "Mr Honky" was "a shy, native Los Angeleno in his mid-fifties who began his love affair with sound as a teenaged janitor at the Capitol Records studio in 1959." The invented story went on to describe how Honky had landed an engineering gig at Reprise Records working for Frank Sinatra before eventually retiring from music to focus on pottery. But he couldn't give up his first passion, eventually returning to "his huge vinyl record collection to create massive sound collages and virtually inventing a new genre of music he calls 'self help rock'." Honky's daughter attended an Eels concert and slipped E a tape of her dad's tunes, which prompted the songwriter to produce *I Am The Messiah* and bring the recluse's music to the masses. There were no photos of Honky, only cartoon illustrations, which made the tall tale both more ludicrous and, somehow, more plausible — maybe the guy *was* just that shy that he didn't want his picture taken.

Adding to the fun was E's resolute insistence to curious journalists that he and Honky were two separate people.

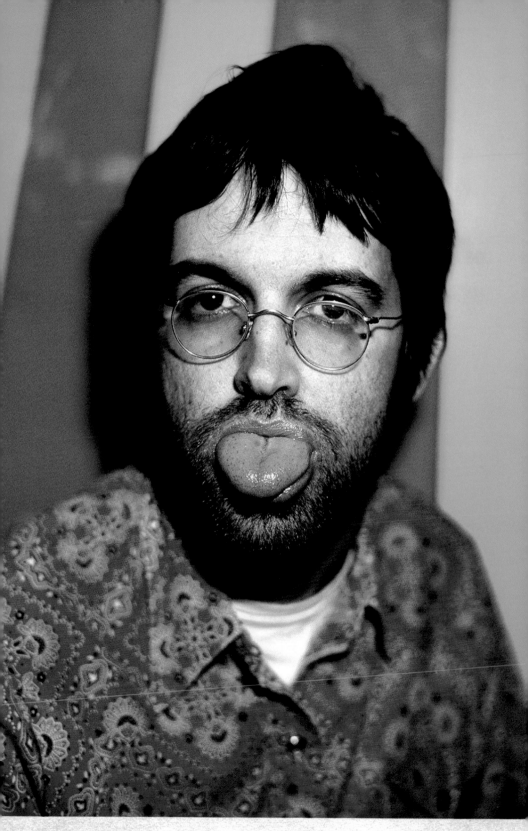

E in a pensive moment. PATRICK FORD/RETNA UK

Eels playing dress-up during the 2000 tour for *Daisies Of The Galaxy*. COURTESY PROBYN GREGORY

E performing during the band's after-show encore when the group members would come back on stage in their pajamas. TINA MCCLELLAND/RETNA UK

rocks the keyboard at the Reading Festival, 2001.
ROB WATKINS/RETNA UK

on guitar. CAMERA PRESS/MEL LONGHURST

Eels performing live at the Lowlands Festival in
Biddinghuizen, Netherlands on August 30, 2003.
MICHEL KOOLEN/CYBERIMAGE/LFI

Big Al hands E the phone during Eels' 2006 Live And In Person! tour. AWAIS BUTT/LFI

Eels performing live at Le Bataclan in Paris, France on February 18, 2008.
LAETIZIA FORGET/DALLE/RETNA UK

Top left: E and The Chet take photo shoots very seriously. Top right: A BBC promotional shot for *Parallel Worlds, Parallel Lives*, an award-winning documentary that found E coming to terms with his father's scientific legacy. ADAM SCOURFIELD

(L-R) Physicist Max Tegmark, musician Mark Everett and physicist Michio Kaku speak at the panel discussion "Parallel Worlds, Parallel Lives" at the World Science Festival held at the Paley Center for Media on May 29, 2008 in New York City. AMY SUSSMAN/GETTY IMAGES FOR WORLD SCIENCE FESTIVAL

E hanging out in his backyard at home. ROSS HALFIN

E shares a quiet moment with Bobby Jr. ROSS HALFIN

For Eels' 2010 world tour, E took to the stage hidden beneath a bandana, sunglasses and beard, as seen here at the Manchester Academy on September 4, 2010 in Manchester, England. CHRISTOPHER STEWART/REDFERNS

Mr E feeling those beautiful blues during a 2011 show. SIMONE CECCHETTI/CORBIS

"Most DJs, they sample a record like anyone can," E told *Metro Times* writer Fred Mills, "that three seconds or whatever of a whole song. But MC Honky was a recording engineer in the Sixties and Seventies and still has access to a lot of old tapes that, um, he probably shouldn't have, master tapes to unbelievable albums. I'm sure it's all completely illegal. I shouldn't say any more. But he can actually go in and isolate and sample individual tracks from songs off these records, which nobody else can do. So it's a whole new ball game."

Even more cleverly, E started giving Honky distinct personality traits. "The *NME* in England does this article that says, 'E puts out solo album under the name MC Honky'," he told Mills. "Which, of course, isn't true. I mean, why do I need to make solo albums? I make Eels albums, which are solo albums, really. I'd have to break up with myself to do that! Anyway, MC Honky heard about this article — and the press pretty much copied it, calling his album my album — and he got angry about it."

When Joey Waronker finally heard the record, he was disappointed, saying that there was "maybe one layer too many of irony or something going on. To me it felt sort of derivative and half-baked." But even if *I Am The Messiah* failed to match the primal release of Fatboy Slim or The Chemical Brothers, that was in part the point — and the charm. Any listener who knew that E and his band of merry men were behind the record could instantly appreciate the home-made quality of its indie-hipster aesthetic, which was both an homage and a send-up of the popular sound. (This was no more apparent than on the scratch-heavy '3 Turntables & 2 Microphones', about an angry rapper who loses a freestyle competition and plots his revenge. The title was a nod to Beck's *Odelay* hit 'Where It's At' with its iconic line "I got two turntables and a microphone".)

And while most of the vocals were samples of obscure vinyl — including a yoga record of Waronker's that ended up on the single 'Sonnet No. 3 (Like A Duck)' — there were great performances from, for instance, Koool G Murder, who smoothly intoned the positive messages of the New Age-y 'A Good Day To Be You'. Plus, the record was consistently hilarious and fun, somehow making room for a track built around a demented answering-machine message ('Soft Velvety 'Fer'), while another ('The Baby That Was You') proved to be one of E's most joyous. And as the bogus press release had suggested, *I Am The Messiah* flaunted its self-help rock, churning out the groovy hypnotism of 'The Object'. Magically, E and his cohorts had succeeded in producing a record that mocked the clichés of big-beat rock while still being viable as a piece of music itself. In the history of throwaway side projects, *I Am The Messiah* is one of the most consistently rewarding and entertaining.

When E wasn't trying to sucker journalists into buying the Honky sham, he was busy working on a proper Eels album, one that has in some ways been marginalised as much as *I Am The Messiah* was. Because of the speed in which it was written and recorded, and because of its straightforward sonic and thematic approach, *Shootenanny!* tends to get overlooked a bit in the Eels catalogue, generally considered a transitional record lacking the artistic heft of *Electro-Shock Blues* or the stylistic curveballs of *Souljacker*. But in retrospect, this seemingly laid-back, dashed-off album marked a period of major changes for Eels that contained both domestic contentment and a significant personnel shift. If *Messiah* was a lark and a parlour trick, *Shootenanny!* was a sombre statement hidden behind an ironic exclamation mark in the album's jokey title.

In the spring of 2002, Eels were wrapping up the *Souljacker* tour (which had been dubbed Bus Driving, Band Rocking) in the States. It had been a lengthy tour and, at least for one band member, exhausting. "On the *Souljacker* tour I lost 35 pounds because it was full-on," Butch told *Rhythm*. "I couldn't eat three hours before a gig, I was exhausted." The band's final show for the tour was a TV appearance on April 22 in Las Vegas, where they played as part of a special episode of the late night talk show *Last Call With Carson Daly*. It was a memorable three-song set, if for no other reason than because it presented one of those truly odd television moments in which you could watch the impossibly photogenic and vapid Carmen Electra instructing a Vegas crowd to "make some noise!" for the scruffy, bearded E and his cohorts. But the date will go down in Eels history for another reason: it would be the last time E and Butch would play together as Eels. Not that anyone tuning in that night could have known.

Returning home from the road, E refocused his energy on an ambitious album he'd previously shelved but which would eventually become the double-record *Blinking Lights And Other Revelations*. But that album's intricate, ornate design started making him fantasise about an entirely different record he wanted to make first. "I was inspired by listening to Muddy Waters," he told a journalist later. "I really wanted to do something succinct, direct and no bullshit."

"I remember I was actually in New York and he e-mailed me and said, 'What are you doing in November?'," says Greg Collins, who served as the primary recorder and mixer for *Shootenanny!* "'I want to do a record live-band style, everyone playing in the room.' I think he wanted to do that when he still had the budget to go in and use a good studio."

But for this idea of a garage-rock album to work, he was going to need Butch. And by comments Butch has made since leaving the band, it's clear that the drummer had already departed Eels by the time E started mapping out the recording sessions that were slated for November 2002.

In the summer of 2003, Butch discussed with *Rhythm* his reasons for exiting. Calling his decision to leave "a business thing," he explained that he'd had to file for bankruptcy. "The Eels were a great, creative, wonderful musical outlet," he said, "but my partnership deal was not taking care of my family." (He had met his wife, Lynn, at Cal Arts, and they have two sons, Nathan and Nicholas.) "I told management three years ago that this day was coming: 'We need to restructure, I'll give up my partnership if I can get a retainer or something.'" But Butch's request fell on deaf ears. "I got a call from E's accountant who said, 'E doesn't want to change the structure.' I said, 'Well, I made an offer for a retainer.' He said, 'That's way too much money,' so I said, 'Well, why don't you come back with an offer?'"

The two sides apparently couldn't come to an agreement. Still, E wanted Butch to be part of the band for *Shootenanny!* "I was a musician for hire on that one," Butch told *Drumhead*. "He decided to keep with his original plan and we worked out an agreement for me to do the record. I was broke and needed the session."

"For *Shootenanny!*, we actually went into a real recording studio," E told Douridas later during an interview in his home studio, "'cause we needed more room to all play like a live band, [which] is what I wanted to do. As you can see, it would be hard to do in here — the songs tend to be built up piece by piece here because you can only do one thing at a time. But I wanted to play together like a live band. It's essentially a live album."

With a plan in mind for the album, E started writing feverishly, trying to emulate the approach of Muddy Waters and other older blues artists. "I really admire that kind of writing," he later told *The Omaha Weekly-Reader*. "The old blues singers tell it like it is and the name of their songs wasn't something like 'Strawberry Letter No. 58', it was 'Mannish Boy'."

Collins, who has worked on albums with everyone from U2 to Gwen Stefani to Kiss, had supervised the "Climbing To The Moon" session on *Electro-Shock Blues*, so it made sense that E went with Collins on this new project: "Climbing To The Moon" had sought a live-band feel, which was the vibe for this new record as well. "I came from a background of being a recording engineer," Collins says. "To me what was most fun at that time was recording a live band in the studio and getting great sounds of everything and having something that's really natural that's a result of people playing with each other. I think that was something E got in his head — that *Electro-Shock Blues* track went well, and he just thinks of me as the guy who can handle a session of live players and he doesn't have to think about it. He knew that I had a background in working on big sessions with live players. And he knew that I could handle the technical aspects and get sounds that he's happy with — that way, he's free to play and not have to worry about that stuff."

But if it was Collins' job to handle the technical considerations on *Shootenanny!*, that didn't necessarily mean the sessions were completely carefree for E. According to Butch, there was tension between E and the drummer during the 10 days they spent recording the album at Hollywood's famed Ocean Way Studios. "There were photos of that session, but I didn't make any of the final cut," Butch told *Drumhead*.

"E didn't want me associated with Eels any more, and I had a huge sore in one of my eyes. Things were very tense between us, and the physical manifestation of our tension decided to travel to my eye. It was painful and gross. Funny how the universe works."

Shootenanny! was the last time the two worked on an album together, although tracks from previous Butch sessions showed up on later records.

Those who know E or Butch are hesitant to say much about their split, but it would seem that the drummer's departure was surprising although not entirely unexpected. No one interviewed for this book blamed either man for the break-up, instead citing the financial realities of life in a band.

"I was pretty surprised to find out he left," Parthenon Huxley says. "I mean, touring is a grind. There's an old expression: 'If you wanna hear a musician bitch, give him a gig.' It's so true — I don't know why it is, but it's a really common thing for musicians to talk about the travel and what a grind it is. The hour and a half or two hours onstage are 8,000 percent the best part of touring, but if all you're doing is going from town to town in a bus and you don't have any time at all to live like a human or walk around or see anything, the glamour goes away pretty quickly." Huxley adds that he had no inkling that Butch was planning on leaving or what his reasons were. "It's hard to stay in a band forever," Huxley says. "There's gotta be a lot of compelling reasons to do it. There's lots of reasons not to do it if you have family at home or the money's not good enough or you're bored or the travel sucks. When people leave bands, I'm never really surprised."

"It was brewing," Joey Waronker says when asked if he was surprised by Butch's exit. "I think that was something that was probably in the works for a while." Waronker and Butch didn't have any prior conversations about Butch maybe leaving Eels, but Waronker says he was "picking up on tension" between E and Butch. "They were moving in different directions, that kind of thing," Waronker says. "Butch had a family, and it's really hard to maintain that kind of lifestyle when you've got growing kids."

As part of Butch's exit from Eels, he signed a confidentiality agreement that prohibited him from being interviewed for this book. But he has talked to a few publications since his departure, and journalists will ask him about his feelings regarding his legacy with the group. In 2009, long after Butch had moved on from Eels and was now Lucinda Williams' drummer, he was asked about his best memories with Eels. "The entire journey and process will always be a positive memory," he replied. He went on to list several highlights of his time in the group — including first hearing the songs that would end up on *Beautiful Freak* and making the 'Novocaine For The Soul' video — but he concluded by citing the opportunity "to be able to work with an amazingly gifted and talented guy, E." As for the worst memories, Butch's response was, "I always felt bad that E was frustrated with me for my lack of intellect. I could never match his, and I dare say that not many people can. He is of the genius type, always was and always will be." In the same interview, he talked about playing in Williams' band, which prompted a comparison to his time in Eels. "You need to have all kinds of personalities in a band," he said. "Not everyone thinks alike. This was a problem when I played with E... because it was hard for him to understand that not everybody thought the same way he did. A family is not made up of people who all think alike, but you're still a family. A band is the same."

Not surprisingly, the person who perhaps best grasped what it must have been like for Butch to leave the band was someone who had gone through the same experience: Tommy Walter. "I think after [Butch's departure] went down," Walter recalls, "Butch reached out to me and was basically, like, 'I'm in your shoes now.' Or maybe he kinda understood [where I was coming from] more. He said, 'Well, I stuck it out longer than you, but I get it in a way what you were [feeling].' I think Butch took it really hard. Even more than me, Butch *really* invested his time, really put himself into it, and he felt like he was unappreciated and wasn't making a living from it. Even before the Eels, Butch toured on the solo stuff. Butch had been there for E from the get-go — super-supportive and his yes man and his support. He was that guy. So Butch really put his time in, and I think when it went down he was sorely disappointed."

★   ★   ★

Shootenanny! — the final album Butch made with Eels — was both commercially successful and critically tarnished because of its simple, stripped-down aesthetic. With its plain cover (yellow-and-white lettering on top of a black background), casual in-the-studio photography, lack of printed lyrics and jokey title, the album's presentation seemed to suggest a record that was more tossed-off than divinely inspired. Released on June 3, 2003, it looked and sounded minor after previous Eels albums' conceptual and sonic boldness. And yet it proved to be a "hit" of sorts, charting as high as number 145 on the *Billboard* album chart, the first Eels record to chart since *Beautiful Freak*. This was due in part to the first single, the rollicking and poppy indie-rocker 'Saturday Morning', which was warmly inviting and a fun little sing-along tune.

"He's a master of working with the simplest little chord sequence and making it something really cool," Collins says of E. "He's got all the Beatles tricks in his head that he obviously has studied from the time he was a kid. All those pop tricks of the trade are in his brain, and he knows how to filter them into his own sort of weird, cool little constructs."

Despite its modest trappings, *Shootenanny!* represented a weird twist on one Eels tradition: the album was more commercially embraced in E's home country than in the UK, where his albums have sometimes been released before making their way to the States. "We've been much more appreciated in Europe [than in the US]", E told me shortly after its release. But he observed that *Shootenanny!* "seems to be received a lot better in America than the previous ones were, where I get the feeling it's not their favourite in Europe compared to the other ones. I can't explain it." Indeed, in France, Germany and the UK, *Shootenanny!* did not chart nearly as highly as earlier Eels records, although reviews remained strong.

In the US, no matter its commercial standing, *Shootenanny!* represented the first time E got a series of truly bad notices. Whereas past records generally found favour with critics, *Shootenanny!* provoked some shrugs and a few outright dismissals. Calling the album "a rather mediocre mofo", *Spin's* Rob Harvilla lamented, "[t]his is the kind of bedroom folk pop E's done prettier — and weirder — before." *Pitchfork* elaborated on that sense of disappointment but reacted even more angrily, with reviewer Chris Dahlen commenting: "E coined the word 'shootenanny' to describe a fun shooting spree, but this pathetic title turns out to be 10 times more clever than anything else on the album." But Dahlen wasn't done yet: "Musically and lyrically, E is spent — out of ideas, out of innovation, unable to cough up anything but by-the-numbers pop in the 14 originals he wrote for this disc." Apparently, Dahlen's rancour blinded him to the fact that the album contained only 13 songs, unless he was counting the between-song snippet that bridges 'Wrong About Bobby' and 'Numbered Days'. Still, Dahlen insisted: "I'm not slamming this album to diss the man behind it, but to tell him he can do better. Much, much better." Granted, these negative reviews were in the minority, but *Shootenanny!* didn't inspire the sort of gushing praise that had greeted other Eels efforts. Ironically, Harvilla used *I Am The Messiah* as the tool with which to bludgeon *Shootenanny!*, declaring the "loose and lazy" MC Honky album "more fun" than the Eels record. (Perhaps the most surreal moment was when the hip-hop magazine *Vibe* put *I Am The Messiah* on its list of "Droppin' Dime" recommendations in its October 2003 issue: "Who's got the stones to call himself MC Honky? Only a hugely confident artist.")

And yet despite these complaints, *Shootenanny!* succeeded largely because of its perceived limitations. After years of heavily conceived and constructed records, *Shootenanny!* was a legitimately intimate and candid affair, featuring some of the most direct lyrics of E's career to that point. He may have wanted to make an album that sounded "like a band wailing away in the garage", but with the exception of the record's first two cuts, 'All In A Day's Work' and 'Saturday Morning', *Shootenanny!* was largely a gentle and reflective album in which the usual angst and self-doubt were somewhat undercut by a fragile domestic contentment.

"It's a little bit of a head fake," Collins says about E's decision to open the record with the raw, ornery blues of 'All In A Day's Work.' "It's like, 'Check out this darkness, and then if you've got the stomach to stay through that, then here's a reward of something much, much different [that's] much more pleasing and beautiful.' You got to be a real legit artist to pull those kinds of moves and to even think that way."

But even the album's more pleasing-sounding tunes had their share of dark worries. This idea was hammered home in an interview E did with *KCRW*'s Chris Douridas a few months after the record's release in which the two hung out at E's home studio, a rare allowance by the intensely private songwriter. Discussing the spare 'Lone Wolf', an unapologetic ode to being a loner, E talked about how acquaintances had misinterpreted its meaning.

"One of my friends did think 'Lone Wolf' was a joke of some sort," he told Douridas, "and I thought, 'Wow'. Because when I wrote it, I felt like that's the most honest song I've ever written... A lot of people ask me, 'You're married now, how can you write a song like "Lone Wolf"? This must be one of your songs written in character'. But it really was very autobiographical. I think getting married you are forced to learn things about yourself that you might not learn otherwise. And I learned that I really am essentially a loner." But rather than resisting that tendency in his married life, he decided to embrace it. "I just realised, 'Well, you know there's nothing worse than being in a relationship with somebody who hasn't accepted what they essentially are in some ways'," he said. "They're at war with themselves, and it just makes it hell for them and for you and for everybody involved. There's no winning in that situation."

More so than on *Souljacker*, in which he tried to hide love songs underneath feedback, *Shootenanny!* is as close as E will likely ever get to a "marriage album." And much like his hero John Lennon's *Double Fantasy*, the record reflected the edgy balance between ardour and lingering worry that most marriages generate — an anxious push-pull between allowing oneself to be happy while wondering if the happy ending can last.

In interviews for the album, E tended to create a bit of distance between the subject matter and his marriage, but on vulnerable, guardedly hopeful tracks like 'The Good Old Days', 'Love Of The Loveless' and 'Somebody Loves You', E seemed to be writing relationship songs from an up-close perspective in plain-spoken language. Speaking with The Rev Charles M Young, E said of 'Somebody Loves You': "I wrote that song after being alone in the basement for a week. I don't even know what I meant by it. I was just singing it to comfort myself. I think it's like 'Love Of The Loveless'. You've got to learn how to take care of yourself. The somebody who loves you might have to be yourself." But even if E was being completely honest, it was hard not to interpret the album's comparatively warmer glow as an indication of a more loving home life, which allowed a lyrical nakedness to emerge. This, matched with the quick writing and recording of *Shootenanny!*, arguably contributed to its unvarnished, unself-conscious honesty.

"He loves to surround himself with guys who are incredibly well-versed in their instrument and then tell them to dumb it down, if you know what I mean," Collins says. "A lot of great artists do this — take people who are great players and play complex, cool things but whittle out everything that is ornamental and keep the important stuff. That's what he did during *Shootenanny!* with Joe Gore and Koool G — if someone plays something he likes, he'll say, 'That's great, do it, keep that, that'd be amazing.' And if someone plays something flowery, he'll make some incredibly funny and possibly insulting comment about it being too much like, uh ...." Not wanting to name any specific bands E would use as derogatory comparisons, Collins changes course and says, "E's about the vibe and the impact, the way a song comes across — he never wants it to seem like he's trying hard to do anything."

But that didn't mean that *Shootenanny!* was boring, brainless bliss. For instance, the acoustic ballad 'The Good Old Days' opened with E admitting that he knows his limitations as a mate. A snapshot of the small hopes and fears that greet each new day, 'The Good Old Days' was an attempt to cobble together the shards of contentment that keep people going, not just for himself but also his relationship.

"I think it often gets interpreted quickly by the lazy of mind as some sort of nostalgic song," E told Douridas about 'The Good Old Days', "and it's really the opposite of that. It's about trying to appreciate the moment right now. This could be as good as it gets, and you might look back on this time with nostalgia. But [the song is] not about looking back, it's not about looking forward — it's just about looking at now."

"When I think of E's stuff," Collins says, "I think — in terms of construction — it's simple. And that is so hard to do — you either can do that or you can't. To make a song with three elements and have it be just totally absolutely beautiful — like, 'The Good Old Days' is one of my favourite songs and it's so incredibly simple. It's utterly just restrained. With the production, I wanted to hear more of the pedal-steel guitar stuff that Joe Gore was doing, but E was so happy to have all this space. There were moments that were just nothing but an acoustic guitar playing. If you can achieve that kind of simplicity and keep people's attention and then have it be great, that's a gift. There's people who can do it, and he's in that club."

Another seemingly simple tune, 'Rock Hard Times', appeared to speak to a post-9/11 atmosphere in which the foundations of life had been permanently altered by terror attacks and war. But a closer examination of the lyrics, which took aim at the phoniness and hypocrisy of Hollywood, revealed that the song was, in fact, a gentler and more rousing version of the anti-industry tracks he'd first started writing around the time of *Daisies Of The Galaxy*.

"It was actually inspired by living here in Los Angeles," he admitted to Douridas. "Everybody knows that it is pretty impossible to do anything of substance any more in the entertainment industry. There's all these forces working against you constantly. You have to be willing to be thought of as difficult, and you have to be willing to not be friends with everyone that you work with. Really, your best friend is your vision or your song. You just have to make these choices — otherwise, people will pull you into a really bad place, I think."

But where these complaints used to come off as huffy, 'Rock Hard Times' reflected an acceptance that this battle between art and commerce was going to be an ongoing struggle, one that E was happy to take on. If anything, he'd adopted a sense of humour about his problems with the machinations of the music business: *Shootenanny!*'s penultimate track, 'Fashion Awards', was a funny, pissy little throwaway (sung in mocking falsetto) about a soulless red-carpet frequenter who loves attending the endless parade of award shows.

(As a brief digression, despite E's many misgivings about Los Angeles, the city does provide opportunities for him to work with filmmakers, such as screenwriter Ed Solomon, who for his 2003 feature directing début *Levity* approached E to write the score. "I really just wanted to see what it was like to have a real grown-up job," E told *Music Connection* at the time, "and to see what it was like to have to answer to someone other than myself. I'm used to being the boss, you know? And I found out that I'm not very good at taking direction." Still, he was quite pleased with the soundtrack, which was credited to Mark Oliver Everett. "It's good music for getting a massage to," he stated. "Very sleepy and atmospheric — don't operate any heavy machinery after listening to it.")

Shootenanny!'s generous air, occasionally lacerating self-examination (like on 'Agony') and enjoyably cheap jokes (the pathetic, heartsick stalker of 'Restraining Order Blues') lacked the urgency of E's earlier discs, but, as *Rolling Stone* suggested, the album's "Zen-like self-realization" was a welcome new wrinkle to the songwriter's record-making strategy. "I think *Shootenanny!* is a really beautiful record," Collins says. "It's got a lot of emotionally direct songs, and the vocals are just big and out there on the whole record. That's what helps you get that sense that he's revealing himself — his voice is the big centrepiece of the whole thing."

And even if critics were a bit dismissive of the record, at least one of his idols took note: Tom Waits nominated *Shootenanny!* for the 2003 Shortlist Music Prize, a short-lived American equivalent of Britain's Mercury Prize. "I remembered he was really psyched when he found out that Tom Waits liked the band," *Shootenanny!* touring guitarist Shon Sullivan (who records under the name Goldenboy) says. "I remember he was just really excited about that."

It was a time of new beginnings for E, but it was also the end of his run with Butch. When E hit the road to promote the record a few weeks after its release for what would be dubbed Tour Of Duty, the official word was that Butch had previously committed to touring with Tracy Chapman and would therefore be replaced by his cousin Puddin'. And while it was true that Butch was drumming with Chapman, the new Eels drummer was not related to Butch. But he was linked to the band in another way. Puddin', whose real name is Daren Hahn, was childhood friends with Kelly "Rusty" Logsdon, aka Koool G Murder, Eels' bassist. Likewise, Sullivan became the band's touring guitarist because he had been in a group whose accountants were Murder's in-laws. Murder went to see the group, and soon after Sullivan got an invitation to audition.

As for the Puddin' nickname, "that was definitely an E thing," Hahn says. "He's definitely about nicknames." Recalling the origin of the Puddin' name, Hahn said: "I believe the Eels were doing an interview on TV and the interviewer called Butch Puddin'. And E was like, 'Aw, I wished I'd have given you that name instead of Butch! I like it so much better'. So then when I got the gig, E came up with this whole story about how I was Butch's little cousin filling in for him and my name is Puddin'."

"I felt bad [for] Daren," Sullivan says, laughing. "'What the fuck's Puddin'?! What the fuck?! I want to score with girls and he called me Puddin'."

"We're all about creating our own world here," E once admitted. "And when I say 'we', I mean 'me'. I create my own little fantasy world, and I live in it, and everybody else must play along."

That spirit of camaraderie carried through the tour, with just about everyone picking up a nickname along the way.

"The guitar tech, you're not gonna believe this, but his nickname was Tea Bag," Sullivan recalls. "I don't even remember his real name, but he had all these stories from [working with] heavy metal bands. The tour manager [Jim Runge], we called him The General. He was the tour manager for Alice In Chains, so every time someone would get nicked off the tour, there would be some guy from Alice In Chains' entourage that would join us. Their soundman joined us, then we lost our monitor guy and Alice In Chains' monitor guy joined us. It was gradually turning into this full-on serious rock thing!"

Tour Of Duty was indeed a "serious rock thing", although it lacked the full-blown antagonism of the *Souljacker* tour. E would later describe it as a sort of "midlife crisis" tour: "I decided it was time to really live like a rock band." But the tour took inspiration from both *Shootenanny!*'s stripped-down aesthetic and Elvis Presley's 1968 comeback special, which featured The King's back-up band decked out in red suits. For Tour Of Duty, E instructed the band to wear similar red suits. They made the band look pretty cool onstage, but the outfits got oppressively warm as the show went on, causing the players to sweat buckets.

But before Eels took the stage, the night would open with a set from MC Honky. Prior to the tour, the Eels' website promised that Honky would be performing at the shows, seemingly to perpetuate the myth that Honky was a real person. But a few days before the band's warm-up gigs at The Roxy in Hollywood, E spoke to me about Honky's prickly nature, saying, "I'm so angry at him right now... I hope he dies of SARS." Shortly after our interview, an announcement on the band's website said that the chances "appear to be slim" that Honky would play. "According to an about-to-be-published story... EELS main man E said, 'I Hope MC Honky dies of SARS!'" (If all of E's world is a stage, I'm pleased to have played my small part.)

But eventually the hatchet was buried and Honky showed up on opening night — or, rather, a guy dressed in a button-down sweater, horn-rimmed glasses, fedora and pipe who'd been made up to look like MC Honky did. For about 20 minutes, Honky would stand onstage behind some turntables and play tracks from *I Am The Messiah*. He never acknowledged the crowd until he tipped his hat when his "performance" was over. (Later in the evening after Eels finished their set, Honky would return for a final bow and stand with the rest of the band, again as a ploy to "convince" fans that he and E weren't the same guy.)

So who was "Honky"?

"There was definitely a big air of mystery," Hahn says, "and really if I told you about it I would have to kill you. In fact, I'm contractually obligated to remain [quiet]."

"MC Honky is my bud," Sullivan says. "I did the most hanging out with him when we were doing the tour."

The importance of keeping up the mystery even extended to the band's printed daily tour itinerary. Several band and crew members are listed, complete with their real names and nicknames, but "MC Honky" is merely called "Special Guest." E didn't want anybody finding out who this guy was. As best as can be determined, he was a pal of someone who worked in the crew, his "Honky" get-up (when he was in costume

194

and full make-up) closely guarded so that no one would see him before or after the show.

Not that the theatricality ended with the Honky ruse. Eels would start their set with E coming through the crowd to the stage while the rest of the band mercilessly repeated the opening riff from 'All In A Day's Work'. Decked out in short hair and aviator glasses, E was a striking presence, demonstrating his growing ease with being a front man for a rock'n'roll band. Now, years after the personal heartache he captured on *Electro-Shock Blues*, he was able to turn that album's greatest songs ('3 Speed', 'Last Stop: This Town') into enduring snapshots of family memory. "For a couple of years, I didn't want to play 'Last Stop: This Town'," he admitted to me at the time. "Now I really love playing that song. It really feels good." Asked if he ever considered not bringing the songs back for Tour Of Duty now that he had some distance from the pain associated with them, he replied, "That kind of thing you never get over, and you can't just bury it. You gotta keep it alive for the sake of your emotional well being. It sorta feels to me like a healthy way to live with the painful memories."

Near the end of most nights, E would talk to the crowd during the instrumental section of 'Love Of The Loveless', saying that while he could sometimes be accused of being a sourpuss he wasn't sad right now. It would get a huge, roaring response, and while it might just have been simple stage banter, Sullivan believed there was some truth buried beneath E's deadpan delivery.

"I think that was a really positive time," Sullivan says. "Just from what I was gathering from some of the other people, like John Broms who did lights on that tour and did previous ones — I remember him saying, 'This is my favourite band that I've seen of the Eels. This is the coolest and most fun'. I think that album and that tour was a really good time for him. I think he really, really enjoyed touring that album and that band, because it was a very easy thing — no headaches at soundchecks, every show we just got out there and the band was solid and tight. There was nothing to worry about. It was just like going back to some of the early days of rock'n'roll where it was about just going out and playing these songs." Indicative of the laid-back vibe, the band would convene for "martini hour" before each show, and certain nights would end with an additional encore in which Murder would take over on the drums and Hahn would show off his break-dancing skills.

That slight mellowing was also exhibited in E's personal habits. While he remained someone who didn't enjoy the grind of the road, he had learned how to adapt to the endless travel and demands on his time. "I have to separate myself as much as possible, honestly," he said. "I need a door between me and everyone else." He laughed. "I'm like a classic introvert personality. Introverts get energy by being alone, and extroverts are the people that get energy by being around people. I lose all my energy when I'm around people. I can be around people, but I need time to recharge my batteries and I need to be mentally prepared that this is coming, that I'm going to be around people a lot. I need a place to hide away from everybody... It's all in the name of trying to have a good concert. I know what I need to do and it's pretty simple. I need a tea kettle and somewhere that I can go and be alone, and then I can put on a good show."

Plus, he had turned 40 that year, which prompted him to take up whisky and cigars. "I thought it's time for some fun old-man activity," he told *Mojo* seven years later about that period in his life. "At the time I couldn't believe I was this old; middle age in my family is often old age. If my family genes were like Keith Richards', I'd be drinking a bottle of Jack Daniel's and doing heroin every day, but my family genes are the opposite."

Interviewers couldn't help but note the milestone birthday. Asked if he was worried about being a more mature musician in ostensibly a young person's game, he was philosophical about the road ahead. "I feel like I've been slowly improving over the years," he told writer Tim McMahan. "A lot of people by now are doing some of their worst stuff and I feel like I'm doing my best stuff lately." And then he made a curious comment: "I feel like I have one more album in me and that's it. It remains to be seen."

The tour ended in November 2003, by which time Sullivan was already focusing on other projects. But the usually stay-at-home E left the house to catch a show of Sullivan's in Silver Lake, which allowed them to catch up and for Sullivan to hear about E's project now that the so-called "midlife crisis" tour was over.

"I was talkin' to him," Sullivan recalls, "and he says, 'Yeah, I got this album, and I don't even know who's gonna put it out. I gotta find someone to put it out'."

If it was, indeed, going to be E's last album, he was going to be sure he made the most of it.

Chapter Twelve

B efore it was an album — and before that album morphed from a one-disc orchestral record to a four-disc behemoth before finally becoming a 33-track double album — it was just a song. In 1997, E came up with a tune called 'Blinking Lights'. "I was writing the song to comfort someone that was close to me that was going through a hard time," E recalled, "and I was looking out the window one night. A plane was flying over the sky, and I was thinking about people that were scared of flying. And I thought, 'Well, wouldn't it be nice if that little light on the end of the wing was flashing a Morse code signal that when you decoded it, it spelled out *Don't worry: everything's going to be OK?*' "

The song — delicate, simple, comforting — was intended for a soundtrack to a Wim Wenders film, but the movie never happened, so E put the track on the shelf and focused on other material for what eventually became *Electro-Shock Blues, Daisies Of The Galaxy* and *Souljacker*. However, during the years he was promoting those records in interviews, he would also mention the albums he had in the can that he couldn't decide what do with. ("It's just getting confusing," he told me in 2003 about those unreleased records. "I've got to figure out what I'm going to put out next.") During this time, his relationship with Wenders continued, leading to the filmmaker directing the band's 'Souljacker Part I' video. But Wenders did E a bigger favour a few years later when he approached him about an acting gig, one that would help the musician find a home for 'Blinking Lights'.

At some point before Eels' spring 2002 US *Souljacker* tour, E took a train from Los Angeles to New York to see actress Jennifer Jason Leigh. He had given music to her 2001 ensemble film *The Anniversary Party*, and in return she had invited him to visit her on the East Coast to give him acting lessons. When Wenders asked him to act in his film, E's only previous thespian experience had been as "Indie Music Guy" in the 13-minute 2001 short film *The Girls Guitar Club*, which starred comediane Mary Lynn Rajskub as part of a talentless musical duo. (Rajskub went on to play Chloe on TV's *24*, while the film's director, Ruben Fleischer, later helmed the zombie comedy *Zombieland*.) *The Girls Guitar Club* was hardly an auspicious début for E, so it's understandable that he would look to Leigh for guidance. (What advice did she give him? "I'm not sure she'd want me to reveal her secrets," E told an interviewer. "She told me never to rehearse my lines in front of the mirror, because it makes you self-conscious. I think I can tell you that. I don't think that's the whole basis of her success.") E ended up passing on the Wenders film role, but as would often happen when E took a break from music, ideas simply came to him. And just as *Souljacker* was inspired by a trip to a meditation retreat, *Blinking Lights And Other Revelations* came together when E decided to take a train to and from New York when he went to meet Leigh.

Ironically, the reason E was on a train at all was because, post-9/11, he had developed a fear of flying. ('Blinking Lights', which had been written years earlier about other people's flying phobia, now hit home in a much more profound way for him.) But while on the trip, he became friendly with the train workers, most of them older men. Their conversations about the dying railroad industry got him thinking about the parallels with the industry he worked in. E had always admired older artists and had become increasingly disillusioned with modern pop music. Plus, he'd just gone through a series of battles with *Daisies* and *Souljacker* as he tried to sell his label on albums that lacked clear alternative-rock singles. No doubt he felt antiquated, just like the railroad itself.

And so he wrote 'Railroad Man', a country-ish ballad in which he imagines himself working the titular profession at a time when train travel had long been surpassed by faster modes of transportation. (Suggesting that he still held Lenny Waronker in high regard despite his problems with DreamWorks, E would later subtitle the track 'A Song For Lenny And Me', acknowledging their kinship in quality-over-commerciality.) Back in 1995 when Lonn Friend had been hanging out with E, desperate to sign Eels to Arista, they had spent a night listening to *Pet Sounds*, prompting Friend to ask E if he ever felt like Brian Wilson singing 'I Just Wasn't Made For These Times'. Friend couldn't remember what E's response had been, but in a way 'Railroad Man' was E's bittersweet answer to both Wilson and Friend.

But it wasn't just the song that made the train trip worthwhile for E. Heading home from New York, he pondered the long-gestating album he'd worked on over the years that he never could quite crack. He thought about 'Blinking Lights', wondering if the song's warm, helpful tone might provide a possible direction. Then he hit upon an idea for the nascent album: "I [wanted] it to feel like a friend to the listener," he explained later.

But despite the fresh inspiration, E still couldn't entirely flesh out the concept when he got back to Los Angeles, eventually deciding to postpone it and focus on the blues-rock simplicity of *Shootenanny!* in late 2002. By the time Eels had completed the *Shootenanny!* tour a year later, E had gotten loud, uncomplicated rock out of his system and was ready to get back to *Blinking Lights*. But in a further sign of how much this album reflected E's displacement from contemporary popular music, his inspiration came not from other songwriters but from movies.

While on the *Shootenanny!* tour, "I started to think about [*Blinking Lights*] more like a film than a record," E told *Magnet* around the album's release. "Whenever I read biographies about certain filmmakers, I always seem to identify with their personalities a lot more than musical guys." The films of Ingmar Bergman held special meaning for him during the downtime between shows, in particular *Wild Strawberries*, which tells of an aging professor who travels to his old college to receive an honorary degree, bumping into memories of his past along the way. "I wanted it to kind of feel like a Swedish car trip of an album," he explained to *Flaunt*, "like you're taking a drive one Saturday, thinking about your life and what it's going to add up to."

But perhaps *Blinking Lights'* most important influence was another film: Stanley Kubrick's seminal *2001: A Space Odyssey*. Speaking with *Harp*, he explained: "The most remarkable thing about that film was that when it came out no one really knew what to make of it because it didn't have the usual linear narrative thread that you follow. It was really asking you to feel it rather than think about it. That was really key for me. I want to feel something here. I don't want it to be so cerebral." (Kubrick was a filmmaker both he and his dad admired — not surprisingly, considering the work his father did for the government calculating nuclear-war scenarios, Hugh's favourite film was *Dr. Strangelove*.)

After returning from Tour Of Duty, E essentially went into hiding in 2004, committing himself to the vision of *Blinking Lights*. Aside from an appearance at UCLA's Royce Hall on January 24 for a tribute concert to Randy Newman — where he performed 'Living Without You' and 'I Don't Want To Hear It Anymore' and joined Vic Chesnutt for 'Mr President (Have Pity On The Working Man)' — he stayed out of sight, sticking to a strict recording regimen. For two weeks, he would record. For the next two weeks, he would review what he'd worked on during the previous two weeks, sequencing tracks together and deciding what could be tossed out and what gaps needed to be filled.

"It's actually a great way to do it," he told *Hot Press*, "if you can afford to work on that kind of schedule." Pretty soon, he realised that earlier versions of the album — which included an all-orchestral edition and (as he described it to *Hot Press*) "an obvious, birth-to-death kinda narrative" storyline — didn't work for what he was going for. It was going to need to be a double album. And it was going to need instrumental passages to give the album, as he phrased it, "more space" between the traditional songs. But that sense of space didn't just apply to *Blinking Lights'* pacing and running time — it could also be an indication of the years of material culled for the final record.

Most Eels albums are intentionally vague in the liner notes when it comes to who played what on specific tracks. "I like the credits in albums to not spell out too much," E once explained to Chris Douridas. "I find when I'm listening to a record and I read the credits and it says who does exactly what on everything, it takes away some of the magic for me. I like when you hear sounds and you don't know exactly what instrument it is." Lumping all the musicians who worked on *Blinking Lights* together in the liner notes served to highlight the Eels eras that helped make the record.

In fact, some of E's associates aren't quite sure what tracks they collaborated on — or if they're part of the final version of a particular song. "'Old Shit/New Shit' might be something that E and I started — I'm not even sure," Greg Collins says. "There was a period between *Electro-Shock Blues* and *Shootenanny!* where I'd be free and he'd want to be recording and I would come over to his place and we would just record a bunch of stuff." (Equally confused by which *Blinking Lights* tracks he worked on, *Daises* producer Wally Gagel said, "When you work that fast and you're recording all these ideas, sometimes you almost just have titles like 'Untitled Number Five'.") Meanwhile, E was bringing in newer associates. For instance, Daren Hahn flew in from Colorado to add drums to two existing tracks, 'Son Of A Bitch' and 'If You See Natalie'. The latter is one of two *Blinking Lights* tracks to feature guitar from Peter Buck, although whether those songs originated from the *Daisies* sessions remains unclear.

E also recruited another musician from the *Shootenanny!* period, The Chet, to add guitar, lap steel, and saw. The Chet, aka Jeff Lyster and Chet Atkins III, had auditioned to be the guitarist on the 2003 *Shootenanny!* tour. Living in Portland, he received a call about the tour, but had to get to LA immediately if he wanted to try out. "So I borrowed an amplifier from Guitar Center because of their 30-day, no-questions-asked return policy and flew down," The Chet recalls. The audition went well, but E chose Shon Sullivan instead. ("I always tell myself that it was because he was a local and they didn't have to fly him in and pay the extra amount," The Chet says.) But after Sullivan left the tour in July, The Chet's moment arrived. "They called me and I flew into Lawrence, Kansas," he says. "We had two afternoons of rehearsals to bone up on all the material, and I finished out the tour with them." The Chet remembers feeling a little out of place, "being the new guy coming on in the middle of a very long tour. I joke with E about it [now] — he barely spoke a word to me the entire time I was on the road that first tour. He was already in his own zone. So it was funny — I didn't feel like I got to know him at all until the very last night of the tour. He pulled me aside after a show or something and said he really enjoyed it, and did I want to come back. I was pretty stoked."

When the time came to work on *Blinking Lights*, The Chet was very much part of the Eels family. "He had recorded a whole bunch of that record already," The Chet recalls, "and I was at home in Portland. He called me up and said, 'There are some songs on this that I think are very Chet-friendly and I want you to come down and play on them'. In addition to my sort of rock'n'roll background, I also have done some country and some finger-picking stuff."

That style came in handy on tracks like 'Railroad Man'. "He doesn't do things a lot of bands do," The Chet says. "They go to the studio and they do all of the rhythm tracks all at once, then they go back and they lay down all the vocals or whatever. But with 'Railroad Man', for example, I didn't come down and play to a track. I came down and we recorded the entire song. We'll sit down, he'll say, 'Here's a song', and he'll go sit in front of the mic and play it. And then, we'll all do what we need to do on it. And we'll sit right there and mix it and be done with it. I think that's why you get this interesting thing on [*Blinking Lights*] — each song is its own little unique piece of art. *Blinking Lights* was like a collection of little stories and tidbits and stuff."

The album's higher-profile collaborators reflected E's range of influences and heroes. John Sebastian, founder of The Lovin' Spoonful, co-wrote the instrumental 'Dusk: A Peach In The Orchard'. "I had a friend who'd grown up on a commune with John Sebastian," E told *Clash*. "I went to Woodstock and ended up going over to his house and meeting him. This was probably around 1997. I stayed there for a couple of days and just had the best time staying up all night talking to him, getting stories out of him about hanging out with The Beatles." (Incidentally, during this time he also met Nic Harcourt, who, before joining KCRW, was a DJ for a Woodstock alternative-rock station that played 'Novocaine' pretty regularly. "He was in town visiting John Sebastian's son," Harcourt recalls. "They just walked into the radio station to say, 'Hey, thanks for playing the record'.")

E also roped Tom Waits into performing on 'Going Fetal', about an imaginary dance craze which involves rolling into a ball and giving up on life. "I was talking to him on the phone one day," E told writer Rob O'Connor, "and I just wouldn't... I just thought... well, he's such a great guy and he really loves music. He pays attention to a record the way most people pay attention to a movie. He really immerses himself in it and gets into it." E knew Waits liked Eels, so it emboldened him to ask his hero to participate on *Blinking Lights*. But what song would really benefit from the Waits touch? "This 'Going Fetal' thing would be interesting to put him in a situation he's not usually in," E recalled thinking, "basically having him on *American Bandstand* in 1965. I sent him a little letter with detailed instructions of what I wanted him to do and he completely ignored it." Accidentally erasing E's lead vocal from the temp track, Waits recorded wails and screams and sent it back, inspiring E to further develop the *American Bandstand*-parody element by adding the sounds of smitten young girls screaming in ecstasy in the background. The resulting song was funny and creepy in equal measure.

After the battles with DreamWorks over previous Eels albums, E shouldn't have been surprised when the label was none too pleased with his ambitions for *Blinking Lights*. "They weren't very happy I was off making a double album without their input," E told a Dutch reporter after its release. "They said, 'You know, we make *collaborative* records here, E'. And I said, 'Well, great, let me know when Bob Dylan or somebody I respect wants to collaborate'." Of course, it wouldn't be entirely fair to heap too much scorn on DreamWorks. By that point, the label was under the thumb of Universal, which put E in the weird position of being part of a parent company, Interscope, that he had rejected back in 1996 when he signed with DreamWorks. One might say that Interscope eventually got its revenge: E's Universal A&R rep let it be known that the company wasn't interested in putting out his 93-minute double album.

Depressed and stressed because he had spent all of his own money on the record — which, to extend the album-as-movie metaphor further, any film producer would warn was a cardinal error — E realised he needed to find another label to release it. "The sad irony of the making of this record," he said in the same Dutch interview, "is that I was trying to make a record that reflected what it's like to live, and a lot of the good experiences in particular I wanted to make sure were represented. I wanted something that had compassion for the world and for the listener and all that. But the irony is that making this double album and everything I've had to do to make it and get it out has just made me much more cynical as a person." He laughed ruefully. "It's been a really difficult process. I've been confronted with people and sides of humanity in the process that have me lose more faith instead of gain more."

In the end, E went a similar route as indie-rock darlings Wilco, who a few years prior had battled with their label, Warner Bros, over the experimental sound of *Yankee Hotel Foxtrot*, only to wind up on another label owned by the same conglomerate. E got out of his contract and landed at Vagrant, an artist-friendly label that was also owned by Interscope. "In a way I was fortunate that that happened," he would admit later, "because the new company kinda understood, 'Here it is — this is the album. It's not going to change. If you want to put this out, it's this or let's not bother talking'."

For Vagrant president and co-owner Rich Egan, it was a no-brainer, citing the label's previous relationship with former Replacements front man Paul Westerberg. "[Westerberg] came in our door going, 'I've got a double record and I'm not cutting anything!'" he told *Magnet*. "And I'm not gonna tell Westerberg to cut anything, so I'm certainly not gonna tell E to cut anything, either. I thought it was really important to present the Eels record as a whole, because it's such a journey."

The world got to experience that journey when *Blinking Lights And Other Revelations* was released in April 2005, a couple of weeks after E turned 42. And perhaps not surprisingly, one of its most glowing reviews came from a film critic. Ty Burr, writing in *Entertainment Weekly*, rated the album 'A', calling it "the absolute stone masterpiece fans have always known lurked inside his dour heart." Though incorrectly labelling *Blinking Lights* a "cradle-to-grave journey through one unlucky man's life" — a concept E had flirted with before rejecting it — Burr praised the album's "measured ascension toward grace that is almost unbearably moving."

Richard Cromelin of the *Los Angeles Times* declared that E had "never before traced the trajectory of transcendence with the meticulous detail and shaded gradations afforded by the expanded canvas of these two CDs."

The words "masterpiece" and "ambitious" were included in a few of the album's most ecstatic reviews, but that latter adjective proved to be a double-edged sword. The less sympathetic complained about the record's instrumental interludes or overall length. Summing up these reactions succinctly, *Pitchfork*'s Rob Mitchum observed: "Here's the part where I fulfill my critic's duty by proclaiming that, as always, *Blinking Lights* would've been better as a single album." But even those who groused about the album's bulk had to acknowledge its achievements. "There's a good album underneath all the filler — probably the Eels' best since *Electro-Shock Blues*," Mitchum concluded, "but it'll take some editing to excavate it."

(Asked his opinion of *Blinking Lights*, Carter replies: "It is unfortunate that whoever he's working with is not the brutal asshole I was, 'cause he shouldn't be putting out double albums. I don't want to be, you know, put in that fast-forward, judging-things-by-the-first-verse syndrome that you get when you have a mountain of material like that.")

But E seemed to anticipate his album's reviews while he was promoting it, drawing comparisons again to *2001*. Speaking with *Hot Press*, he talked about how Kubrick's movie inspired him to "be brave enough to make something that you might not get on the first listen. If you have to write about this album on a deadline, it's probably going to be a negative review, I would guess. It's probably going to say that it's boring, or that it doesn't go anywhere or whatever. But like *2001*, it's designed to get under your skin. The first time you listen to it, it might not fully register, but by the third or fourth time, hopefully it'll take you by surprise and you'll really start to get it."

That sense of a puzzle requiring multiple listenings to fully absorb is crucial to appreciating *Blinking Lights*. As E suggested, it is an album that can't quite fully be understood the first time through — not necessarily because it's so thematically or intellectually deep, but because of the plethora of moods and tones it contains. Both kind and unkind reviews made comparisons with *Blinking Lights'* most obvious antecedent, *Electro-Shock Blues* — positive notices generally hailed it as a bold improvement on the previous effort, while mixed reviews preferred the former record's more manageable length — but beyond certain superficial sonic and conceptual/thematic similarities, those comparisons simply don't hold water. For good or ill, *ESB* was a feverish, immediate response to all the death that seemed to be raining down on E's head. Death asserts itself on *Blinking Lights*, but it's merely one character among many that occupy E's time.

When *Harp*'s Paul Nolan compared *Blinking Lights* to Robert Altman's multi-character Los Angeles epic *Short Cuts*, E responded by saying, "I've always been a Raymond Carver fan", referring to the short story writer whose work inspired the film, "and I do like those little slices of life." And indeed it's the fragmented, ensemble nature of *Blinking Lights* that gives the album its hypnotic hold. Put simply, no Eels album has such an abundance of incidents and vignettes. Plus, E wilfully bounced between autobiography and fiction in such a way that one had to give up the "is this song based in fact?" game that had been the primary sport of every Eels record since *ESB*.

The album's introduction sets the tone: After the instrumentals 'Theme From Blinking Lights' and 'From Which I Came', the first song with lyrics is 'A Magic World', a joyful story of a newborn's first moments — E's, to be exact. But this is immediately followed by the satire of 'Son Of A Bitch', detailing a lousy childhood in which the narrator is taken in by his grandmother. Some of the lyrical details seemed to correspond with E's own biography, specifically the mention of an alcoholic father, but it was purely a work of fiction. "I thought he was talking about his father," Hugh biographer Peter Byrne says of 'Son Of A Bitch'. "So the first time I met E, I said, 'What about that song about your father being drunk in the doorway?' And he goes, 'That wasn't my father — that was one of my characters. That was some guy's father from down the street'." From the first few tracks, *Blinking Lights* established that it would be a blending of the real and the imaginary, but what soon became clear was that the characters, fictional or not, were simply extensions of E's own personality.

"I think an awful lot of these songs really are me saying things that I wish someone would say to me," he admitted at the time. "It's sort of like when you go to sleep at night and you have a dream and they say that all those characters in your dream are really some aspects of you, it's coming from your mind."

And the album reflected that half-remembered essence of dreams that are more about feeling than pure logic. If *Souljacker*'s 'Woman Driving, Man Sleeping' had been his most successful stab at creating a Carver-esque mini-scenario to that point, *Blinking Lights* had a bounty of them. 'In The Yard, Behind The Church' was an impossibly pretty glimpse of a couple walking through a graveyard that ached with a melancholy which the lyrics never quite spelled out. Kicking off with a howl from E's beloved dog Bobby Jr, 'Last Time We Spoke' echoed the moody, ghostly-carnival spirit of indie band Sparklehorse for a vague tale about someone close to the narrator who is gone. (Much like the ballads on *Daisies*, it was impossible to know for sure if it was a paean to a former lover or a dead family member.) And then there was 'Understanding Salesmen', a story so rich with evocative details that it could take a lifetime to unravel the larger narrative. Subtitled 'Know Your Enemy', the acoustic-guitar-and-mournful-strings track painted a portrait of a man haunted by his own insignificance. The song's incidents don't add up — there's a card game, a drive on a country road, a knock on the door, a ring of a phone — and the title phrase never appears in the lyrics. But as E had strived to do, he constructed a superb song that provoked an emotional rather than intellectual response.

With many of the non-instrumental songs clocking in around three minutes or less, it could be said that *Blinking Lights* is filled with slight, insubstantial songs, except the shorter tracks help give the album a sense of short but powerful bursts of melody and feeling which juxtapose, and occasionally complement, each other. And as for the complaint that there were too many instrumentals, it's interesting to refer to an interview E gave after the release of *Electro-Shock Blues*, when a reporter asked about the importance of balancing music and lyrics in a song. "To me they are equally important," he said. "The reason I like to do popular music, because there is something about — if it was the lyrics, if it was just poetry, or if it was just instrumental music, both of those things are fine, but when you put both of those things together, it changes the meanings of the words, so it become[s] something of itself. That's what I like: the marriage of the two. Though I really do think all music is better without words. It's much more effective. It's maybe closer to the pulse of, oh, God, or whatever you want to call it." For an atheist like E, this was as close to a sense of the divine as he could muster.

Not that there weren't plenty of songs that stuck to the ears — in fact, some seem to have haunted listeners.

Lonn Friend, who had kept up with Eels ever since the Arista deal collapsed, fell in love with *Blinking Lights* while taking long walks with his iPod. In particular, he became entranced by the slow, mournful 'I'm Going To Stop Pretending That I Didn't Break Your Heart'. (If that title wasn't enough of a mouthful, it also had a subtitle: 'The Ballad Of Too Little & Too Late'.) "When I got divorced," he says, still somewhat in awe, "that song really got me."

When pondering 'I'm Going To Stop Pretending', it's impossible not to think of E's idol Randy Newman's song 'I Miss You', which similarly was about a singer addressing a fondly recalled lover who had long since left. When the comparison was brought up by *Harp*, E responded cheekily, saying "His song doesn't have anyone playing saw on it", a reference to The Chet's spooky-sad performance on the antiquated instrument. Years later, E offered more insight into the song, saying in the *Meet The Eels* best-of liner notes: "The person who inspired this also inspired another song on this collection. Let's face it: the girl is good for my catalogue." But unlike any of the earlier love songs in his arsenal, 'I'm Going To Stop Pretending' rippled with a sad, honest regret that's unabashedly adult and weary. Minus the fancy turns of phrase or ironic wordplay that marked his earlier confessional lyrics, 'I'm Going To Stop

Pretending' finds E owning up to his shortcomings with a grace that left no room for whining or petulance. And it featured one of his best plot-twist endings: the singer is thinking about these things on Christmas Eve because he's alone. The holiday would be significant for anyone, but it has special agony for E who, as he mentioned in his memoir, tends to miss his family most during the yuletide season. E has written about his personal life in numerous songs, but it's hard to think of many other tunes that are as deeply candid as this one.

Another person affected by a particular *Blinking Lights* track was, oddly enough, the song's co-writer. Around 2002, Jim Jacobsen and E worked on 'Dust Of Ages', the melancholy and pensive tune that became the album's second disc's opener. But it seems that Jacobsen has yet to wrap his head around the song's lyrical power. "The philosophical slant is not something that you hear in a lot of songs in that territory," he says. "The kind of existential edge [it] has... it's like, I have friends who have been listening to [it] for years and who still say, 'I can't get over that song, I still listen to that song'. It's just something so — 'wistful' sounds too light. But it's sort of like a big sigh. I can't even put my finger on it because it's like poetry. You can analyse poetry and talk about the symbolism, but that still doesn't get at the thing that's really going on."

When E was making *Blinking Lights*, he understood fully just how out-of-step a two-disc set was in the age of the iPod. "I know it's a tall order to expect anyone to listen to a double album now," he told *Magnet*. "But when I hear talk about the death of the album as a form and how everybody's just downloading their favourite songs, it kind of sends me in the opposite direction. Like, 'All right, it's time for a double album. Somebody must need it more than ever now'." Even more than its length, though, *Blinking Lights* stood in opposition to its era by being a record that you had to absorb in its entirety to appreciate. E was wary of having *Blinking Lights* labelled a concept album — "When you say 'concept album', you immediately think of a Genesis rock opera or something," he told one writer — but *Blinking Lights* nevertheless honoured their spirit of thematic unity in which individual songs all contributed to the album's emotional whole.

E may have abandoned the idea of a purely orchestral record, but *Blinking Lights* was a far more contemplative and sedate album than anything he'd attempted before. And it was a deeply comforting one as well. Beyond 'Blinking Lights (For Me)' (with its caustic subtitle, 'Or How I Learned To Stop Worrying And Love Airplanes, Car Accidents, And Psychic Pain'), there was the warm hug of piano and strings that buttressed 'If You See Natalie', the sweet indie-pop of 'To Lick Your Boots' (which was dedicated "To My Friend, Whose Name Has Been Unjustly Thrown Around"), and the jubilant mixture of autoharp and saxophone that form the heart of 'Hey Man (Now You're Really Living)'.

Not that everyone thought 'Hey Man' was as sincere as its composer did. When asked by an interviewer if 'Hey Man' was meant to be taken ironically, E responded: "[People think] I'm really saying, 'Ha ha, doesn't life suck?' I'm not at all: I'm just saying there's things in life that people say 'yes' to and there's things in life that people say 'no' to, and I'm just saying you have to say 'yes' to all of it if you want to really live. It's not a joke."

(Even if it wasn't a joke, those who knew him well could still appreciate its dark humour. "I'm always excited when he busts out and does something like ['Hey Man']," Parthenon Huxley says. "That sounds like him, but it's just got this kind of energy to it, and it's funny as shit.")

If the album's first disc contained some jokes and snotty/ironic flourishes — beyond the goofy 'Going Fetal', there was also the *Daisies/Souljacker*-era 'Mother Mary' that's more petulant organ piece than compelling tune — *Blinking Lights'* second disc grew increasingly more poignant and heartfelt. Even 'Whatever Happened To Soy Bomb', which might ostensibly be funny (it's a name-check of performance artist Michael "Soy Bomb" Portnoy, who leaped on stage during Bob Dylan's 1998 Grammy performance), was, in fact, a cogent look at the dangers of celebrating pop-culture minutiae at the expense of what truly matters in life.

That spirit of refocused priorities played out beautifully on the album's final two tracks. If *Blinking Lights* could not escape the *ESB* comparisons, then 'The Stars Shine In The Sky Tonight' was a deeper, sadder companion piece to that record's 'Dead Of Winter'. Both tracks find the singer addressing the departed (or nearly departed) while looking up at the night sky. But while 'Dead Of Winter' struggled with the possibility of living without the loved one — placed on an album where those feelings were still so fresh and raw — 'The Stars Shine' recognised that such wounds never quite heal, that one simply has to learn to live with those emotions.

Discussing the album's examination of the lingering effects of mourning, E turned to a metaphor. "When it's all happening, everyone's there to help you out and bring over a casserole after the funeral," he told *Clash*. "Then afterwards is when the hard part really starts, when you've got to get on with your life. It's the kind of thing that's always gonna be there — in my case to such proportions that it's hard to shake it off."

'The Stars Shine' was a collaboration between E and Jim Lang, and began when Lang sent him the piano part which ended up being the foundation for the tune. "That's pretty much verbatim what I sent him on the piano," Lang says of the track. "It was me kinda tryin' to do E — in a way it was kinda like, 'OK, well, I'm gonna do me, but I'm really gonna try and do something that E could sing over'." With typical modesty, Lang adds, "It came out pretty good."

After 'The Stars Shine', E turned, at long last, to his father for the album's finale. It was inspired by a trip to the bathroom, when he looked in the mirror and all he saw was Hugh staring back. No matter one's relationship with his father, it's a phenomenon that visits all men — that shocking moment of recognition that we have physically turned into our dads, a moment which makes us wonder how much of our emotional and spiritual DNA might resemble his as well.

The resulting song was by no means *Blinking Lights'* most striking or gorgeous — it's really just a strummed acoustic guitar with a little lap steel in the background. But just as *Shootenanny!* had greatly benefited from its simplicity, never allowing the music to clutter the lyrics' directness, 'Things The Grandchildren Should Know' was really about E's vocals, which were spoken more than sung. As with 'I'm Going To

Stop Pretending', he laid himself bare to describe the person he was: he goes to bed early, he doesn't like leaving the house, he doesn't enjoy interacting with people. The honesty was quite charming, but it was the song's fifth verse that put it in the pantheon of Eels' most indelible tunes. It was here that he came to terms with the fact that the man he hardly knew in life was still with him years after his death. Not only did he see the old man in the mirror, he was beginning to understand the guy — and understand that he was turning into him. None of this angered or depressed E, who was making peace with his father at last.

Twenty years earlier, John Mellencamp dedicated his album *Scarecrow* to his grandfather, writing: "There is nothing more sad or glorious than generations changing hands." And while there may be little else that connects the two songwriters — with the possible exception that they've both worked with Lisa Germano — 'Things The Grandchildren Should Know' echoes that sentiment. Furthermore, E admitted in interviews that it was a song he wished his dad had written so that E could have learned more about him.

But if 'Things The Grandchildren Should Know' was about making peace with some turbulent family history, it was also about finding perspective on his other great lyrical occupation: love. He was now several years into his marriage to Natasha, and although her existence came up in interviews to promote the record, it's interesting how few overt songs there were about their relationship on *Blinking Lights*.

"She likes the songs I wrote about her and periodically complains that there aren't enough about her," he told a journalist at the time. "Of course I tell her they all are." But if E can be taken at his word — always a dicey proposition — the pattern of their relationship (first hinted at in 'Lone Wolf') was now firmly entrenched. Asked by *Magnet*'s Tom Lanham if he and Natasha "participate[d] in typical married-couple activities," E responded: "No, not really. I stay in the house, and she goes out and does stuff without me." Elaborating, he said that Natasha "has some fundamental understanding of me that no one else does, as far as how I live my life and my method of working. And that's the nice thing about my situation. It's pretty well understood at this point that I do disappear" down to the basement studio to make albums.

But he doesn't just make albums, of course — then he goes out and tours them. Except now he wasn't sure if he wanted to ever again. The quiet hours spent watching movies during the *Shootenanny!* tour may have helped inspire *Blinking Lights'* structure, but the gruelling schedule took its physical toll, forcing him to have painful surgery to remove a cyst from his sinus. (But as proof that there's no situation that can't provoke a song out of E, the ordeal helped spur the acoustic number 'After The Operation', which ended up as a B-side on the 'Hey Man' single.) He changed his mind about touring while sitting in his backyard smoking a cigar, wondering if he could do a show in which he smoked a cigar. From there came the idea for a string section, players who were dressed up, and, as he wrote later in his memoir, a "gentlemen's EELS concert". The last album and tour had been a self-described midlife crisis for E — why not do a tour now that reflected his more content and reflective headspace? And so Eels With Strings was born.

That more gentlemanly approach turned out to be sorely tested by the logistics of putting together a rather complex road band: three violinists (who occasionally helped out on percussion); one cellist (who also played a vibrator); a guitarist (who also played the saw, lap steel, trash can and suitcase); an upright bassist (who also played autoharp and keyboards); and E. "Pretty much everybody in the band plays more instruments than they thought they could," he said near the end of the tour. "People will say, 'Well, I don't know how to play that' or 'I barely ever played this', and I just keep pushing them beyond their limits."

But it didn't come easy at first. "That was a really, really complicated scenario," The Chet remembers. "[During rehearsals] we had some problems with personnel, and we had some problems getting string arrangements done. It was going really, really poorly. E was losing his mind." With Koool G Murder unable to participate in the tour, they had to find a bassist at the last minute — not to mention someone who could finish the tour's string arrangements. Chet proved to be the hero, suggesting two fellow Portlanders: string arranger Paul Brainard and bassist "Big Al" Hunter. "I made a few calls," The Chet says, "and we pulled in some extra people and managed to miraculously pull the strings tour together in about five days... I called Big Al that night and told him the low-down and said, 'Do you feel like you can learn 30 songs in two days and get your ass to LA and be ready to go out and tour in like five days?'" The Chet laughs. "He said, 'Let me think about that'. He called back an hour later, and he says, 'Let's do it'. Yeah, it was a tiny bit of a rocky start, but it worked out great."

With The Chet the only returning Eels member for the With Strings tour, they also had to recruit the four female string players in a hurry. Ana Lenchantin, a cellist who has played with everyone from Gnarls Barkley to Billy Corgan, still remembers her audition.

"I went to E's house," Lenchantin says. "Very small living room, tiny, in Los Feliz. It's very dark, he's sitting at the piano. He and Koool G Murder were there. They were making it out to be an audition, but I had already had prior knowledge that they had no other strings. They didn't know any other — they were kinda scrambling." She laughs. "That was what I was told, it was never confirmed to me. But it was funny having this knowledge and sitting there and having them behave like it's an audition."

Before the band went out on the road, E noted the irony that he was going to be touring without drums, the instrument that had gotten him into music in the first place. "It's nice to know that a drummer can grow up and go out on a tour when there's not even a drum set on stage," he joked to writer Kyle Buchanan. In fact, it was in some ways a return to when he opened for Tori Amos 13 years earlier, which also didn't feature drums.

"The With Strings tour was extremely technically difficult," The Chet says, "because you're trying to have these very delicate instruments — like a string quartet and all these acoustic guitars and pianos and so forth — and putting them in a live, sort of rock'n'roll, loud setting. Just the technical aspects of pulling that off were really hard. Soundchecks were super-long, and the monitor guy was pulling his hair out the entire tour."

Shon Sullivan recalled asking how the tour went after it was over. "It was really tough," he remembered being told. "Like, four-hour soundchecks and stuff like that. It's, like, how do you mic a cello? It's almost impossible — even if you do have the pickup, they still just don't come through. And then every venue is going to be different, and those are rock clubs — they're not set up for the acoustics of a classical kind of thing where you have more air around the stage, so you're going to get less feedback."

"During the rehearsals when we put it together, clearly we ran out of time and we weren't ready for it," E reminisced four years after the tour. "We did the first show and we came out and I just told the audience, 'Look, I've got to level with you: we're not ready for this'. And at that moment, we all relaxed and it was great... So maybe that's what I should do with every show — just apologise up front."

As the tour rolled along — moving from some warm-up shows and TV appearances in Southern California in May, then heading to Europe before returning to the States in mid-June — E realised that logistics weren't going to be the only obstacle. There was also a question of finances.

"What people might not understand about the Eels," E told a radio journalist in the midst of With Strings, "is that if anyone ever thought that I do any of this stuff just for the pay cheque, they'd be very sadly mistaken, 'cause all I do is lose money to go on tour. I can't even tell you — you'd be *amazed* if I told you how much money this tour loses. Everything that we're doing is *way* more expensive than the business climate can accommodate for us. We're always doing things that are beyond our means, and you just have to find ways to pull it off. But it's really difficult, really a lot of work and a lot of stress... If anyone ever complains about 'Why didn't you come to my town?' [it's] 'cause there's just no money." He laughed. "That's the reason why. We'd go everywhere if we could 'cause we just want to put on a good show. That's really what it's about. And when I say 'we', I mean 'I'." He laughed again. "I want to put on a good show, but there's a lot of people that have to get paid. And there's just not enough money to pay 'em, and that's the problem."

While these concerns were going on for E, one of his string players was floundering through her own tough time. When Lenchantin had signed up for the gig, she generally knew the Eels' catalogue but had mostly concentrated on learning the music in preparation for the tour. Only when the tour began did she fully grasp E's lyrical content. Normally, dark subject matter would hardly be a problem for her, but she was still getting over the suicide of her brother, who had taken his life less than two years earlier. "I think I shouldn't have taken this tour," she says now. "I was not in the right state of mind. My brother had just committed suicide, and here I am onstage every night... sometimes it was just E and me in the dark. I'm dealing with my brother's passing and hearing about his sister's passing — they both killed themselves in the bathroom. Most of the time that I played on this tour I was onstage balling... I wasn't emotionally ready. E's music is *really* intense."

If With Strings' production woes, financial headaches and personal struggles dampened the mood somewhat, the glowing reviews surely helped compensate. *Variety*'s Steven Mirkin enthused, "[E's] reach has yet to exceed his grasp — no matter what style he assays, Everett makes it work. He is the rarest of all things in today's musical landscape — an original willing to pursue his vision wherever it takes him." *The Hollywood Reporter*'s Craig Rosen commented: "Bearded and bespectacled, E walked the line between pretension and ambition... With his gruff vocals and rich orchestrations, he mined lyrical terrain abutting Brian Wilson's bedroom and beaches, Tom Waits' Hollywood lowlife and Randy Newman's wry cinematic visions. While it might seem premature to put E in the company of such LA singer-songwriter elite, his set made it clear that's where he's headed."

Indeed, if anyone could complain about *Blinking Lights'* occasionally hermetically sealed chamber pop after the dynamism of *Souljacker* and the full-band intimacy of *Shootenanny!*, then the With Strings tour helped add a warmth to songs that sometimes succumbed to a gorgeous sterility on record. Perhaps just as memorable were the reworked versions of older tunes like 'Bus Stop Boxer' and, as always, superb live covers, like The Left Banke's 'Pretty Ballerina' and Bob Dylan's 'Girl From The North Country'. And perhaps as a sign of E making peace with the past, he even resurrected a song from his E solo days, pulling out 'The Only Thing I Care About' from the out-of-print *Broken Toy Shop*. (Parthenon Huxley, who wrote the song with E, attended the With Strings show in Washington, DC and got to hear the revamped, pump-organ-heavy new version of the tune. "The first feeling is, 'Oh, good, he's playing our song'," Huxley remembers thinking. "I was very happy that he performed that song again — I thought it was nice to go back and play it and acknowledge that good stuff.")

And then there were the fun encounters that happened while out on the road. The show in San Francisco on June 15 that kicked off the US leg proved particularly memorable when Tom Waits stopped by the band's Great American Music Hall gig.

Lenchantin, a huge Waits nut, first noticed him during soundcheck. "I'm onstage actually texting my sister," she remembers. "I'm like, 'Oh my god, I'm watching Tom Waits watching me onstage right now!'" Later in the evening when the band changed into their pajamas for the after-show encore, she literally bumped into Waits backstage. "I don't get star-struck," she says, "but I just lost it."

In a radio interview five years later, The Chet recalled his own Waits moment, complete with a fantastic impression of the iconic artist. "I had a musical saw that I was playing," The Chet said, "and he said, 'Chet, great job on that saw!' And I said, 'Thanks. Tom, is there any chance I could get you to autograph my musical saw?' And he said, 'Ohhhhh, it's not going to change the tone is it?' That was awesome."

Even the Eels' leader — just as he'd done when he embarrassed himself meeting Neil Young — had been taken aback by the presence of Waits. "The moment I actually met him in the flesh I awkwardly hugged him," E admitted. "And I'm not a hugger. He just kinda went rigid and went, 'RRRRRRRRR!' Like a Frankenstein noise."

All of that tour's warmth and elegance were documented on a DVD called *Eels With Strings: Live At Town Hall* released in February 2006. Shot around the band's performance at New York City's Town Hall on June 30, 2005 — which was near the end of the US tour — the DVD offered fans a chance to relive the show while seeing some behind-the-scenes moments with E on the bus and walking around New York. The film was directed by photographer Niels Alpert, who had previously made concert films for Beck and Rufus Wainwright. E had seen the Beck film and been impressed. E's management called Alpert to gauge his interest, and soon the two were discussing ideas on the phone.

"When you get into doing these things," Alpert said, "so often you don't have a lot of prep time to sit down and discuss how [the film's] gonna be and plan things out and create a vision. You know, it's kind of like, 'OK, well, can you start tomorrow or in two weeks and join the band on tour?' You just kinda get your resources together and you just go. And that's pretty much what happened with the Town Hall documentary. We didn't get a chance to talk to E a lot before we started shooting — I think we had one or two brief phone conversations, and then it was just, boom, dive right in."

Alpert met up with the group on June 28 at their DC show and travelled with them to the following night's performance in Boston. During those days, Alpert shot E as he gave viewers a look around the tour bus and talked about how the shows were going. "They were all really crammed into that bus," Alpert remembers of the 13 band members and crew who took part in the tour. "That was something that really surprised me — how they got everybody onto that thing. Men and women stuffed into that little tour bus — I mean it's a big tour bus, but it gets little very quickly."

The Boston show had been a particularly good one, but E felt confident that the Town Hall performance would be memorable as well, even though they also had to cram in an appearance on *David Letterman* the same day. But E wasn't counting on what would be waiting at Town Hall when he arrived. "My advice to any artist playing the Town Hall for the first time: don't walk around the halls during soundcheck and look at all the people that have been on that stage," E told *Billboard* later. "Because then you get really nervous." Indeed, everyone from jazz legends like Dizzy Gillespie and Louis Armstrong to singer-songwriters like Bob Dylan have played Town Hall. Nonetheless, the band acquitted itself quite nicely, and *Live At Town Hall* captures that evening with a wonderful intimacy — thanks in part to a trick Alpert had developed while making concert films.

"I don't know if everybody does this," he said, "but we did it once before and it worked, which is that we shoot the soundcheck as a full performance rehearsal. We get the band to play in full costumes, what they're gonna be wearing with all the lighting. And we get them to play as many of the songs that they're gonna play at the show that night in soundcheck from beginning to end. We get the cameras on the stage and we can then cut some of that footage into that night's [performance]. So you know, we're kinda cheating a little bit, but we can get shots on the stage and up close with the musicians in a way that we are not able to when the actual show is going on."

Because they were shooting on a tight budget, Alpert didn't have the extra personnel or equipment to coordinate between the six cameramen during that night's shoot. "You're sort of hoping and praying," he says, "'cause you don't have a lot of time and not a lot of money. And so it's like, well, we'll just see how this whole thing kinda turns out."

If the concert shoot was nerve-racking, the following day's filming was much easier. E was doing radio press, and Alpert tagged along with a camera. "I had a bunch of ideas for New York," he said. Alpert had recently moved back to New York after living in Los Angeles for 13 years and wanted to capitalise on E's fish-out-of-water status in the Big Apple. "You know, E's from LA, and they're playing Town Hall, they're playing New York City. It just is a great, amazing thing for any band to do. And so I was like, I wanna shoot him on the Brooklyn Bridge, in Times Square, down in the subway. I just wanted to surround him with New York — you think of pictures of John Lennon in his New York City tank-top, or iconic artists' pictures on the streets of New York. What I had in mind was making sure that we weren't just shooting in the dressing room while we were in New York City."

And while E was at first hesitant about being filmed riding the subway, feeling uncomfortable at being surrounded by so many people, his naturally funny demeanour quickly shone through, creating a deeply amusing visual portrait of the rail-thin, bearded musician clutching his guitar case with so many onlookers milling around. "He has an incredible sense of what's funny," Alpert says. "You know, he's very savvy about his image and how to present his image."

Of course, those images are all the more iconic because they're in black and white, which is juxtaposed by the colour photography for the concert. According to Alpert, that wasn't an intentional choice but was stumbled upon during post-production. "We were looking at the

[E in New York] footage," he recalls, "and I turned the colour off. And suddenly it just looked really beautiful. It looked like great Robert Frank or Garry Winogrand photographs. I'm a big fan of the great classic black-and-white photographers: Robert Frank, Garry Winogrand, Elliott Erwitt — these people who defined the look of black-and-white street photography in the 20th century. When we turned [the footage] black and white in post, it was just like, 'Wow, OK, this is magic, so let's keep it like this'."

When the time came to cut the film, E was very specific about wanting to strip it down to its essence, removing anything that didn't feel honest. And for a tour supporting an album that was inspired by filmmakers, it wasn't surprising that E paid special attention to the movie that documented its performance. For Alpert, it was a gruelling ordeal that turned out to be richly rewarding.

"E is kind of like legendary for being incredibly difficult and so demanding and exacting," Alpert says. "He tends to exhaust people. And I was a little bit nervous about working — well, I wouldn't say 'nervous', but I was like, 'OK, I'm working with E, and he's tough and demanding'. And he was. But part of the reason why the film is as good as it is, is because he demands the best and he won't settle for anything less. We edited and re-edited and looked at stuff over and over again. And he listened to the sound mixes over and over again. And we worked and reworked and re-reworked stuff. My producer and my editor, they were all at their wits' end. We were over budget — I hardly made a dime on the film considering the amount of hours that I put into it. But he pushed it, and I was so glad that he did. I would bring the editing system over to his house, and we would sit there, and we worked and worked and worked, and he pushed. And I loved that, and I'm grateful for the fact that he wanted the best — I was not going to call the job done until he was satisfied that we had done the absolute best that we could do. I think the film turned out well, and so much of it is because of his dedication to excellence. I absolutely was inspired and loved the process of working with him."

At first glance, such a testimonial might provoke the more cynical to dismiss Alpert's words as the excited ramblings of a victim of Stockholm syndrome. But for Alpert, the commitment came from a desire to live up to E's expectations. "E believed in me to bring me on the job and let me do things like bring him into the subway and run the show my way and shoot the soundcheck," Alpert says. "So, in post-production, I said, 'OK, we have the raw materials here — let's make this work. I'm not gonna let laziness or exasperation or time or money get in the way of making something great because that's what E wants to do. And I wanna do that with him'."

Alpert admits that he knows he's but a small part of the Eels' story. And yet he seemed to understand what so many before and after him recognised in E, that he was a perfectionist who expected the best out of himself and those around him and thus inspired such dedication in others. In fact, he sounded like E himself, who was asked by a journalist about the financial prospects of *Blinking Lights* and the With Strings tour. E's response was realistic but also emblematic of a true artist. "I won't make money from this album," E responded. "I will only lose money from the tour. But that's OK. I'm used to it. It's all right — it's worth it."

Chapter Thirteen

For Eels fans, there are two places in E's house that are of particular interest. The first, of course, is his basement, where he makes his albums. The other is his backyard. For those in his inner circle, it's where he plays croquet on the weekends with friends or on breaks while recording. "He had this terraced backyard," Wally Gagel recalls fondly, "so it was kind of ridiculous. We had these rules, like if it went down this thing, it counted, because how the hell are you going to get the ball back up? It was funny." (And the croquet isn't just for fun — the best players get trophies at the end of the season.)

The backyard has also been the scene for some of E's greatest inspirations, such as the night he was smoking a cigar on the patio and dreamed up the idea for the Eels With Strings tour. But the place also contains what E has referred to as a "little cabin". It was this tiny standalone residence where John Parish stayed while working on *Souljacker*. And it was also the hideaway where E spent a good chunk of 2006 and 2007, doing something he'd never attempted before: write a book.

2006 had been, in some ways, a continuation of the previous year's promotion of *Blinking Lights And Other Revelations*. February saw the release of the CD and DVD *Live At Town Hall*, but in May Eels returned to the road with a tour billed as No Strings Attached. Leaving the string section behind, E went out as a rock trio with The Chet on guitar and new drummer Derek "Knuckles" Brown. As with his recruitment of Big Al, The Chet was instrumental in finding Knuckles, another fellow Portlander. "We needed a drummer for the tour," The Chet remembers, "and E was doing some travelling and had stopped through Portland. We got together in the basement of my house — me, E and Knuckles — and just played some tunes and had some fun. And E liked him, so he came on board for that tour, and then he ended up moving [to LA] and he's still on board." The trio were complemented by Big Al, who didn't play an instrument during most of the concert but instead performed the role of a menacing security guard who also happened to dance during the songs. Well, maybe dance wasn't exactly accurate: he mostly punched and kicked the air around him and strutted around like a boxer in the ring before a fight.

The band wore flight suits and sunglasses, donned thick beards, and generally enjoyed turning the Eels catalogue into a distortion-drenched assault. "It was a heavy rock thing," The Chet remembers. "Super-loud intense." During the No Strings Attached dates, E explained to former Sex Pistol guitarist Steve Jones, host of LA's *Jonesy's Jukebox* radio show, what prompted the guitar-barrage tour. "By the end of [With Strings]," E said, "I started having these dreams on the bus at night where I was *smashing* a violin with an electric guitar. It just became clear to me that it was time to rock." It also allowed him an opportunity to play that August's Lollapalooza, the first time he'd played the festival in nine years, and a chance to appear in front of a huge audience similar to those he enjoys when he's in Europe.

"I hadn't seen or talked to E in like maybe a year and a half," Greg Collins recalls, "and I saw that [tour] and I was just dying in hysterics, laughing so hard. It was such a cool thing. Only he could come up with that. At his heart, he thinks more like a comedian." Collins is far from the first person to talk about E's comedic gifts, but for the producer the analogy extends further. "Some comedians every year throw away their act and they start a new one. E almost thinks that way — every year he would throw away the conception of what the band was live and bring out something completely different. Who does that?"

So, naturally, once E got this desire to rock out of his system, he immediately started getting hungry to go in a completely different direction. "[I] really had the desire to do something that just relied on myself for a while," he later told *The Sunday Times*. So he went to the cabin in his backyard and, without a publishing deal, started writing his memoir in longhand. "One of my best friends has been pestering me to write a book for years," he said, "so I thought this would be a good time. Writing sounds so easy, but it turned out to be the hardest thing I've ever done. I've learnt now why all the great writers are alcoholics."

When the memoir, *Things The Grandchildren Should Know*, was published in January 2008 in the UK, readers learnt that the friend who encouraged E to write the book was Anthony Cain, whom E had met in the second grade and was nicknamed "Ant". But that was just one of the more minor revelations contained in the autobiography.

In spare, conversational language, E traced his life up through the With Strings tour, spending the first 30 percent of the book on his Virginia upbringing. The style of his memoir was patterned after *Brother Ray*, the autobiography of Ray Charles. "I was really struck by how it just felt like he was sitting there talking to you," he told writer Michael Tedder. "That was the thing that I wanted to do." E also hoped that it might help young people who were as directionless as he was during his adolescence. "There have definitely been times when I was angry when I was younger," he said in an interview with *TheBookseller.com*. "I'm really fortunate because I've had a load of amazing experiences to go with all the horrible experiences, and the amazing experiences have been really amazing — I mean, I'm a rock star! That's one of the reasons why I wanted the book to come out. It could be inspiring in the way that it's about this clueless kid from Virginia that has all sorts of weird and wacky and horrible adventures, and somehow ends up making something out of his life."

And while some of the details contained in the memoir were familiar to Eels fans, readers were also treated to some fresh, candid glimpses into his childhood: his earliest memory (falling down the stairs in his house while his dad reads the newspaper); or the girl who inspired 'Jeannie's Diary' (she worked at the post office, went on a date with him the day of the Space Shuttle *Challenger* explosion, and told him she was engaged). Written from the perspective of a man coming to terms with his difficult past, the memoir methodically traces his relationship with his three family members and his developing interest in music. With a minimum of self-pity, E simply related his Virginia years as best as he could in the most direct way possible.

Just as rewarding for Eels fans was trying to spot potential inspirations for future E songs within the prose. For instance, in a passage about his McLean neighbourhood, he mentioned a church graveyard "full of old gravestones with names like 'George Washington' and 'Abraham Lincoln' chiselled on them", a conscious (or not) nod to the setting of *Blinking Lights*' 'In The Yard, Behind The Church'. Later, an acknowledgment of his boyhood fascination with his mother's breasts led to a comment that because she "could unwittingly be cruel and overly critical", he never felt that he had a proper mom. "I needed a mother," he wrote, "and, as a result, still do", an issue he would later confront head-on in *End Times*' stark piano ballad, 'I Need A Mother'.

In equally unvarnished language, E charted his career history, from the early days of struggle before meeting Carter to the E solo albums and then Eels. "I wasn't interested in writing a typical rock star biography," he explained to *Flyp* magazine, "because I don't think anyone is knocking down the door for the Eels-backstage-tell-all memoir."

But while *Things The Grandchildren Should Know* seemed to be a wholly forthright memoir, there were aspects of E's artistic journey he failed to mention. For instance, his Virginia effort, *Bad Dude In Love*, received nary a mention, just as the MC Honky album passed by without comment. (As for Butch's departure from Eels, he writes, "We agree to keep working together but on a more casual, less permanent basis.") Also noteworthy was the change of his wife's name to Anna in the book — by the time he finished writing his memoir, they had already divorced, and perhaps not surprisingly the chapter devoted to her is one of the book's most emotionally guarded.

But if there were certain elements obfuscated by the author, E also took pains to be diplomatic about those who had wronged him, save for a particularly cruel first-grade teacher he dubbed "Mrs Bitch" and R&B pop star John Legend, who pissed him off at a British TV show when one of Legend's underlings demanded he put out his cigar, even though the smoke was going nowhere near Legend. (Speaking of Legend, Ana Lenchantin remembers that after the TV show incident the Eels tour discovered that they were playing certain US dates right before Legend was. E took the opportunity to leave "John Legend sucks" graffiti in the dressing rooms so that Legend would see it when he arrived.)

Looking back at his initial reluctance to write a memoir, he summed up his hesitation to reporter Fiona Sturges: "Why would anyone want to read such a catalogue of misery?" Once he gave it a shot, though, "I began to see there was a story there, and it wasn't that depressing. I think people are surprised to find out how optimistic I am and how I enjoy life. I'm one of the lucky people who is making a living doing something I would be doing anyway. At the very least, I hope the book might inspire some kid who thinks his life is screwed and can't see a way out."

Speaking with *USA Today*, Thomas Dunne Books senior editor Rob Kirkpatrick described the book as being "closer to *The Ice Storm* than a rock autobiography. I often call it *Singing With Scissors*. It's a very literate memoir that happens to be written by an indie-rock star. He's heartbreaking and hilarious on the same page, and it's written with great emotion and intimacy. For someone to achieve that on a first book is miraculous."

But perhaps some of the book's most intriguing reviews came from those who know him or who have worked with him.

"I'm surprised he left some musical stuff out," Carter says when asked about his reaction to reading the book. "I'm surprised, as revealing as it was, that he didn't talk a little more about the girls in his life. The fans would love to know about the real Susan [of 'Susan's House']. Certainly from my point of view, songwriting has to do with experience, and far, far too many [of E's] songs are about love, or loss of love, or lack of love."

Parthenon Huxley was struck by the aspects of E's family life that he learned from reading in the book — and by the connection between the death of E's mother and the death of his own wife around the same time. But beyond that, Huxley notes how the memoir showed fans a window into E's personal feelings without necessarily offering the full picture. "I think it's really cool the way he wrote it," Huxley says. "You can read that book in about an hour — it's a really quick read, but it's funny that he's not giving up a whole hell of a lot about what he *thought* he was thinking [at the time]. It's, like, 'This happened, this happened, this happened'. In terms of revelations about E, I don't think there was a lot of that in there. I think it was kind of like, 'Here's what happened and you can guess how I feel about it'."

"My initial reaction to the book was, like, I could write a book too," Tommy Walter says, "and all that stuff is not in [E's book]. I think he was just picking the things that he wanted to put out there in the book — anybody would do that. Obviously Butch is in a lot more [of the book], but my initial thought was how much [Butch and I] were downplayed and how little was shown [of] the impact we had or the contribution that we made or the fact that we did work hard."

"I, of course, have picked up little stories about him along the way," The Chet says, "but the memoir was awesome because it filled in the whole — not the entire 100-percent story, but the bulk of the story. I learned a lot about him, and it ended up opening up a lot of conversations that were interesting about the past and how it went down. It gave me more understanding of him for sure."

Folks from E's McLean days hadn't read the book but were in general surprised to hear the musician badmouth his Virginia youth. Mike Kelley, The Toasters' keyboardist, in particular expressed frustration at the drubbing McLean received from the songwriter. "From what I've heard and what I've read [E say about McLean], it doesn't jibe with what I remember," says Kelley, "and I've got a pretty good memory. I don't know, man. I don't know what's going on. I'd have to talk to him and hear him. He had fun while he was here."

Professional reviewers were generally impressed with E's candour and brisk writing style. In a profile piece in the *Los Angeles Times*, Geoff Boucher said, "The memoir... is nothing like the lurid rock-star confessionals that crowd the bookstore shelves. Instead it is, like the music of Eels, intellectual, wry and unflinching as it conveys complex emotions with simple, graceful language." *The Independent*'s Ben Thompson wrote, "The title... suggests one of those supposedly inspirational but horribly cloying collations of the kind of conventional wisdom which the author vainly hopes readers will wish to pass on from one generation to the next. Yet *Things The Grandchildren Should Know* is the opposite: it's a mordant and ornery little book, outlining one man's personal road-map through the desolate landscape of familial absence." But while Thompson praised the memoir as "entertaining," he took E to task for his "lack of perspective on which elements of his life story are remarkable and which are mundane," commenting that "the quiet dignity with which he responds to the myriad tragedies of early middle age... is somewhat undermined by the relentlessness with which he moans about everything else."

Thompson could be accused of being as grouchy in his review as he charged E with being in his memoir, but his criticisms touched on what has been the danger of E's career since he began writing songs about his personal pain: the possibility that it would simply feel like self-pitying whining. What has saved E has been his leavening humour that, unlike the angst-mongers he disapproves of in bands like Korn, has kept his material largely free of forced melodrama. But Thompson raised a point that was echoed by writer David Hajdu who, in an essay called "The Blogging Of American Pop," mocked a wave of new American singer-songwriters (including E, Sparklehorse's Mark Linkous and Aimee Mann) "whose aesthetic is based upon having no particular place to go and nothing in particular to say." Whereas Dylan had given pop music a literary ambition, his heirs, Hajdu complained, "are writing not just about anything, but about everything. As such, they tend to communicate nothing except self-absorption."

For E's part, he's often referred to the musical mapping of his family trauma as "an ongoing art project," and he spoke about its benefits after the book's release. "This has been an amazing time in my life, really," he told the *Los Angeles Times*. "It's weird enough to write a book about your life, but it's even weirder to then be talking about it... But it does have a value as an artist. You dig into all of this and when you're done, you've cleared the decks. I know I'm a lot more carefree than I ever thought I would be. I have answers to things now."

More answers came as he was finishing the book and was approached by the BBC to be in a documentary about his father, which was set to coincide with the 50th anniversary of his Many Worlds theory and the 25th anniversary of his death. "When they first came to me," he said in 2008, "the idea gave me a pain in the pit of my stomach." Yet he decided to go through with it in late June and early July of 2007, taking two weeks to travel from Los Angeles to McLean, Princeton and the Pentagon to meet with Hugh's colleagues and old friends.

Director Louise Lockwood recalls that even as they were about to begin filming, E was still a bit reticent. "It's like before you go on holiday," she says. "You don't really believe you're going on holiday till you actually get to the airport. I think it's that kind of thing — it was like, 'All right, this is actually happening now'. He kinda knew that it was coming at some point, this trip. And it was now."

Followed by a three-person crew, including Lockwood, E heard stories of his father's struggles to bring recognition to his Many Worlds theory, and he spoke with physicists who tried to make the theory understandable to a guy who hadn't taken a math class since ninth grade.

One might think that E would have been comfortable by that point with digging through family history. After all, he had already been deeply enmeshed in writing his memoirs. (In addition, he'd also tapped filmmaker Jesse Dylan — Bob Dylan's son — to begin filming a documentary about his life, a project that seems to have been put on the shelf for the time being.) But Lockwood understood that those endeavours wouldn't be comparable to what he was about to undertake. "There's something about going on a journey and going and physically meeting people," she says. "It was almost like going on a Hugh pilgrimage. It makes things much more emotive and much more immediate. You can sit at home [and think about your family], but if you're standing there in a bedroom in Princeton, it's much more evocative. I think [the film] took him somewhere that he wouldn't necessarily have predicted that he would have gone."

Lockwood recalls their first night in Virginia being a difficult one as memories started flooding back for E. "We were staying at this place called The Wolf Trap Motel," she says. "And we didn't know this, but when he was a teenager, this was where all the teenagers would go to get drunk and shag. It was a dive — bloody awful it was. And I didn't realise how hot Virginia is in June — it was like walking in soup." Wanting a drink to take the edge off, he and the rest of the crew went around town in a futile search for a bottle of whiskey. "We ended up at this diner or whatever, and we just sat and got very drunk. It was a very good bonding moment. He was feeling particularly vulnerable that night — he'd just come back [to Virginia], it was hot, it was all a bit random. He'd walked past the funeral parlour that he had to deal with [for his] mother. So that was kind of the last time he'd been back there. I think he was finding that quite emotional, so, yes, we hit the bar."

The resulting one-hour film, *Parallel Worlds, Parallel Lives*, aired on BBC4 on November 26, 2007. It is quite an odd documentary, particularly for those well-versed in E's adorable curmudgeon persona. Narrated by Annie Mac's cool British voice, the film uses E as the story's central figure on a journey to get to the bottom of his father's theory and legacy. For someone who insists on a high degree of creative control, E legitimately feels like a traveller navigating through uncertain emotional waters in the documentary, with the result that fans were allowed to see a more vulnerable version of the musician, despite his clutching of cigars and dispensing of some wonderfully wry lines. In addition, the juxtaposition of caustic, jean-jacket-clad E and the ivory-towered professors is a delight throughout the movie. Filled stem to stern with Eels songs, *Parallel Worlds* is also notable for its inclusion of B-sides and even a track from *A Man Called E*, the sort of songs you tend not to hear in an Eels project.

As for its investigative qualities, *Parallel Worlds* is inevitably a mild exploration of the Many Worlds theory, its implications and its scientific and cultural repercussions. The viewer learns the basics of the theory and the conflicts it provoked in the scientific community, particularly simplifying Hugh's post-theory life as one in which he was hopelessly bitter and withdrawn almost until his death. (It would take a few more years for Hugh biographer Peter Byrne's book, *The Many Worlds Of Hugh Everett III*, to uncover the real reasons for his leaving academia: although Hugh was certainly displeased that his theory was not more widely embraced, he was also disinterested in the institution and realised he could make a fortune by working for the government.) And due to the short running time, the film can't help but seem a little rushed as it strains to poignantly illustrate E's reconnection with his father's memory.

But that doesn't mean *Parallel Worlds* lacks its genuinely affecting moments. Returning to Virginia is never easy for E — he often talks about the smell of death he encounters when he's there — but the trip had an added degree of difficulty when he unearthed a series of recordings his father made when E was just a boy. They were found in E's basement among all the other items he had saved from his parents' home, and at first it seemed they might be inoperative. But in a hotel room, the camera crew filmed E after the tapes had been successfully transferred. It was to be the first time he would hear them, and for once you see him legitimately nervous, laughing awkwardly as he tries to make himself hit the "play" button. Once he does, his head jerks with shock at the first sound of his father's voice. It's one of the few moments where anyone has seen E look less than totally composed in his pubic life.

"I did feel kinda ambushed," he later told *The Boston Globe* of the *Parallel Worlds* experience. "The whole time I was shooting that was just like having a camera crew follow you around trying to make you cry: 'How does that make you feel, E?'"

"I know he found it uncomfortable," Lockwood says of the scene in the hotel room, "and I know the bit, especially where he hears himself, he totally blushed — you don't think of E blushing. It was really very endearing. It was very sweet. All I can say is that I'm very thankful that he trusted us to be in a room with him filming while he did that. I don't know for him how that makes him feel now [but] it certainly helped to make a better documentary."

In addition, the film follows E as he visits his family members' graves, an intimate scene that Lockwood says he had no problem doing for the cameras. He did have one request, though. "He didn't want to go back to his house, to his home, in Virginia," Lockwood says. "He didn't want to do that, which was fair enough — we didn't need it. He was happy to go to the cemetery, so I was perfectly happy to respect somebody's request on that."

As they were finishing the shoot, Lockwood, E and the rest of the crew had become pretty close, and E seemed very happy that he'd agreed to go on the trip. "I remember him saying, 'You know, Lou, I think we shot some really great stuff'," Lockwood recalls. But always one to deliver the perfect comic zinger, E then added, "Better not fuck it up!"

The film won several awards, including the Grierson Award (no relation) for Best Science Documentary. But for E, the rewards seemed to be based on things other than prizes. In an interview with *The New York Times* which coincided with the documentary's premiere in the States on PBS in October 2008 — which happened the same month as the US publication of *Things The Grandchildren Should Know* — he described watching the film as "transformative". Admitting that the movie "really changed me", he added that it was "kind of embarrassing to say, but I liked both the guys that were in the film, my father and myself, a lot more" after it was over.

In conjunction with this strategy of "clearing the decks", E also invited investigative journalist Peter Byrne into his basement to go through the boxes from his McLean home. Left virtually untouched since he and Spider had packed up his family's house after Nancy's death, the boxes' contents served as the invaluable source material for *The Many Worlds Of Hugh Everett III*, Byrne's exhaustive biography of Hugh that was published in the summer of 2010. "Peter managed to dig through the smell and bring the people buried in the boxes back to life," E wrote in the book's foreword, judging it to be a work that was "[a]lternately enlightening and troubling, like any good book should be". If *Parallel Worlds* helped start E's process of bringing attention to his father and forgive him, then *The Many Worlds Of Hugh Everett III* hopefully worked as a form of closure for him.

Simultaneous to his work on the memoir and film, E was also putting together two compilations of Eels material: one, a greatest-hits package called *Meet The Eels: Essential Eels Vol 1*; and the other, a two-disc collection of rarities entitled *Useless Trinkets: B-Sides, Soundtracks, Rarities And Unreleased*. "Universal has wanted to do a best-of for a while," he told *The Sunday Times*, "but I wanted to wait until I had time to do it properly." Consequently, 2008 turned out to be a year in which Eels fans took a trip through the past with E. And in turn, it allowed listeners (and critics) an opportunity to reassess the band's legacy.

Meet The Eels presented the challenge of what constitutes a "hit" for a group who's really only had one in its native land. Focusing on singles — though excluding 'Cancer For The Cure' — the compilation also made room for the band's dive-bomb cover of Missy Elliott's 'Get Ur Freak On' and the *Shrek 2* track 'I Need Some Sleep'. And while *Meet The Eels* was a strong overview, *Pitchfork* writer Jason Crock got to the heart of its nagging limitation. "You can glean the Eels' M.O. from these songs," he wrote, "but picking democratically from a career with some serious peaks and valleys makes for a set that sounds like a frustrated and failed novelty act. Until you listen to one of their records in full, you'd never understand how they've built the cult status that justifies these kinds of releases."

Truly, *Meet The Eels* was an introduction for people who would wholly miss the point of E's record-making strategy by purchasing this best-of. A man who stubbornly insists that the album remains an art form in the download age, E was powerless to make a greatest-hits collection that didn't feel somewhat artistically inconclusive, as well as inevitably lacking the thematic through-line that powers his individual studio efforts. Unfortunately, *Meet The Eels* also allowed the less generous, like Will Hermes in *Spin*, to needlessly simplify E's career as "a more romantic, less high-concept version of fellow LA *guero* Beck."

As for *Useless Trinkets*, although it wasn't the first time Eels had put out such a platter — a one-disc rarities collection came out on iTunes in 2005 — it was a massive gift to fans who hadn't scoured the record bins for every single Eels B-side in existence. Culled over a span of two years, *Useless Trinkets* is by no means exhaustive — "There was a lot of stuff to sift through," E told writer Andrew Mueller after its release — but its 50 tracks contain more than enough sterling moments to justify its heft. One could quibble about the amount of remixes and live versions of famous songs, like 'My Beloved Monster' and 'Novocaine For The Soul', but to hear *Electro-Shock Blues* outtake 'Funeral Parlor', the wistful pop of 'Dog's Life', a magnificent cover of 'Dark End Of The Street' and the stark anguish of 'Animal' was to understand just how deep the Eels catalogue stretched. And that was just the first disc — the second included, among other gems, a Peter Buck collaboration ('The Bright Side'), the joyously rollicking 'Eyes Down' and the soulful 'Estranged Friends' that was part of the *Shootenanny!* sessions. ("'Estranged Friends' is the song that I begged him to keep on *Shootenanny!*," the album's mixer Greg Collins says. "While we were recording it even he was like, 'Oh, this is great, I love it.' It's him trying to make an R&B song, and I think he finally felt it was a little too on-the-nose in that respect. He tried a bunch of sequences with 'Estranged Friends' in it, and he was just like, 'Yeah, it doesn't work.'")

"I really don't like to look back," he told Mueller about *Useless Trinkets*, "and it has been weird because all I've been doing is looking back." Still, the process had its advantages: "If you're not cringing at some things you've done you haven't grown." But what was so remarkable about *Useless Trinkets* was just how little was cringe-worthy. Around the time of the double-disc *Blinking Lights*, E insisted to interviewers that he wasn't someone who thought that every song he wrote was brilliant and deserving to be thrust upon the public. But *Useless Trinkets* argued that perhaps E was being a little too stringent in his quality control.

To promote the retrospective collections and memoir, E went on a tour that kicked off in Europe in February 2008. As was E's practice, though, the band first did a warm-up show at The Galaxy Theatre in Santa Ana. Fans in attendance at that Valentine's Day concert saw a stripped-down affair that featured just E and The Chet, who in addition to his usual array of instruments also read passages from *Things The Grandchildren Should Know* during the concert. "During rehearsals, E was talking about wanting to read from it, and I was like, 'Oh yeah, I'll sit onstage and read from your book'," The Chet recalls. "I was doing characters onstage from the book and, you know, it was kinda trippy standing in front of sometimes 5,000 people with a single spotlight with a pair of silly glasses on reading from a book. But, it went really well, and we both dug it a lot."

And in a further sign that E was making amends with the past, he brought on a special guest during the encore at that Galaxy show.

Sitting at the piano playing the opening chords of 'Beautiful Freak', he reminisced about the band members that he used to have with him for that album. "There was a big fat guy on the drums," he mused aloud, "and a bass-player guy — what was his name?" The crowd shouted "Tommy", which prompted E to say nonchalantly, "Tommy, right." Still doodling on the piano, he said, "I should call Tommy one of these days, say hi," though he wondered if Tommy would "want to punch me in the face". He then started singing the song's lyrics, but as he segued into the chorus, another figure appeared onstage, armed with a French horn. It was Tommy. The audience, recognising him instantly, went nuts at this unlikely duet, knowing the significance of this onstage reunion. When 'Beautiful Freak' concluded, they shook hands and hugged.

Most fans knew that the two hadn't been on speaking terms since Walter had been booted out of the band after the *Beautiful Freak* tour. But unless anyone in attendance at the Galaxy show had shelled out extra dollars to purchase the UK edition of *Things The Grandchildren Should Know* — the book wouldn't arrive in the States for several more months — they wouldn't yet have read the far-from-rosy things E had written about his former bandmate. Though calling Walter a "nice guy", E described him as someone who clashed with the rest of the Eels crew. "He was young," E concluded, "and maybe he was just having a hard time dealing with all the excitement." But at about the same time he was finishing the book and preparing to film the BBC documentary, he also extended an olive branch to Walter.

"He called me or sent me an email and said, 'Hi, do you want to get lunch?'" Walter remembers. "Just out of the blue completely. Then we sat down and he goes, 'So, what have you been doing for the last 10 years?'" Walter laughs at the bizarreness of the scene. He had not communicated with E for a decade, but yet here they were having a meal together. Walter was initially on guard, but soon the bad feelings disappeared. "You know, I have always loved him," he says. "He is such a complex person, but he is just a lovable person, too. We were always good friends, and I truly cared about him. So when he reached out to me again it was, like, 'Yeah, let's hang out'. And then it kind of went from there."

But while E and Walter had let bygones be bygones, E's reunion with his other *Beautiful Freak* bandmate proved less healing. In September of that year, Lucinda Williams played five nights at the El Rey, performing a different album in its entirety at each show. Her September 9 date was in honour of 1992's *Sweet Old World*, and she invited several artists to sit in with her band, such as Chuck Prophet and The Doors' Robby Krieger. One of the invited guests was E, which afforded ticket-buyers a chance to see the musician onstage with Butch for the first time since 2002. (As an added bonus, The Chet was part of Lucinda's touring band as well.)

LA Weekly's review of the concert commented on the evening's vibe as "more like a rehearsal or a house party", with E delivering a solo 'Railroad Man'. But unlike the genial catch-up meal with Walter, the Lucinda Williams concert apparently didn't lead to a thawing of E's relationship with Butch. According to associates, the two men don't hang out or speak. In *Rhythm*'s August 2003 issue — shortly after he'd left Eels — Butch was asked if he thought their hiatus was permanent or temporary. "I think for quite a while," he said. "E and I are taking a break for quite a bit here because we've come to a crossroads, as it were." Six years later, he was asked by a different journalist if he would ever consider playing with E again. "I would," he replied. "I don't know. I don't think E would want to, but who knows what the future will hold. Three years ago I would have said, 'No,' but who knows?"

Greg Collins, who recorded and mixed much of *Shootenanny!*, Butch's last Eels album, has since used Butch on other albums he's produced, precisely because of his experience working with the drummer on that Eels disc. "I learned what he does well, which is pretty much everything," Collins says. "I mean, the man can play in pretty much any style, and he's got a great sense of sound. Butch is like super-music-chops guy. He's got like the Steely Dan chops." And while Collins is close friends with E and hesitant to discuss the specifics of the Butch/E break-up, he will say that, "I think their relationship creatively was really a cool thing. E encouraged this character out of Butch that Butch embraced. To this day it's like you see the guy with the cowboy hat — that's Butch. I think a lot of music fans are familiar with that connection [between

E and Butch]. They see Butch up there [onstage] and they think about the fact that he's a big part of the Eels. They had a really awesome run."

After E's impromptu rendezvous with Walter and Butch, he soon headed off on his own tour that stretched from Europe to Australia to the US within the span of a couple of months, with just E and The Chet manning the stage. "The duo tour that we did was even more intense than [With Strings]," The Chet says. "There were two of us onstage and something like eight instruments, and we were jumping around to all of them. That was the one where we did the whole exchange-drummers-in-the-middle-of-a-song thing", which was done during 'Flyswatter', turning the song into a high-wire act that involved the two musicians seamlessly bouncing back and forth between drums and piano. "You know," The Chet says, "I think I enjoyed that tour more than any just because it was so crazy."

Certainly, it was not your typical rock concert. Instead of an opening act, they showed *Parallel Worlds*. The Chet would perform excerpts from E's memoir. E would read fan mail and reviews. A God-like voice would announce, "Mark Oscar Everett, this is your life", intentionally getting his name wrong. Plus, the tour spotlighted just how integral The Chet had become to the Eels universe, serving as a wry foil and straight man to E's shenanigans. Five years after first touring with the band, he was now one of E's main men, the closest thing to a Butch replacement that the live group ever had.

That relationship was also apparent from the memoir's audiobook. E had declined to read the book during public appearances and signings. ("The book is incredibly embarrassing for me," he told *USA Today*. "The idea of hearing anyone say it out loud is horrifying.") And after the skill and enthusiasm The Chet had displayed performing *Things The Grandchildren Should Know* during the duo's concerts, it simply made sense to have him do the audiobook.

"They had originally been chasing after someone with a bigger name to do it," says The Chet. "But that didn't pan out, for whatever reason, and they called me and asked if I was interested in doing it." The job required him to drive about five hours' south from Portland to Ashland and spend a week recording the book. He wasn't given any direction:

"They stick you in the IsoBooth in a studio in front of a mic with a book and a glass of water. And you just read and read for, like, five hours, which gets a little tough around hour three-and-a-half. Hearing only your voice chattering on — it starts to be pretty weird."

Equally challenging was the realisation that reading E's lyrics, which crop up frequently in the memoir, in a normal voice "sounded really stupid". The Chet called E, who came up with an easy solution. "He says, 'Well, you're just going to have to sing them'," The Chet recalls. "I'm like, 'Great, now I'm singing in the audiobook'." Each night, The Chet would return to his hotel, using a borrowed guitar to practise the lyrics he'd have to sing the following day. "It was terrifying," he admits. "We finished the whole thing and I'm just terrified that E's going to get the final copy and *hate* it. But he didn't — he liked it a lot."

The book (and audiobook) hit American shelves in October 2008, which was perfectly timed to coincide with the documentary's airing on PBS stations. American reporters travelled to E's Los Feliz house to discuss the projects, writing articles about the singer-songwriter's new-found contentment. He had helped give his father a day in the sun with *Parallel Worlds*. And he had found a way to lift the past's burden off his shoulders by writing the book.

His home seemed an appropriate location to conduct the interviews since the house had helped give birth to these very personal projects — the guesthouse was where he wrote the book, and the basement had contained his father's boxed-up affairs. But reporters also discovered why he had to be so careful about his privacy.

"Those are for the stalkers," E told Geoff Boucher of the *Los Angeles Times*, indicating what Boucher described as "a bank of security-camera screens in the kitchen". "It's nice when something you have written or recorded means so much to people," E said, "especially since you never thought about that happening when you're working on it. But I prefer letters to unannounced visitors." Boucher mentioned that the back cabin also contained "another set of security cameras".

He was asked if this concentrated look back into his family life had influenced his thoughts on starting a family of his own. Having kids "is on my list" he told *USA Today*'s Edna Gundersen, "but I'm definitely terrified because of my family and the sense of doom that surrounds it." Gundersen was able to pry out of E that he did have a girlfriend, but E let fly with one of his wry, self-deprecating comments: "She could break up with me at any time."

Other creative endeavours presented themselves in the autumn and winter of that year. Eight years after he escorted his new love Natasha to the premiere of *How The Grinch Stole Christmas*, E contributed several songs to another Jim Carrey film, the Echo Park-based romantic comedy *Yes Man*. Most of the tracks came from previous Eels albums, but there was one, admittedly minor, new song: the *Shootenanny!*-style intimate 'Man Up'. More intriguingly, there was also a play that ran for about two weeks in September and early October at The Vineyard Playhouse on Martha's Vineyard in Massachusetts. Written and directed by Tony- and Pulitzer Prize-winning theatre director James Lapine, *Mrs Miller Does Her Thing* had been in the works since the early Noughties, inspired by a meeting between Lapine and E. They'd been put together by the manager they shared. "We were just sort of having breakfast and trying to find something to talk about," Lapine told *The Boston Globe*. "Mark started talking about Mrs Miller. He adores Mrs Miller."

Mrs Miller was Elva Miller, a matronly, middle-aged California choir singer who became a minor celebrity in the Sixties with her off-key renditions of pop standards like 'Moon River'. In an age before embarrassingly inept *American Idol* tryouts could launch the talentless hordes toward 15 minutes of ironic fame, Miller released four albums between 1966 and 1968. She died in the summer of 1997, a forgotten punch line in the history of pop vocal music.

E had originally hoped to turn her story into a film. "Nobody was really clear if she was in on the joke," E said in the same *Boston Globe* piece. "I was so obsessed with her that I ended up tracking down and talking to her family members. It seems that she wasn't in on the joke at the beginning, but she started picking up on it during her Capitol recording sessions, when they were picking her worst takes." For a songwriter who had always embraced outcasts in his tunes, it was obvious why E gravitated to her story. "I really want to give Mrs Miller her shred of dignity that was taken away from her," E declared at the time. "People have a memory of her as the little old lady who ruined 'Downtown'. But she really believed in what she did. I want people to understand her a little more."

Lapine took the idea and ran with it, eventually crediting E as co-creator of the resulting jukebox musical. After initial readings in the summer of 2005, *Mrs Miller Does Her Thing* had 14 shows in Martha's Vineyard in 2008. And that was that.

But E had long since moved on, as he always does. After all, he hadn't released an album of new material since April 2005, the longest span between new records in the band's history — even longer than the gap between the final E solo record and the first Eels disc. But he was about to make up for lost time — and in a pretty big way. He certainly wasn't going to let a sense of closure with the past affect his future music.

"The conventional thinking is that I will go soft and start writing lame mid-tempo anthems," he told the *Los Angeles Times*. "Don't worry, that's not on the horizon. I have a lifetime of angst stored up."

Chapter Fourteen

On March 3, 2009, the Eels website, which had been dormant for almost three months, displayed the following headline: "Eels return with first new album in four years". There were few details, except that it would be called *Hombre Lobo*, was recorded in E's home studio and would be coming out in June.

But while fans wondered what the follow-up to *Blinking Lights And Other Revelations* would sound like, E was thinking beyond *Hombre Lobo*. He didn't have just one album in mind — he was thinking of three.

"I learned early on never to talk about stuff before it's gonna come out for sure because I don't like to paint myself into a corner," he would later tell *FasterLouder*. "If I'd said at the beginning, 'Here's the first instalment of a trilogy', then everyone would expect it — which also takes a lot of the fun out of it — but also I knew that it was going to take long enough for me to put out these three albums and that I might change my mind along the way and decide there was only going to be two or it needs to be four or whatever."

Audiences had no way of knowing E's master plan when *Hombre Lobo* arrived, but from its first seconds the album signalled a new direction for the songwriter. Opening with a howl and the grungy garage-rock feel of raw guitars and crude drums, the album kicked off with a rollicking stomp. It was a song called 'Prizefighter', in which the narrator lets the listener know that he'll always be there for her, and with its pleasing, straightforward groove the invitation could be interpreted as both cocky and friendly. But the slightly distorted vocals (especially during the howls and shrieks that came later in the song) suggested darker impulses. 'Prizefighter' was one of Eels' most deceptively insignificant album openers, and yet it perfectly set the mood and intent of the record that followed — one that was subtitled *12 Songs Of Desire*.

E explained his intentions to *Interview* shortly after *Hombre Lobo*'s release. *Blinking Lights* had featured "all this sweeping orchestration," E said, "and it's only natural after doing something like that that you would want to do something more stripped down and immediate, something more succinct. The idea of desire appealed to me, something about playing guitar in a garage that's different than sitting down with someone orchestrating at a computer. It's just rocking."

The press release preceding the album indicated that *Hombre Lobo* was provoked in part by the massive beard E had grown, prompting him to write the album in the voice of the fictional Hombre Lobo (or wolfman) character. "I was thinking 'what happens when the young 'Dog Faced Boy' [character] grows up?'" he said in the press release, adding later, "it occurred to me that the best a dog faced boy could hope for would be to grow into something that can just squeak by in society with some semblance of dignity." (Dutifully reporting that the record was on its way, *Billboard*'s story was headlined "Eels Ready Beard-Inspired Album", not the sort of grabber that stokes the curiosity of the music-buying public.)

With an album cover that paid homage to the black-and-gold packaging for Cohiba cigars — a constant prop during the With Strings tour, as well as during press promotion for the documentary, book and Eels compilation albums — *Hombre Lobo* was a record that, like *Souljacker* (which contained 'Dog Faced Boy'), was about hiding in disguises, aural or otherwise. Tellingly, *Hombre Lobo* was the second Eels record to feature E on the cover — and like *Souljacker*, he was concealed behind shades and a beard, as if to say it was him, but not quite him.

"There were a couple of the songs I had written ahead of time for my own purposes," he told me right after *Hombre Lobo* had come out, "then I decided to go into the [Hombre Lobo] character. So everything after the first couple of 'em were written specifically to be from this character. And the other ones fit into that." And just as 'Things The Grandchildren Should Know' had been provoked by E seeing his father in the mirror, this Hombre Lobo character was inspired by E's own reflection. "I was working on some other music," he explained in an interview with NPR's *Weekend Edition*, "and I looked in the mirror one morning and I saw this werewolf staring back at me. And I thought, 'You know, this beard doesn't really suit the music that I'm working on currently — I should cut it off'. Then at the last minute it occurred to me, 'Well, why don't I just make some music that suits the beard and I'll keep it'."

(There might have been another, subtler influence going on as well — one he wasn't even conscious of at the time. "I was at E's house," Peter Byrne remembers, "and I went to the bathroom at his studio. He had this picture on the wall, a drawing, that [belonged to] his grandfather — his father's dad, Hugh Everett Jr. Somebody had given it to [his grandfather] when he was in the army. It depicted Hugh Everett Jr going through four stages, from human all the way to werewolf with a big beard. And I think I said something to Mark: 'Hey man, did you base your album on this picture?' And he said, 'Oh my god, I've been staring at that thing for years without seeing it. I'd even forgotten it was there'.")

E started plotting out a narrative arc that would constitute 12 songs, thinking about each track both musically and lyrically. "I wanted it to be [a look] at the frustrations that arise from his passions and desires — from different angles," he told me. "I think of [the songs] as like sales pitches from this guy who's trying to convince the object of his desire that he is the one. He takes different tacks in each song — sometimes he tries a more gentle, human approach, and other times it's a little ugly."

And the music matched that schizophrenic strategy, the lyrical indie-pop of the wistful, yearning 'That Look You Give That Guy' butting up against the horn-dog garage-funk of 'Lilac Breeze'. And although he's long admired Prince, he either was unable or uninterested in mimicking The Purple One's sexy, seductive pop. (In an interview, E once listed the gloriously filthy 'Erotic City' as his favourite Prince track.) Instead, the character's sexual desire came out in other ways: pretty ('In My Dreams'), frustrated ('What's A Fella Gotta Do'), eternally optimistic ('Beginner's Luck') or borderline craven ('Tremendous Dynamite'). But *Hombre Lobo*'s two most striking tracks were a study in contrasts — and a further demonstration of just how musically dexterous E can be when the spirit moves him.

With 'The Longing', E came up with his most gently upsetting side-ender since the quiet anguish of 'Agony' on *Shootenanny!* In contrast to the more striking musical moments on *Hombre Lobo*, 'The Longing' was minimalist, with just a modestly plucked electric guitar carrying the tune. And likewise, E's vocal lacked the violence or beauty that he employed elsewhere on the record. And yet, it may be *Hombre Lobo*'s most stubbornly riveting track, a long, slow exploration of the quiet moments that stretch out into eternity while you pine for the one you love (or lust after). On *Shootenanny!*, E wrote a caustically funny, tongue-in-cheek tune called 'Restraining Order Blues' about a clueless (though genuinely heartbroken) stalker. Six years later, there wasn't anything humorous about 'The Longing' — the spare, delicate, resilient guitar melody hinted at the explosion of need and desire that percolated just below the surface. It was an astounding performance, E singing nonchalantly about the little things that make his lover so wonderful, such as her smile and her laugh, before calmly expressing the depths of his devotion: yes, he would sacrifice his own life for her if that's what was required.

In 'The Longing', E brilliantly captured that sense of loneliness that occurs when the actual pain becomes a comforting companion — if you can't be next to your beloved, then the agony of the unrequited love produces its own sense of exquisite emotion. Subtly increasing the volume as the song builds, E and his echoey guitar never oversell the drama of the situation, which makes it all the more arresting and frightening — the song's narrator might do something desperate at any moment, or on the other hand perhaps he's entirely harmless.

Asked about the benefits of writing in character, E once told me: "You become more fearless — and less vulnerable — if you feel like you're not being yourself. But at the same time, you have to really identify with the character in some ways for it to work." But he was more explicit when he talked to *Vanity Fair*. "When I was working on the album," said E, "I described the concept to a friend of mine as basically 12 songs from the point of view of a horny old werewolf. And she said, 'Oh, so it's your most honest album to date'. So, I'll have to get back to you on this in a few years, but it might be more autobiographical than I think."

That horny old werewolf really showed his teeth on the album's next track, the eerie, propulsive 'Fresh Blood'. "That one came very early [in the writing process]," E told me. "It felt good. It had the feeling you want to have when you're making a new song, like 'Oh, here's something new'." And while it ostensibly shared some qualities with the more menacing textures of *Souljacker*, 'Fresh Blood' was a legitimately sexy, cocksure rock song. Mixing deranged howls, funky drums, a bluesy guitar moaning off in the distance and some horror-soundtrack keyboards, the song managed to convey throbbing desire without ever winking at the audience. "I wanted to do something that was what I would call dark and spooky," E said at the time. "Spooky music is fun." And for E, it was also a winning change of pace. He understood that as well — in fact, he seemed to be getting off on it a little. "I like the challenge of dealing with things like lust and sexual desire in songs," he told me, "because it occurs to me that something that seems to be lacking from so-called indie rock these days is the element of sex and danger. And that's where rock'n'roll comes from — I wanted to bring some of that back in. The sex and the danger in rock'n'roll has been replaced by this awful earnestness and literary references — it's like no one will know what to make of good ol' rock'n'roll where a guy's actually howling after girls."

The album was recorded in about a month with Koool G Murder and Knuckles, and the process was filmed for a promotional documentary, *Tremendous Dynamite: Making 'Hombre Lobo'*. Casually intimate, the 30-minute black-and-white film showed the trio laying down tracks for some of the album's songs in E's home studio, later observing as E and Murder mixed the record. Since Murder tends to shun interviews, the documentary was one of the rare instances where fans got to see him interacting with E.

"If you want the true odd-couple story," The Chet says, chuckling, "it's E and Koool G Murder. Those guys, while they have a great thing going, they couldn't be more different in terms of the kinds of people they are. It's pretty awesome to watch. E is definitely Felix, and Koool G is definitely Oscar."

Though he's never had the high-profile prominence in the band that Butch enjoyed, Murder has been working with E since *Souljacker* and *I Am The Messiah* — only Jim Lang has enjoyed a longer professional relationship with the singer-songwriter. Tall with a red beard, Murder enjoys cultivating his air of mystery, so much so that in a 2007 interview with Eels fan site *Rocking Eels*, almost all of his answers were put-ons. (Sample response: "I've been working with a great band from Belgium called Daddy's Urinal and another really cool band from Brazil called Buenos Nachos." He also said that he and E met because they go to the same bathhouse.) What is known about Murder is that he was part of a rap group around the turn of the century called Scapegoat Wax and studied music composition and theory at the University of Colorado at Boulder. (One wonders if the pluses and minuses of music school ever come up in conversation between E and Murder.)

Explaining the inter-band dynamics between himself, E and Murder, The Chet says: "Murder does a whole lot of recording and some writing with E, so my role is more 'live Swiss Army knife' and Murder's role is more 'studio Swiss Army knife'. Koool G has lots of keyboard skills and lots of sequencing skills and drum machine skills and all that stuff, and he lives practically around the corner from E. I live in Portland, so Murder tends to be his studio go-to guy."

"He's just very gifted musically," E explained to *Q* in 2010 about Murder's longevity in the band. "He's very versatile, a great player of several instruments."

A sense of Murder's importance to the *Hombre Lobo* project was clearly communicated in *Tremendous Dynamite*, which, for the obsessive Eels fan — the people that necessitate E's home-surveillance system — also featured shots of E's backyard and laundry room. With cameo appearances by Bobby Jr and a cardboard cut-out of The Chet, *Tremendous Dynamite* conveyed a loose-but-businesslike vibe of record-making that certainly backed up what E had told interviewers about the album: where *Blinking Lights* had been a gruelling, painstaking process, *Hombre Lobo* was a simple, direct affair. Not unlike *Shootenanny!*, it was an album that was intentionally not fussed over.

Summing up the recording experience, E told *Tiny Mix Tapes*: "It was about three or four weeks, and most of the songs were actually written during the three or four weeks of recording, with a few exceptions. And what was unusual... is that it was only these 12 songs. I didn't whittle it down to these 12 songs. I had a very clear idea of what I wanted each song to sound like and be about, and I kept track of the sequence as it was going along and filled in the spaces as I went along. Once I was done with 12 songs, I knew I was done."

In other words, it was a very different, less obsessive process for E, who is used to recording a bunch of different tracks and then picking the best ideas to build from. Subconsciously, there might have been more going on for E than simply changing up his approach, which he alluded to at the time. "I felt like I painted myself into a corner after I made *Blinking Lights*," he admitted to *Interview*. "It was the type of record you make at the end of your life." And although he has always joked about the short lifespans in his family, which has prompted a sense of making the most of his time on Earth, there had to be a worry that following up the ambition, scope and achievement of *Blinking Lights* would be a daunting task. And he clearly wasn't in the mood to try to repeat (or outdo) that double-disc affair.

It's not uncommon for musicians and filmmakers to follow up a perceived magnum opus with an intentionally modest effort — a lighter, less challenging project that helps reduce expectations to reasonable levels. (Ironically, Beck proves to be an apt example of this, releasing the stripped-down and sad-eyed *Mutations* after the world-beating *Odelay*.) For Eels fans, who weren't yet aware of E's grand plan for a linked trilogy of records, *Hombre Lobo* couldn't help but feel like a calculated palette-cleanser.

This is not to suggest that the album was tossed-off or lazy — indeed, 'That Look You Give That Guy' and 'In My Dreams' are two of E's most affecting examples of sunny indie-pop. But after those early highlights and the stunning one-two punch of 'The Longing' and 'Fresh Blood', *Hombre Lobo* started to noticeably sag, delivering solid songs that nonetheless echoed earlier triumphs. By the time we reached the poppy 'All The Beautiful Things', the concept of a wolfman trying to woo his girl started to feel superfluous, a predictable back-and-forth between tender and aggressive. (And in perhaps a sign that E was enjoying the casual, less-than-urgent approach to making the record a little too much, he broke character a bit with 'All The Beautiful Things', including his aborted countdown at the beginning of the track and saying, "I'm not gonna count, sorry." Or perhaps he was simply acknowledging that, really, there was no difference between this fictional guise and his creator.) With several of *Hombre Lobo*'s best songs co-written with Murder, it was hard not to get the impression that, for his first album in four years, E needed a little help regaining his sea legs.

Hombre Lobo received its share of positive reviews, but even those recognised that this wasn't a new high watermark for the band, instead pointing out how the album refined and returned to past Eels melodic and lyrical touchstones. But *A.V. Club* critic David Wolinsky got to the heart of *Hombre Lobo*'s inescapable problems in his mixed review. "It took Mark Everett seven years to record 2005's *Blinking Lights And Other Revelations*," Wolisnky wrote, "so it's understandable that the man might be drained." Unfortunately, he observed, that only produced an album that "sounds so tired... Sure, a back-to-basics vibe permeates the album, but it sounds more by-the-numbers than refreshed."

NME critic Jamie Fullerton continued in that same vein: "Last year E subscribed to the unwritten rule that a greatest hits release marks the point after which all acts apply the artistic handbrake. From there on in, acts go gannet-grabbing from their back catalogue to create music that fans will adore and the rest of the world will ignore. As if to prove the theory, there's nothing on *Hombre Lobo*... that couldn't be constructed by breaking down the DNA of the previous six Eels albums and re-piling the strands up in some melodically fresh but warmly recognisable way."

E had talked about *Blinking Lights* being an "end of your life" record, which presented artistic challenges going forward for him. But it also created a problem for fans and critics — how else could he surprise or wow us? E continued to produce great songs, but beyond the Hombre Lobo conceit, there wasn't much new about *Hombre Lobo*. He was, in essence, being accused of making the exact same great songs as he had done before. The most striking example of this odd predicament came when E performed 'That Look You Give That Guy' (his favourite track off the album) on David Dye's *World Café* radio show. Dye was a great fan of the album, putting it in his top 10 of that year, but after the song was over, he commented (seemingly in an attempt to give a compliment): "E, I dunno, that sounds like a song you could have written for *Shrek*." E's best new material was being praised for sounding like his old stuff.

Still, *Hombre Lobo* proved to be somewhat successful in the States, peaking higher (number 43) than any previous Eels records. It might have done even better if Eels had kept with tradition and toured around the album's release, but E declined. "I'm just not feeling it really," he told me at the time. "I don't want to disrespect the audience by doing something I'm not fully invested in right now. There's no lack of inspiration as far as how I would do it — I just don't feel like doing it at this moment." The "disrespect the audience" line was one he would use on a few interviewers who asked him about his touring plans, making it clear that it was his choice. But perhaps another issue might have been that his guitarist The Chet was already committed to touring around the same time.

"There was a little bit of talk about a tour after *Hombre Lobo*," The Chet says. "I was out with Lucinda Williams' band. There was a kind of lull in Eels touring that had happened, and I had to make a living, so I had stumbled on this other gig and was doing that for a while. So I was approached about the possibility of doing a tour for *Hombre Lobo*, but I couldn't do it because I was already committed to another thing. I don't know how much bearing that had on whether they decided to do it or not, but they ended up not doing the tour."

In the absence of a proper tour, E found other ways to entertain his fans. He produced clever, low-budget videos for the singles 'Fresh Blood', 'In My Dreams' and 'That Look You Give That Guy'. 'Fresh Blood', helmed by Jesse Dylan (who also directed the video for *Blinking Lights'* 'Trouble With Dreams'), was a creepy/funny tour of a rundown section of the warehouse district of downtown Los Angeles, with E playing the Hombre Lobo character as he slowly followed a fetching beauty while battling Mexican wrestlers. 'In My Dreams' was an impossibly sweet narrative about a young boy who wakes up to discover he's covered in fur and meets a nerdy-cute young woman looking for her missing frog. Then with 'That Look You Give That Guy' he delivered what was arguably his finest video since 'Novocaine'. It hilariously tells of a first date between E and *Top Chef* host and model Padma Lakshmi. E, still with the long beard, has dressed up for the occasion and has invited her to his (fictional) mansion. She is, of course, stunning, but his attempts to seduce her — showing off his memoir, making her watch the *Live At Town Hall* DVD, playing the guitar for her — all prove unsuccessful due to her clear infatuation with adorable Bobby Jr. The video allowed E to show off some fine nebbishy, Woody Allen-esque comic timing, and director Gus Black threw in a great twist ending — we at first think that Lakshmi has changed her mind and run back to the house to kiss E, but in fact it's all a dream and E has instead been French-kissing his dog in bed.

Beyond the video's comic brilliance, though, it inspired perhaps the greatest rumour in Eels history. A month after the video débuted, Lakshmi announced that she was pregnant, although she would not name the child's father. Lakshmi, who had only recently divorced author Salman Rushdie, generated significant scandal-sheet buzz because of her news, and rumours soon circulated that E was the father. (*The Boston Globe*'s celebrity blog breathlessly reported that "she has been linked to Eels singer Mark Oliver Everett of late", while *NME* published a headline that truly made one wonder about parallel worlds: "Eels' E the father of Salman Rushdie's ex-wife's baby?" In the end, Lakshmi revealed that the father was, in fact, Adam Dell, an American venture capitalist.)

When he wasn't setting the gossip rags aflame with his purported romantic exploits, E also made time for a few one-off appearances. Shortly after the album's release, he and Knuckles flew to New York to play 'In

My Dreams' on *Late Show With David Letterman*, where, incidentally, he first met Lakshmi, who was also on that night's programme. Then, about a month later, he drove over to *Jimmy Kimmel Live!*'s Hollywood studio to play a particularly ragged and brawling version of 'Tremendous Dynamite' with Knuckles, Koool G Murder... and Tommy Walter. The former Eels bassist's appearance at the previous year's warm-up show turned out not to be the last time the two would share a stage.

"He just called me," Walter remembers of the invitation. "'Hey, do you want to do *Jimmy Kimmel*?' And I'm like, 'Great'." More surreal was that when the programme came back from the night's final commercial, Kimmel had the band play the show out, and Eels launched into 'My Beloved Monster', the first time Walter had played the song with E in 12 years. Walter recalls thinking at that moment, "This is kind of fun — I'm singing these backups I used to sing."

The joint appearance didn't lead to any sort of formal return to Eels for Walter, but it did re-establish their friendship. "After we did the Jimmy Kimmel thing," Walter says, "I started hanging out with him on Sundays with this group of friends that we have." Of course, croquet is part of the weekly-hangout festivities, just like volleyball had been when E was a kid in McLean. And where before the two would bicker over E's control issues, now Walter easily shrugs them off. "One time I had tweeted something about croquet at E's house," Walter recalls, "and he sent me a stern email saying, 'Don't do this'. He's like, 'This is not people's business'. I mean, that's what friends can do — he can say, 'Stop, I don't want you doing this, this has to stop'. And I'm like, OK, and then we move on, and everything's cool. He's a very private person." As further proof of their deepening bond, E volunteered his house as the site for Walter's wedding when he tied the knot in October 2010. "We're buds," Walter says simply. "He has really gone out of his way to embrace me again. I like to hang out with him. Now he's one of the most kind, generous people I know, and I totally support him musically, too." Walter pauses, hearing himself go on. "So in the end," he adds with a laugh, "it's kind of a beautiful love story."

E and Walter's relationship may have had a happy ending, but E was also focused on another tale, one that proved much bleaker.

Seven months after the Eels website announced *Hombre Lobo*, a news item appeared on October 14: "End Times Are Coming". There was a new album on the way, called *End Times*, and it would be arriving on January 19, 2010 in the States. In November, a more detailed press release laid out the vision for the record under the none-too-subtle headline "Apocalyptic Heartache: The State Of The Broken Union."

"The eighth Eels studio album, *End Times*, is the sound of an artist growing older in uncertain times," the statement began. "An artist who has lost his great love while struggling with his faith in an increasingly hostile world teetering on self-destruction." Intriguingly described as "a 'divorce album' with a modern twist", *End Times* was said to have been recorded in E's basement mostly on an old four-track, a return to the approach of his earliest recordings when he was still dreaming of becoming a signed musician. Evoking *Broken Toy Shop* — a rare mention of a pre-Eels album — the announcement draped the record in stark, desperate tones: where *Hombre Lobo* was written in the voice of a character, *End Times* was "pure real life". "The subject matter is so personal that he won't be interviewed on the subject," the announcement warned. "He'll only offer that it's all based on a true story. This is a raw and real state of the broken union address." If all of this wasn't enough of a gauntlet being thrown down, the press release closed with a final quote from the artist: "This will be some people's favourite Eels album and some people's least favourite Eels album," he said. "I'm prepared for that."

Break-up albums are a very special breed of record, especially in the internet age when journalists and fans can seemingly learn everything about a star's love life. Consequently, such albums aren't just discussed in terms of their artistic merits but also by the details they reveal about the actual relationship. Hence, Kanye West's *808s & Heartbreak* isn't just a nervy experiment to use Auto-Tune and electronica to personify the dehumanising aspects of lost love — it's also an opportunity to gossip about his ex-fiancée Alexis Phifer. Similarly, Beck's *Sea Change* can't simply be judged on its attempts to integrate Nick Drake-style folk and British psychedelia into his world of sonic collage — we must waste time discussing the particulars of Leigh Limon, the costume designer whose relationship's end prompted the album. By refusing to do press or a tour for *End Times* — and by working so strenuously to keep Natasha's identity a mystery — E forced his audience to judge the record on its own terms.

"The less we know about an album that's as intimate as, say, *Blood On The Tracks* the better it is for our listening pleasure," he told *Mojo*, the only publication to which he gave an interview for the album. "We can paint our own pictures." But even though he allowed *Mojo* to visit him at his Los Feliz home, he remained tight-lipped about the album and its making. "A lot of what I've read is wrong," he said, "but I'm OK with that." But he realised that this was part of the by-product of keeping quiet. "*End Times* was a tough one," he said. "I understood it was pretty bleak and not for everybody, but I felt it had something to say. Whatever subject matter I'm going to explore, I'm going to go for it all the way. When I listened to the album I thought, I don't want to talk about this, I don't want to be selling this. I'm just going to let it go out there and do what it's going to do."

End Times was yet another album in the Eels canon to receive the "masterpiece" tag by critics. But unlike the stylistically ambitious *Electro-Shock Blues* and *Blinking Lights*, *End Times* was consciously lacking in any sort of overtly bold musical touches. Quite the contrary, it was an album that was meant to sound spiritually drained — some reviewers had disliked *Hombre Lobo* because it seemed tired, but *End Times* paraded its exhaustion as a hallmark. Written and produced entirely by E, the record featured, as it indicated in the liner notes, "a little help" from previous collaborators like Koool G Murder and Jim Lang, but after the garage-rock aesthetic of *Hombre Lobo*, the bare construction of *End Times* felt stripped of disguises, personae and attitude.

Loss of love haunted the record, but in a sign of how much he had matured as a songwriter, *End Times* bore little resemblance to *Broken Toy Shop*, his previous attempt at such a record. With a minority of its 14 tracks running longer than three minutes — and only the album-closing 'On My Feet' clocking in above six — there was a sense that the songs were more fragments of moods and memories than proper tunes. And where *Broken Toy Shop*'s romantic despair could feel wimpy, *End*

Times had a directness that seemed uncensored, providing a peek into the songwriter's mind-set as he floundered between different emotional states.

The opener, 'In The Beginning', featured a guitar line that bore similarities to John Lennon's White Album ballad 'Julia', providing a delicate glimpse into a happier past between the narrator and his lover. But at only 137 seconds, the song stopped abruptly, as if to suggest that the memory was too painful or too far away to remember for long.

From there, E seemed to build on the unfussy candour he'd sought for *Shootenanny!* — and carried over into his memoir — by writing lyrics that often felt like secret communications to his ex. "I've worked hard over the years to trim away as much of the fat as possible to get to the point," he told *ArtistDirect* about his songwriting approach. "I'm really trying to tell a very succinct story: sometimes in 10 or 15 lines. Writing's successful in a short story or song because someone gets to the heart of the matter more quickly... When I was younger, I used to write songs that were too many minutes long, and they had all sorts of stuff in them that they didn't need. I just tried to pay attention to that as I went on. I think that's why a lot of my songs are really short. I've noticed my songs rarely break the three-minute mark."

End Times quite often attacked the listener lyric-first. The 146-second 'Unhinged' was a simplistic keyboard-and-guitar rave-up that allowed E to rant at his lover for her wild mood swings and otherwise unconscionable behaviour. The 155-second 'Little Bird' married some quiet electric guitar picking to melancholy lyrics in which E resorts to talking to a bird in his backyard to deal with his loneliness. The 160-second 'I Need A Mother' was built around a ghostly piano figure, but its arrangement wasn't nearly as spooky as E's downbeat declaration of the title phrase, drawing quick, universal parallels between romantic affairs and the complex relationships we have with our parents which inform (and, in some ways, damage) our future relationships. (Naturally, it was hard not to think of E's own mother and the obsession he had as a child with both her approval and her breasts.)

And then there was the title track, which, at two seconds shy of three minutes, was positively epic for the album, a stripped-down guitar figure forming the track's heart as E observes a raving-mad homeless man screaming about the end of the world. Deftly and eloquently, E used this all-too-commonplace character as a springboard for a rumination on the similarities between loss of love and a sense that the entire planet is falling apart.

There were those who complained that E's misery on *End Times* wallowed in an unreflective self-pity, but such dismissals missed the point of E's approach. The songwriter who scolded his lover in 'Unhinged' was the same guy reduced to talking to birds and, in one of the album's more daring moments, comparing his ex to a suicide bomber in 'Paradise Blues'. By writing and playing these songs as simply as possible, E honoured each track's emotional purity without offering any commentary or editorialising. In essence, each song was "true" for that moment in time, and yet all the other tracks on *End Times* contradicted and argued with that truth.

This isn't to say that *End Times* was without its lapses. Recalling the four-track starkness of Bruce Springsteen's *Nebraska* — a raw, acoustic-guitar-heavy album meant to reflect the desperation of the songs' hopeless characters — *End Times* was sometimes too monochromatic for its own good, hitting at the same miserable tone without much relief.

In addition, the forced metaphor of 'Paradise Blues' couldn't help but feel a little too glib at a time when real suicide bombers were never far away from the news. As a clue to his thinking on the track, one could return to E's memoir where he talked about his affinity for "crazy girls". To give his readers an idea of what he meant, E referred to Woody Allen's 1992 comedy-drama *Husbands And Wives*, in which the Allen character dubs them "kamikaze women". "I've always had this penchant for what I call 'kamikaze women'," Allen's character admits. "I call them kamikazes because they, you know, they crash their plane, they're self-destructive. But they crash it into you, and you die along with them."

If that was the intention behind 'Paradise Blues,' the song still seemed clumsy and vaguely insensitive, no matter how honest its sentiment. It also highlighted just how rare it was in the Eels catalogue for a song to comment on current events, no matter how tangentially. In a radio interview around seven years earlier, he talked about his total uninterest in politics. "When I was younger," he said, "you're naïve... Every time someone new is running for president, you think, 'Yeah, things are gonna change and it's gonna be a better life!' But nothing ever changes, it just seems to get worse. So, I gave up on politics many years ago." Such quotes, of course, will just fuel those who grouse that introspective songwriters like E are mere navel-gazers incapable of interacting with the world outside their domiciles. But while he has proved consistently capable of turning his personal dramas into captivating art, 'Paradise Blues' suggested a downside to such an approach.

Since *End Times* was advertised as a "divorce album" — and because its author refused to discuss the record's inspirations — fans took it upon themselves to scrutinise its lyrics for clues about E's failed relationship. (Later, he would allow that "most of it was [autobiographical], but not all of it.") Several songs provided seemingly personal details, and one of the most impressive tunes was the piano-and-strings number entitled 'A Line In The Dirt'. In the song, E sings in the present tense about a domestic scene in which his lover has "locked herself in the bathroom again," forcing him to pee in the yard and, later, try to convince her to come out. In frustration, he finally abandons their home and drives away, wondering if he'll ever return. In between, Eels fans latched onto a verse that sounded like a perfect encapsulation of E's lone-wolf issues: "So I am knocking on the door again/I say 'Do you want to be alone?'/She says 'No, I don't wanna be alone/ but I think that you do'." One of the album's most lush, confessional and heartbreaking tunes, 'A Line In The Dirt' had all the intimacy and pain of a diary entry. The listener would understandably assume that the song's characters were E and Natasha — but, in fact, the song was more than 10 years old.

The track originated from the *Daisies* sessions with Wally Gagel, who hadn't heard 'A Line In The Dirt' since they worked on it in 1999. "That's a great song," he says, listening to the finished song on *End Times* for the first time. "God, how come they never released that earlier?" Lost in thought while listening to the track, he adds, "I do remember... I think I know who that's about, too." He laughs. "But I can't say."

And it wasn't the only *End Times* track to originate during *Daisies*. Jim Lang, who's credited with recording the folk-song-with-strings 'Nowadays', believes it too came about from that album's sessions.

As for those who would accuse E of being dishonest for adding 11-year-old songs to an album purportedly about his ex-wife, Gagel praises the artist for being "good at recycling things". Indeed, 'A Line In The Dirt' in particular demonstrated what a remarkable amount of good material the *Daisies* sessions had spawned, with *End Times* being the third studio album since that record to include songs from that period. "There was a wealth of material," Gagel says, adding, "It's kind of interesting [to see him] constantly go back to this real productive time, just letting all this stuff out." And the origins of the song didn't hamper its emotional impact on the record — whether it was fictional, based on someone else's life or about a previous girlfriend, 'A Line In The Dirt' resonated because it felt real. It was just another fabric in the album's overall design in which E was not only laying out his sadness, but also trying to make sense of it all.

And for the first time since *Daisies*, E closed an album with a wistful but not quite hopeful track. With a reflective melody vaguely reminiscent of 'Valentine's Day', the final track on Bruce Springsteen's disillusioned-relationship album *Tunnel Of Love*, 'On My Feet' broke from E's tradition of going out on an optimistic note.

Strumming a guitar and addressing his departed lover one last time, E balanced personal recollections of their time together with an uncertain outlook for his own future. Some of the details in 'On My Feet' were simply devastating in their simplicity — he moves his bed up against the wall to eliminate the idea that there's a "his" and "her" side to it — and although he vows at the conclusion that one day he'll be OK again, there's no doubt that he won't be the same person afterward, that something has been permanently lost. It was a theme continued from an earlier *End Times* track, 'In My Younger Days', which acknowledged the crucial difference between a failed relationship in your twenties and one in your forties: the realisation that more of your life has passed, which can make the heartbreak more pronounced and feel more permanent. *End Times* finishes with E declaring that he'll pick himself up again at some point, which then leads into more than a minute of soft, melancholy strumming that slowly fades into nothingness, closing on the same diaphanous note on which the album began. Artist Adrian Tomine's front-cover illustration of the title tune's homeless loony seemed clearly intended to be a representation of the songwriter, trading E's long black *Hombre Lobo* beard for a long white one. *End Times* reeked of spiritual, but not creative, exhaustion — of a man now decidedly middle-aged who, after years of being nicknamed Grandpa by his associates, genuinely felt old and worn out.

Several months after the release of *End Times*, fans were left with only that gentle strumming as the final word from E. But then some festival dates were announced in April, with the band set to play in Japan, France and Switzerland later in the year. Then, on May 18, the Eels website's home page changed to a light pink background with one word in dark pink announcing: "tomorrow". The following day, the word changed: "morning". One day later, the cryptic design became clear with an official announcement: "Eels are set to release a new album entitled *Tomorrow Morning* August 24, 2010 and embark on a world tour August 3." It would be the third new Eels record in 14 months and, as the announcement went on to explain, their close succession was intentional: "E calls the 14 track album the final instalment of a trilogy that began with HOMBRE LOBO (June 2009) and END TIMES (January 2010)." Elaborating further a month later, another announcement included a quote from E, who called the album: "The redemption... A new beginning and another chance. The blooming of all new possibilities. The hope that was always there coming to fruition."

When E started doing promotion for *Tomorrow Morning*, he talked about the tonal shift from *End Times* to the new record. "[E]verybody's reaction [to *End Times*] was so, 'Oh God...'" he told *Q*, "and it was funny for me because I already knew what was going to happen after that, and I knew there was a happy ending to it." Not that the knowledge made it easier for him to make *End Times*. "That was probably the hardest one to make [of the trilogy] — partly because of the subject matter and also partly because of the loneliness," E told *Clash*. "With *End Times* I was in a similar situation as to when I first decided to write a book. I naïvely thought that because I was going to do something alone it would be easy. Then it turns out that those things are the hardest to do. I thought like, 'oh I'll just sit down with my old four track recorder and sing some songs'. At times it was difficult to record."

But *Tomorrow Morning*'s positive outlook wasn't the only noteworthy twist in the Eels playbook — there was also its sound. This was an album of drum machines and electronic keyboards. Speaking with *Spinner*, E explained that "originally my idea was I wanted to do a very warm album, a celebration of the things I like about life and the world. I also had always wanted to make an album that was pretty electronic, but I always thought that would be a colder kind of album because of the nature of the sound — the kind of music that is normally made with those instruments. And then one day it occurred to me: what if I combine these two ideas? The electronic idea and the warm, celebration idea. And then I got excited because then it kinda becomes its own thing."

In the same interview, he discussed how he felt the three albums worked together as a trilogy. "*Hombre Lobo* was the spark that ignites everything," he said, "even on like a physical level, planting the seed or the need to plant the seed. Then *End Times* is kind of the opposite of all of that, in dealing with the loss. And then, for me, the most fun part is what comes next, hopefully: a new beginning. So the whole thing ends with a beginning and the end is in the middle. Which, by following the title *End Times* with the title *Tomorrow Morning* — that changes the meaning of the title *End Times*. How can it be the end if there's a morning coming tomorrow?"

Beyond thinking of the albums as a linked trilogy, E also carefully considered when to release each of them. "[I]n the Eighties, I remember Prince would put a record out every spring," he told *PopMatters*. "And, especially when I lived on the East Coast, that was a real part of the listening experience, what time of year an album comes out. And I'm very conscious of that. I specifically wanted *End Times* to come out in the winter and *Tomorrow Morning* to come out in the summer...the thing I really notice is that if I hear some song that I liked a lot when I was younger, the first thing I think about is what the weather was like when I was first listening to it."

To promote the tour and album release, E flew to London in the middle of June. When I interviewed him a year earlier for *Hombre Lobo*, he had just returned from New York after performing on *Late Show With David Letterman* and had been delayed at the airport. I asked if he experienced problems with security because of his long beard as he had during the *Souljacker* days. He laughed. "No, this time it was because LaGuardia was flooded," he said, "and all the flights doubled up at JFK, where I was. Ever since Obama got into office, I don't get hassled as much at the airport." But the hassles returned once he got to London. An *NME* story on June 22 reported that "E from Eels was questioned by police in London's Hyde Park after they mistook him for a suspected terrorist. The singer… was taking a break from a day of interviews when police approached him thinking he fitted the description of a suspicious person they were looking for."

E later elaborated. "It was one of the strangest things that has ever happened to me," he told *American Songwriter*, "which I guess says a lot. I was doing what I've been doing for 15 years, walking around Hyde Park. You know, you go over and do these press junkets, talk about your album. I got my first break on the first day and I went out and left the hotel, I was just walking around. I sat on a bench, smoked a cigar, and as I was leaving the park I was approached by three policemen. It was unusual that they were London police, and they had guns, and they said someone had called them and said that there was this suspicious character matching my exact description, and it was my description, is the strange thing, down to the clothes I was wearing and everything, but the strange part about it was that I wasn't doing any of the things that were described — standing menacingly in front of an embassy, and peering over the wall at my hotel, and that's eventually how I got them to let me go. They questioned me for about 20 minutes, filed a report, and took all the information, and I showed them my hotel key, and I said, 'why would I be staring back at the hotel that I finally got out of?' And they said, 'yeah, that doesn't make a lot of sense'."

E tried joking about it in an official statement — "Not every guy with short hair and a long beard is a terrorist. Some of us just want to rock" — but the situation clearly rattled him. Recalling the incident to *PopMatters*, he said: "I did tell [the police] at one point, I'm a rock singer, I'm staying at this hotel — I was just trying not to get arrested. They took a police report on me...it was actually really scary, I was shaking by the end of it. Because I started to realise that my freedom was at stake and I don't know if I've ever felt that before. It was a horrible feeling." One wonders if it brought back bad memories of appearing in front of a judge at age 14 pondering the possibility of landing in jail.

Eels played their warm-up show and several of their first festival dates before *Tomorrow Morning*'s release, with the band's rollicking onstage get-up in no way mirroring the sound of the album. Indeed, as *Tomorrow Morning*'s instrumental opening, the atmospheric electronica of 'In Gratitude For This Magnificent Day', suggested, E was serious about marrying stereotypically "cold" sounds to warm, hopeful themes.

Not since *Souljacker* had E so profoundly altered his sonic template as he did on *Tomorrow Morning*. Where even *Blinking Lights'* airier moments had been dressed up with thrift-store instrumentation or strings — familiar weapons in the Eels arsenal — *Tomorrow Morning* seemed practically otherworldly, comforting but also ethereal and experimental. The album's themes were consistent with earlier Eels albums — the hope for a better tomorrow, the search for love — but there was an unmistakably happier tinge to the proceedings.

The last time E had tried to make an "up" album was with *Daisies Of The Galaxy*, which he'd recorded as a reaction to the darkness of *Electro-Shock Blues*. But *Daisies'* attempts to embrace life sometimes meant indulging in stylistic tricks like 'Flyswatter' or succumbing to sadness in 'It's A Motherfucker'. By comparison, *Tomorrow Morning* was resolutely hopeful, avoiding forced joy for a more measured, resilient optimism. Much of that carefully considered hopefulness was reflected in E's vocals. Indeed, like the songwriters he loves whose voices have become battered and weathered over time — Dylan, Newman, Waits — E's raspy singing served as a constant counterpoint to the happy lyrics, as if making clear that these sentiments had come only after a long, dark crawl through unpleasant times. There wasn't sarcasm in his delivery — his voice sounded as ragged as it had on *End Times* — but there was a noticeable lift and tenderness to it.

E wouldn't discuss who had inspired these songs, but *Tomorrow Morning* clearly pulsated with the promise of new love. The sleepy Seventies pop of 'That's Not Her Way', the gentle reverie of 'What I Have To Offer', the touching indie-pop of 'I Like The Way This Is Going', the Casio-and-a-drum-machine swagger of 'Baby Loves Me', the indie electronica of 'Spectacular Girl', the chilly-yet-sweeping soundscapes of 'This Is Where It Gets Good' — aside from the occasional funny lyric, these were unabashedly genuine love songs not heard since the days that a 20-something Mark Everett had serenaded his girlfriend on *Bad Dude In Love*. "I've sung enough about what's wrong with me," he said by way of introduction to a performance of the open-hearted 'What I Have To Offer' during a radio appearance. "Here's what's good about me." But E couldn't resist a typically wry remark. "I still hate myself," he said, "but I'm trying to convince someone else that I'm likeable."

When asked by *American Songwriter* what in his personal life had prompted such happy tunes, E shifted away from specifics. "Hopefully as you get older," he replied, "you start to slowly learn what things to be upset about and what things to be thankful for. I finally felt like I was at the point where I'm starting to look around me and see all the good things about my life, and I couldn't help but express gratitude for it." And when *The Culture Show*'s Sue Perkins mentioned that people would be curious who the subject of 'Spectacular Girl' was, he responded by saying, "Yes, wouldn't they like to know." And then he seemed to have a little fun with his inquisitor. "I don't think it's important that anyone knows *who* she is," he added, "and I'm not saying that it is or isn't a very famous actress that we all know. It's not important because I think it's more important for the listener to project that onto their own spectacular girl." But no matter who the mysterious "spectacular girl" was, it was apparent that she had helped brighten E's world.

In another throwback to his *Bad Dude* days, E took the opportunity on *Tomorrow Morning* to indulge his love for African-American musical styles, specifically gospel on the jubilant call-and-response 'Looking

Up', which found E howling and testifying like an old–time preacher. "That's my favourite track on this album," he said shortly before the album's release, "it might be the favourite track I've ever done." As an indication of just how much he loved that song, he then admitted that the choir of female backup singers was actually just him. "You get away with what you can get away with," he said, "and I can sing in that kind of high falsetto and it sounded good to me so there was no need to get real women in there... there's just nothing more fun than screaming. I mean just really losing yourself. Total abandon." It called to mind *Bad Dude In Love's* 'I Can't Get Next To You' where he first showed off his playful vocal dexterity. And like the young Everett paying homage to Motown half a lifetime ago on 'Too Busy Thinking About My Baby', E on 'Looking Up' was again connecting with music's power to bring about some sort of transcendence. The reason was pretty simple: "I noticed recently," he said, "that if I'm listening to music in my own life, more often than not, it's something that's very uplifting."

That sense of liberation also seemed to open him up creatively in other ways. Whereas *Hombre Lobo*'s theme of lust was easier for E to approach by writing in the voice of a character, 'This Is Where It Gets Good' spoke candidly to his partner in his own voice, looking forward to the moment when he could see her naked again. Later, on 'The Man', he revisited the lyrical conceit he first attempted on *Daisies*' 'A Daisy Through Concrete', in which E walks down the street looking for reasons to be happy. He encounters a skinhead, an old hippie, an angry redneck, a New Age guy, an indie-rock kid, a homeless gentleman, a rapper, and a politician, but the mood is unreservedly upbeat — as opposed to the lyrical run-ins E had had in the past, these peripheral figures were not objects of scorn or anxiety but, rather, part of a shared community. And in perhaps a nod to his failed film project, even Mrs Miller tells E that he's the man.

Reviewers tended to appreciate this new E, although the stylistic change of pace left some nonplussed. "It's not serenity that's the problem on *Tomorrow Morning*... it just feels slack in execution," BBC's James Skinner wrote, "like a series of vaguely pretty sketches or half thought-through ideas. It's a palate-cleanser for sure, and whatever lies next for Everett, you have to hope it's a little more emphatic than what's on offer here."

For others, *Tomorrow Morning*'s electronic sound provided an opportunity to compare it unfavourably to artists who had attempted something similar previously. *Slant*'s Kevin Liedel denounced the record as "borrowing lo-fi electronica themes from decade-old work by Radiohead, Peter Bjorn and John, and Hooverphonic," deeming it meagre in the face of Radiohead's "ambient masterpiece" *Kid A*.

But such complaints failed to understand that E wasn't competing with the Radioheads of this world. (In fact, if E can be taken at his word, he stopped paying attention to much contemporary music long ago.) Rather, like when Portishead inspired his direction for *Beautiful Freak* or he hooked up with John Parish for *Souljacker*, E wasn't trying to sound like other artists but instead was attempting to locate what it is about their approach that could also work for him.

In an interview in *The Huffington Post*, E addressed this, somewhat, when answering a question about what advice he'd give aspiring artists. "I think the best advice I could give a young act is to try not to be tentative about anything that you do," he responded. "Even if you're unsure about yourself or what you're doing, do it like you know what you're doing. That right there is half the battle. Do what you're doing with authority, and you'll be amazed at how much it works just by having that attitude." Then he added, "Even if you don't believe what you're doing, lie to yourself that you believe what you're doing as a start, and eventually, you might start believing what you're doing." People have asked E what his secret is, and that right there may be the answer. Not an artist who grew up a heralded prodigy, he's been a songwriter who just keeps building his tracks a piece at a time and seeing what happens.

"They're all three sort of different," The Chet says about the recent trilogy, "but the main thing I would say about them is that they seem to be more just coming from the gut and less cerebral. Of course, I'm not saying that there isn't thought put in them, but I think that E might be coming out of a place just in his head and going into a place that's more in his gut and heart and stomach. I think he's enjoying life more now. I think he's just kind of cutting loose and enjoying it and going for it.

He's feeling the sex and drugs and rock'n'roll — although E doesn't do any drugs at all. *Blinking Lights* was perhaps his sort of catharsis album — since then he's just been having more fun with it and howling and screaming."

A little more than two months after their warm-up show in Santa Ana, Eels returned to Los Angeles on October 12, 2010 to play The Music Box for the final night of the tour.

The band had made its way around the globe to get to that night's LA date. Starting in Japan, they visited Australia, playing in Melbourne almost exactly 10 years to the day that Spider died in a hotel room there. Then they were off to Europe, where they played large festival shows in between venues whose capacity ran generally from 1,000 to 2,000 people. On September 1, Eels played Brixton Academy in London, no doubt the memory of being detained by the police in the same city back in June still a fresh annoyance. If that wasn't enough, there was a report that the group had to get their beards insured specifically for the Brixton gig, a source telling *The Sun*: "Eels were told by the venue that their big beards are a health and safety risk — and they had to take out a separate policy just for the night. The venue regarded their facial furniture as a potential fire risk." ("England is a weird place," E would later surmise.)

By late September, they were back in the States, hitting most of the major markets in the US and Canada. On September 23, Eels performed in Richmond, Virginia, and three days later the band were at DC's 9:30 Club, the venue *Bad Dude In Love* producer Bobby Read worked at three decades earlier as a soundman when it was just starting up. By early October, Eels were in Seattle, the city where E got the phone call in November of 1998 telling him that his mother's cancer was getting progressively worse and that he needed to come home immediately. E has been touring for so many years now that it seems like there's no city or concert stage that doesn't have some sort of connection to his history. In fact, The Music Box was the location of the Tori Amos show that David Wild attended, only to be so impressed with E's opening set that he ended up missing Amos entirely and instead hung out with the young songwriter, a friendship being born in the process.

Fans at this 2010 Music Box show were first tormented by a ventriloquist comedian who normally does kids' parties. The bizarre form of "entertainment" that had occurred at the Galaxy in early August of that year wasn't a one-time event: E had found local ventriloquists to perform throughout the band's world tour. There was the one in Sydney whose characters included a slutty kitten and a crocodile; there was a gentleman at the San Francisco show who dressed as Captain Jack Sparrow from *Pirates Of The Caribbean*; as for the Washington, DC performance, it featured, according to a tweet from a fan in attendance, "a post-op transsexual 'rock-and-roll' ventriloquist".

When Eels took the stage, there was an instant feeling of connection between E and the crowd. But the Music Box gig was also a reminder of the limits to such a feeling of community. For one, it's an LA concert, which meant that there was also a small, obnoxious minority who felt compelled to yell "witty" things at the performers between songs, including some fool who kept bellowing "bass solo!" and calling out for Koool G Murder. E ignored it as best he could, but when he introduced the band towards the end of the show, he finally had to tell someone near the stage, "Douchebag, stop talking to me."

This onstage behaviour was not entirely unheard of from E during Eels' early years. Jim Jacobsen had seen it first-hand back in the day. "That's one thing that he does that his friends say, 'God, I really wish he learned not to do that'," Jacobsen says. "I mean, it's really a no-no — you don't fucking scold people in the audience. If he feels like people are not paying attention, he will call them out." Jacobsen has a valid point, but in E's defence, on this particular night the jerk deserved it.

But a few loud-mouthed morons weren't the evening's only troubling sign. Although this was the last night of the tour — and was the Eels' first show in their hometown in more than two years — The Music Box (which holds about 1,300) was still selling tickets at the door. Granted, the economy was in a horrible shape, it was a Tuesday night, and many bands play to less-than-capacity crowds all the time. But as the show moved along and Eels garage-rocked their way through their recent trilogy of albums, the audience noticeably thinned out a bit in the back. It was still an impressive turnout, and the crowd was largely an appreciative throng, but it was hard to shake the feeling that Eels are fated to be loved by the margins but never fully understood by the masses.

And yet E couldn't have looked happier onstage.

Thematically, the 2010 tour might have been Eels' least ambitious live iteration. Three guitars, a bass, drums, E back with a long beard, dark sunglasses and a jumpsuit — its sound and design weren't breaking any new ground. But just as E timed *Tomorrow Morning*'s release for the summer, the tour felt very much like a warm-weather show — even though by the time it ended it was October. With The Chet and new member P-Boo backing up E on guitar, and Koool G Murder and Knuckles holding down the rhythm section, this version of Eels was drunk on the sweaty, sexy pleasure of being in a band and making a lot of noise. Earlier tours were about precision and presentation — this one was about the enjoyment that can be had when you bludgeon a musical catalogue with the youthful spirit reminiscent of the first rock'n'roll bands.

Near the end of the Music Box show, Tommy Walter joined the band onstage. He stood near E and pounded away on a tambourine for the rousing 'Looking Up'. The two men — once bandmates, then estranged, now friends — shared a smile. (Eleven days later, Walter and his fiancée would get married at E's house.)

The night soon wound to a close, and E said goodbye to the Music Box crowd, ending with *Tomorrow Morning*'s 'Baby Loves Me', a buoyant celebration about the joy of being loved. He walked offstage and into his future. During the album's press rounds, journalists had constantly asked him what he was going to do next. He always replied that he really had no idea, that it was the first time in a very long while that he had no big strategy to pursue or in-process albums to revisit.

Finally, at one point he offered this: "I think at the end of this tour I'll take a year-long nap and maybe during the nap I'll have a dream that'll tell me where I'm going next."

It was, as is his preference, a funny but noncommittal answer — after all, it wouldn't be the first time that he kept his plans hidden. But perhaps, as he sang on 'Things The Grandchildren Should Know', he was keeping himself open to the idea that no matter how bad yesterday was, a new day can offer fresh possibilities. And the possibility of a happier tomorrow seemed to be of primary importance to an artist who has had many sad yesterdays and wanted to savour a few moments of contentment. It was the reason, he told *Clash*, that he chose a jacaranda tree for the cover of *Tomorrow Morning*.

"Right now they've all bloomed 'round my neighbourhood," he said. "It's a really lovely shade of purple but it's only in bloom for a short time so you have to really appreciate it while it lasts.

"You've got to appreciate the good things while they're there."

Epilogue

On June 1, 2011 at 8.48pm, E takes the stage of The Galaxy Theatre in Santa Ana, California. It's been about 10 months since he was last here. Back in August 2010, he was preparing for his first world tour in a few years. He was in the midst of releasing a trilogy of albums, reintroducing himself to fans who hadn't seen him since he had put out *Blinking Lights And Other Revelations* and combed through his past with an autobiography, a documentary and some retrospective discs. And now he was back at The Galaxy Theatre. No new music, no new product — just a new year and another warm-up show for a new tour.

If the previous year's tour had been about embracing the sweaty joy of old fashioned garage-rock, this year's tour is that with horns. E has added two guys who play everything from flute to trumpet. The only other change is the return of bassist "Big Al" Hunter, whom E tells tonight's crowd is actually "Tiny Al." Koool G Murder won't be playing this tour, but he's in attendance, sitting at a table that seems to be filled with E's friends, including Tommy Walter. They're here to see off the band before they venture to China for the first time. Then it's Europe and North America. All in two months.

Despite the introduction of horns, the warm-up show doesn't feel markedly different from last year's. The set list has changed and some of the songs' arrangements have been reconfigured — and instead of a ventriloquist for an opening act, this time it's a juggler. But that happy vibe remains. Other than a poignant rendering of 'P.S. You Rock My World', the closing track from *Electro-Shock Blues*, there's no mention of suicide or death. And even then, 'P.S.' is about taking stock of the joy around you, not dwelling on the sorrows of yesterday.

Even more than in past years, E's performance of 'Grace Kelly Blues' feels significant tonight, a song awash in guarded optimism that began *Daisies Of The Galaxy*, an album about trying to hold on to the best of life. After surveying four divergent searching individuals — a lousy mime, Grace Kelly, a truck driver, a mall food-court employee — E ends with a look at himself:

> *but me I'm feeling pretty good as of now*
> *I'm not so sure when I got here or how*
> *sun melting the fake smile away*
> *I think, you know, I'll be okay*

Outwardly, not much has changed in E's world since last year, but one of the people from that world is gone. On May 10, 2011, John Carter died of cancer. He was 65. Obituaries mentioned 'Incense and Peppermints' and how he was instrumental in Tina Turner's *Private Dancer* and launching the careers of Sammy Hagar and Eels, among many others, but the most meaningful tributes came from friends and colleagues who knew him best. Industry columnist Bob Lefsetz called him, "A teenager in a sexagenarian's body. With that little soul patch and the twinkle in his eye. He never got old. Unlike so many who put on the suit and went straight, Carter was rock and roll until he died." Even less than a month before his death, he remained a larger-than-life force, boasting in emails to friends like a proud papa that Hagar's memoir had just hit number one on *The New York Times*' best-seller list.

The summer before his death, I met Carter in Los Angeles for the first time to talk about what it was like to manage E. He was fiercely opinionated, chatting passionately about everything and anything before jumping on a plane to San Francisco. And despite his criticisms of some of E's career choices, he remained an ardent fan. "E is prolific," Carter said. "That's the most precious word in the music business as far as I'm concerned. He is without question — times two, times three — the most prolific guy I have ever been around."

People close to Carter had known he was sick, yet his death still shocked them. When Carter died, Butch emailed Walter to let him know. It led to the two former band members talking on the phone, which was the first time in a while. They caught up: Walter was working on new Abandoned Pools material, while Butch was on the road with Lucinda Williams. They talked about the past. And they talked about the future.

"I don't know if E would go for it," Walter said a few days before the 2011 warm-up show, "but [Butch and I] would both be up for a reunion tour of some sort, which I think would be amazing." Had Walter mentioned it to E? "No. E sort of mentioned it to me before, but his comment was he didn't think anyone would even remember the original line-up." Walter laughed. "Thanks, buddy." Of course, before that could even happen, Butch and E would have to start talking again. "They'd have to patch things up, [but] if E and I can, I don't see why Butch and E can't. It's really funny to be in this position. It's really ironic, considering [how I got] fired. Now, I'm the guy who may have to get *them* back together."

But some casual conversation between two former bandmates shouldn't be confused with anything concrete. Though E has made amends with Walter and invited him onstage a few times, he remains an artist who isn't much for nostalgia, reinventing his old songs for new tours so that they remain fresh to his ears. In fact, E has been around long enough now that whole chunks of his discography have to be ditched when he's putting together his set lists. Tonight, for instance, there's no 'Dog Faced Boy' or 'Susan's House', and 'I Like Birds' long ago morphed into a revved-up punk-rock song live, far removed from its indie-pop origins. But while these omissions and changes may disappoint some in the crowd, E has never been about hits. He's after something much larger.

Ask those who have worked with E to name their favourite Eels album, and you'll get a range of answers. *Electro-Shock Blues, Beautiful Freak, Blinking Lights, Souljacker* and *A Man Called E* are all mentioned as possible candidates, which suggests that, really, there is no "best" Eels record. Much like the artists he admires — Randy Newman, Bob Dylan, Prince, Tom Waits, Neil Young — E has tried to produce a body of work which reflects his many different moods and seasons. Consequently, there is an Eels (or E) album that's ideal for any state of mind or musical preference. *Bad Dude In Love* is wonderful Eighties cheese with a knowing sense of humour and real feeling. *A Man Called E* is lilting, perfect pop. *Broken Toy Shop* is loneliness expressed with exquisite, edgy melancholy. *Beautiful Freak* is a time capsule of mid-Nineties alternative rock as it struggled to balance commercial success with personal expression. *Electro-Shock Blues* is all pain and emotion gushing out. *Daisies Of The Galaxy* is pretty on the surface but ugly underneath. *Souljacker* is the exact opposite. *I Am The Messiah* is really funny and really funky. *Shootenanny!* is an early morning looking out the window to take stock of one's life. *Blinking Lights And Other Revelations* is mature and graceful. *Hombre Lobo* is fun, simple rock. *End Times* is all day in bed with the covers pulled over your head while it's sprinkling outside. *Tomorrow Morning* is the stylistic curveball that's as pleasant and undemanding as a day without worry. Each album is very much its own self-contained entity. Individually, not one of them is perfect, but collectively they're an extraordinary achievement.

When E started doing press for *Tomorrow Morning*, he professed again and again that he had reached a new level of contentment in his often-troubled life. One always has to take such comments with a grain of salt — never forget that mere months before committing suicide, Kurt Cobain proclaimed to *Rolling Stone* that he was happier than he'd ever been. But E is a true survivor in a scene that has had too many casualties. Elliott Smith killed himself in 2003 with two stab wounds to the chest. Vic Chesnutt took his life on Christmas Day in 2009, overdosing on muscle relaxants. In March 2010, Sparklehorse's Mark Linkous shot himself in the chest. So to hear E insist that he's reached a happy ending is gratifying, especially when it's backed up by those closest to him.

"My fiancée read [E's memoir]," Walter once told me. "And she was saying to him, 'You seem like a different E these days — you don't seem like that guy in the book'. And he said, 'Well, maybe it is *because* I wrote that book that I'm not that guy in the book'."

E will be 51 in 2014 — the same age as his father was when he died. As a young man driving around McLean trying to figure out what to do with himself, reaching this age was probably impossible to imagine. He's surely smart enough to know that life will continue to have its peaks and valleys, but artistically the challenge will be to keep finding topics as gripping as those that dominated so many of his earlier albums. After he published his memoir, he joked that he looked forward to writing a second, less-harrowing volume that would be "the most boring book ever written". The artistic phase that E now seems to be entering is one in which he'll try to negotiate through life as a relatively happy person who's made peace with the ghosts of his family. It puts his fans in an awkward position: of course we wish him well, but how will contentment affect his muse?

In addition, he might have to contend with the obstacle that faces many veteran artists: too much freedom. *Tomorrow Morning* came out on his own E Works label. "It's still being distributed by all of the same companies — it's still being distributed by Universal in America and V2 abroad — which is the way it's been for the last few," he told a journalist about the record's release. "The only difference is that the home office now is just me. I don't have to answer to anyone saying, 'Hey, why don't you get rid of this song and write another one', or something like that. I just have to say 'no' to myself now and I'm pretty good at saying 'no' to myself." Some of the weaker tracks in the recent trilogy seem to argue against E's claim — moving forward, will his ability to self-govern his creativity lead to strong albums or merely minor and self-indulgent ones?

These are questions to which we can't know the answers yet. Just as we can't fully judge an Eels album upon its release — needing instead to re-evaluate it in relation to the music he makes afterward to see how it all fits together — this new-found happiness and freedom could be a permanent shift or something that gives way to other realities. Along the same lines, we can't even say for sure if this current string of tours is really as inconsequential (albeit extremely pleasurable) as it now appears. Time will offer more perspective on such matters.

But that's what has made the story of Eels so satisfying. As the man himself suggested in 'The Stars Shine In The Sky Tonight', it's not about where you've been but about where you're heading. And wherever it is that he's going, he hasn't arrived there yet. But tonight's final song offers a hint of his mind-set: It's 'Looking Up.' Maybe that's wishful thinking. I'd say he's earned it.

Discography

As Mark Everett:

Bad Dude In Love (1985)
Everybody's Tryin' To Bum Me Out/Gotta Get Out Tonight/History
Baby/Too Busy Thinking About My Baby/Eunice/I Just Wanna
Be With You/Bad Dude In Love/The Girl In My Neighborhood/
Burning Love/Ain't Braggin'/I Can't Get Next To You

As E:

A Man Called E (1992)
Hello Cruel World/Fitting In With The Misfits/Are You & Me
Gonna Happen/Looking Out The Window With A Blue Hat On/
Nowheresville/Symphony For Toy Piano In G Minor/Mockingbird
Franklin/I've Been Kicked Around/Pray/E's Tune/You'll Be The
Scarecrow

Broken Toy Shop (1993)
Shine It All On/Standing At The Gate/The Only Thing I Care
About/Manchester Girl/L.A. River/A Most Unpleasant Man/Mass/
Tomorrow I'll Be Nine/The Day I Wrote You Off/Someone To
Break The Spell/She Loves A Puppet/My Old Raincoat/Permanent
Broken Heart/Eight Lives Left

As Eels:

Beautiful Freak (1996)
Novocaine For The Soul/Susan's House/Rags To Rags/Beautiful
Freak/Not Ready Yet/My Beloved Monster/Flower/Guest List/
Mental/Spunky/Your Lucky Day In Hell/Manchild

Electro-Shock Blues (1998)
Elizabeth On The Bathroom Floor/Going To Your Funeral Part I/
Cancer For The Cure/My Descent Into Madness/3 Speed/Hospital
Food/Electro-Shock Blues/Efils' God/Going To Your Funeral Part
II/Last Stop: This Town/Baby Genius/Climbing To The Moon/
Ant Farm/Dead Of Winter/The Medication Is Wearing Off/P.S.
You Rock My World

Daisies Of The Galaxy (2000)
Grace Kelly Blues/Packing Blankets/The Sound Of Fear/I Like
Birds/Daisies Of The Galaxy/Flyswatter/It's A Motherfucker/Estate
Sale/Tiger In My Tank/A Daisy Through Concrete/Jeannie's Diary/
Wooden Nickels/Something Is Sacred/Selective Memory/Mr E's
Beautiful Blues

Souljacker (2001)
Dog Faced Boy/That's Not Really Funny/Fresh Feeling/Woman
Driving, Man Sleeping/Souljacker Part I/Friendly Ghost/Teenage
Witch/Bus Stop Boxer/Jungle Telegraph/World Of Shit/Souljacker
Part II/What Is This Note?

Shootenanny! (2003)
All In A Day's Work/Saturday Morning/The Good Old Days/Love
Of The Loveless/Dirty Girl/Agony/Rock Hard Times/Restraining
Order Blues/Lone Wolf/Wrong About Bobby/Numbered Days/
Fashion Awards/Somebody Loves You

Blinking Lights And Other Revelations (2005)
Disc One: Theme From Blinking Lights/From Which I Came/A
Magic World/Son Of A Bitch/Blinking Lights (For Me)/Trouble
With Dreams/Marie Floating Over The Backyard/Suicide Life/In

The Yard, Behind The Church/Railroad Man/The Other Shoe/ Last Time We Spoke/Mother Mary/Going Fetal/Understanding Salesmen/Theme For A Pretty Girl That Makes You Believe God Exists/Checkout Blues/Blinking Lights (For You)
Disc Two: Dust Of Ages/Old Shit/New Shit/Bride Of Theme From Blinking Lights/Hey Man (Now You're Really Living)/I'm Going To Stop Pretending That I Didn't Break Your Heart/To Lick Your Boots/If You See Natalie/Sweet Li'l Thing/Dusk: A Peach In The Orchard/Whatever Happened To Soy Bomb/Ugly Love/God's Silence/Losing Streak/Last Days Of My Bitter Heart/The Stars Shine In The Sky Tonight/Things The Grandchildren Should Know

Hombre Lobo (2009)
Prizefighter/That Look You Give That Guy/Lilac Breeze/In My Dreams/Tremendous Dynamite/The Longing/Fresh Blood/What's A Fella Gotta Do/My Timing Is Off/All The Beautiful Things/ Beginner's Luck/Ordinary Man

End Times (2010)
The Beginning/Gone Man/In My Younger Days/Mansions Of Los Feliz/A Line In The Dirt/End Times/Apple Trees/Paradise Blues/ Nowadays/Unhinged/High And Lonesome/I Need A Mother/Little Bird/On My Feet

Tomorrow Morning (2010)
In Gratitude For This Magnificent Day/I'm A Hummingbird/The Morning/Baby Loves Me/Spectacular Girl/What I Have To Offer/ This Is Where It Gets Good/After The Earthquake/Oh So Lovely/ The Man/Looking Up/That's Not Her Way/I Like The Way This Is Going/Mystery Of Life

Compilations:

Meet The Eels: Essential Eels Vol. 1, 1996–2006 (2008)
Novocaine For The Soul/Susan's House/My Beloved Monster/ Your Lucky Day In Hell/3 Speed/Last Stop: This Town/Climbing To The Moon (Jon Brion Remix)/Flyswatter/I Like Birds/Mr E's

Beautiful Blues/It's A Motherfucker/Souljacker Part I/That's Not Really Funny/Fresh Feeling/Get Ur Freak On/Saturday Morning/ Love Of The Loveless/Dirty Girl (Live At Town Hall)/I Need Some Sleep/Hey Man (Now You're Really Living)/I'm Going To Stop Pretending That I Didn't Break Your Heart/Trouble With Dreams/ Railroad Man/Losing Streak

Note: *Meet The Eels* included a DVD of videos for Novocaine For The Soul/Susan's House/Rags To Rags/Your Lucky Day In Hell/ Last Stop: This Town/Cancer For The Cure/Flyswatter/Souljacker Part I/Saturday Morning/Hey Man (Now You're Really Living)/ Trouble With Dreams/Dirty Girl (Live At Town Hall)

Useless Trinkets: B-Sides, Soundtracks, Rarities And Unreleased, 1996– 2006 (2008)
Disc One: Novocaine For The Soul (Live From Hell)/Fucker/ My Beloved Monster (Live From Tennessee)/Dog's Life/Susan's Apartment/Manchester Girl (BBC)/Flower (BBC)/My Beloved Mad Monster Party (BBC)/Animal/Stepmother/Everything's Gonna Be Cool This Christmas/Your Lucky Day In Hell (Michael Simpson Remix)/Altar Boy/Novocaine For The Soul (Moog Cookbook Remix)/If I Was Your Girlfriend (Live)/Bad News/Funeral Parlor/ Hospital Food (BBC)/Open The Door (BBC)/Birdgirl On A Cell Phone/Vice President Fruitley/My Beloved Monstrosity/Dark End Of The Street (Live)/The Cheater's Guide To Your Heart (Live)/ Useless Trinkets
Disc Two: Mr E's Beautiful Remix/Souljacker Part I (Alternate Version)/Dog Faced Boy (Alternate Version)/Jennifer Eccles/Rotten World Blues/Can't Help Falling In Love/Christmas Is Going To The Dogs/Mighty Fine Blues/Eyes Down/Skywriting/Taking A Bath In Rust/Estranged Friends/Her/Waltz Of The Naked Clowns/I Like Birds (Live)/Sad Foot Sign/Living Life/The Bright Side/After The Operation/Jelly Dancers/I Could Never Take The Place Of Your Man (Live At Town Hall)/Mr E's Beautiful Blues (Live At Town Hall)/I Want To Protect You/I Put A Spell On You (Live)/Saw a UFO

Note: *Useless Trinkets* included a DVD of Eels' 2006 Lollapalooza performance of Saturday Morning/Eyes Down/My Beloved Monster/A Magic World/Not Ready Yet/Souljacker Part I

Live Albums:

Oh What A Beautiful Morning (2000)
Feeling Good/Overture (Last Stop: This Town/Beautiful Freak/ Rags To Rags/Your Lucky Day In Hell/My Descent Into Madness/ Novocaine For The Soul/Flower)/Oh What A Beautiful Morning/ Abortion In The Sky/It's A Motherfucker/Fucker/Ant Farm/ Climbing To The Moon/Grace Kelly Blues/Daisies Of The Galaxy/ Flyswatter/Vice President Fruitley/Hot And Cold/Mr E's Beautiful Blues/Not Ready Yet/Susan's House/Something Is Sacred

Electro-Shock Blues Show (2002)
Cancer For The Cure/Fingertips Part III/Going To Your Funeral Part I/Efil's God/Souljacker Part I/My Beloved Monster/Novocaine For The Soul/Not Ready Yet/Last Stop: This Town/Everything's Gonna Be Cool This Christmas/Flower/Dead Of Winter/Electro-Shock Blues/The Medication Is Wearing Off/Climbing To The Moon

Sixteen Tons (Ten Songs) (2005)
I'm A Loser/Packing Blankets/Saturday Morning/Lone Wolf/ Numbered Days/Last Stop: This Town/Rock Hard Times/Sixteen Tons/Grace Kelly Blues/My Beloved Monster

Eels With Strings: Live At Town Hall (2006)
Blinking Lights (For Me)/Bride Of Theme From Blinking Lights/ Bus Stop Boxer/Dirty Girl/Trouble With Dreams/The Only Thing I Care About/My Beloved Monster/Pretty Ballerina/It's A Motherfucker/Flyswatter/Novocaine For The Soul/Girl From The North Country/Railroad Man/I Like Birds/If You See Natalie/Poor Side Of Town/Spunky/I'm Going To Stop Pretending That I Didn't Break Your Heart/Suicide Life/Losing Streak/Hey Man (Now You're Really Living)/Things The Grandchildren Should Know

Live And In Person! London 2006 (2008)
Old Shit/New Shit/Rock Show/Crazy Love (Crazy Music)/Eyes Down/Jesus Gonna Be Here/My Beloved Monster/A Magic World/Not Ready Yet/Dog Faced Boy/Souljacker Part I/I Put A Spell On You/That's Life/I Like Birds/Mr E's Beautiful Blues

Note: *Live And In Person!* included a DVD with the following track list: The Shit/Old Shit/New Shit/The Other Shoe/Rock Show/Crazy Love (Crazy Music)/Eyes Down/Jesus Gonna Be Here/Mother Mary/The Sound Of Fear/My Beloved Monster/A Magic World/Agony/Last Stop: This Town/Not Ready Yet/Dog Faced Boy/Souljacker Part I/I Put A Spell On You/That's Life/Cancer For The Cure/I Like Birds/Mr E's Beautiful Blues

Soundtracks as Mark Oliver Everett:

Music From The Film 'Levity' (2003)
What I Remember Most/Skywriting/Running The Bath/Gravity/Haunted Piano #1/In Manual's Room/Taking A Bath In Rust/Flashback Blues/Post-Flashback Blues/Lonesome Subway/Haunted Organ #1/Sofia Writing In The Sky/To Adel Easley/Trouble In The Alley/Manual's Got A Train A Catch

DVDs:

Eels With Strings: Live At Town Hall (2006)
Going To Your Funeral Part II/Dust Of Ages/In The Yard, Behind The Church/Bride of Theme From Blinking Lights/A Magic World/Son Of A Bitch/Blinking Lights (For Me)/Dirty Girl/My Beloved Monster/The Only Thing I Care About/Bus Stop Boxer/Pretty Ballerina/I Like Birds/Girl From The North Country/Railroad Man/Trouble With Dreams/If You See Natalie/I'm Going To Stop Pretending That I Didn't Break Your Heart/Dead Of Winter/Flyswatter/Novocaine For The Soul/Losing Streak/The Stars Shine In The Sky Tonight/Souljacker Part II/Hey Man (Now You're Really Living)/Things The Grandchildren Should Know/Dog Faced Boy/Mr E's Beautiful Blues

Acknowledgements

I first have to thank David Barraclough at Omnibus, who made my dream of writing a book about Eels come true.

Then, my appreciation goes out to the interview subjects contained in this book. They were extraordinarily gracious and generous with their time, inviting a total stranger into their homes, having long visits at coffee shops, or allowing me to tag along on their walks. I cannot express how much their faith and trust in me meant. Their enthusiasm about my project kept me going when times were tough.

Along those lines, I have to sincerely thank Mark Oliver Everett. E chose not to be interviewed for this book, but he very kindly gave his blessing to those closest to him to speak with me. E, your music has been a guiding light for me for many years — my wish is that in some small measure this book serves as a way of paying you back for all that you've done for me and your many fans.

I would also like to thank those who had a kind word of encouragement for me when I really needed it. Those would include Gwendolyn Martin, Andy Hungerford, Jen Lopez, and Robert Abele.

More specific thanks are due to Bernhard Gmeiner, Russell Brown, Liz Wiley, Norma Jamsheed, Marissa Brooks, Brigitte Lavey, David Briggs, Kevin Gasser, and Stuart MacMillan for technical assistance and guidance. In his own category is Jason Major, who had the answer for every impossible question I threw his way. Jason is the only person

I know who loves Eels as much as I do — I sure hope he likes this book.

A huge thank you to Will Leitch, who has been there from the beginning. What would I do without my old friend?

I also want to publicly acknowledge Bill Holdship, a great music critic, editor and Eels fan. Bill was the first person to take a chance on a certain inexperienced young writer, and I don't think I've ever truly said thanks for what he did for me.

Writing this book has reminded me, as if I needed reminding, how fortunate I am to have been blessed with the family I was born into. My baby sister Lisa is now all grown up with a terrific husband and four impossibly wonderful kids — I don't tell her often enough how proud I am of her because, frankly, she's doing just fine without my encouragement. My parents, Bob and Debbie, have simply given me everything. (Dad, sorry about the dangling preposition at the end of the first sentence in this paragraph.)

And then there's Susan Stoebner. I love you to pieces, honey. Where should we go on vacation?

Bibliography

Books:

Heroes And Villains: Essays On Music, Movies, Comics, And Culture by David Hajdu (2009)

I Was A Cold War Monster: Horror Films, Eroticism And The Cold War Imagination by Cyndy Hendershot (2001)

Life On Planet Rock by Lonn Friend (2006)

Things The Grandchildren Should Know by Mark Oliver Everett (2008)

The Many Worlds Of Hugh Everett III by Peter Byrne (2010)

Periodicals, Newspapers, Radio Interviews and Online Sites:

About.com
American Songwriter
Amplifier
The A.V. Club
Billboard
TheBookseller.com
The Boston Globe
Chicago Tribune
Clash
CMJ
The Current

Drop-D Magazine
Drowned In Sound
Drum!
Drumhead
Entertainment Weekly
The Guardian
FasterLouder
Flaunt
Flyp
Harp
The Hollywood Reporter
Hot Press
The Huffington Post
The Independent
Interview
Jonesy's Jukebox
KCRW
LA Alternative Press
LA Weekly
Los Angeles Times
Magnet
Metro Times
Modern Drummer
Mojo
MTV News
Music Connection
Music Express
The New Times Los Angeles
NME
NPR
The Omaha Weekly Reader
Pitchfork
Playbill
PopMatters
Q

Rhythm
SF Weekly
Slant
Sound On Sound
Spin
Spinner
The Sunday Times
Tiny Mix Tapes
Uncut
USA Today
Vanity Fair
Variety
The Village Voice
VOX Online
Word

Studies and Reports:

Institute For Defense Analyses: "Analytical Support For The Joint Chiefs Of Staff: The WSEG Experience, 1948–1976"
McLean Citizens Association: "McLean Hunt"
National Transportation Safety Board: "Aircraft Accident Report, McLean, Virginia, April 28, 1977"

Liner Notes:

The Who, *Fragments*

Websites

Official Site:
eelstheband.com

Fan Sites:
rockingeels.com
eels.nl
therockhardtimes.wordpress.com

About The Author

Tim Grierson is a film and music critic whose writing has appeared in *L.A. Weekly*, *Yahoo*, *Screen International*, *Revolver*, *The Village Voice*, *Vulture*, *Wired*, *Blender* and VH1.com. He is the Rock Music guide at About.com and a member of the Los Angeles Film Critics Association.

WITHDRAWN